DATE

ECONOMIC STUDIES № 1

TOWARDS A THEORY
OF PLANNED ECONOMY

By Branko Horvat Dr, Ph. D.

Yugoslav Institute of Economic Research

Beograd  1964

Printed by Beogradski grafički zavod — Beograd

FOREWORD

This is a book of a planner for the fellow planners, although it is not a book on planning itself. It has arisen from the need to provide a usable theoretical frame of reference for economists engaged in planning, a need which became particularly urgent for me when, several years ago, I became planner myself.

Originally I intended only to clarify some theoretical problems for myself and for my colleagues in the Federal Planning Bureau. However, as the work was progressing, I gradually came to think that it would be more useful to write a more general study. The purpose of the present study is to examine the issues involved in designing an efficient economic system in given historical circumstances. This task also involves elaboration of a suitable analytical apparatus. Economic efficiency is measured in terms of consumers' valuations. Nothing a priori is assumed about any particular feature of the economy in question or about its institutional set-up. But, in evaluating possible solutions, I draw heavily on the experience provided by the failures and successes of the post-war Yugoslav economy, which I happen to know best, which in the last decade experienced the highest in the world rate of growth, and in which the same question has been posed practically.

My debt to literature, both "Western" and "Eastern", is great. All ideas, of which I am conscious to have influenced my thinking, are registered. Less important references, as well as empirical illustrations, are put in the footnotes; technicalities are treated in appendices. The reader interested in the main argument may skip footnotes and appendices without any loss.

I wish to express my gratitude to the University of Manchester for a generous research grant and to the Federal Planning Bureau for the leave of absence which provided me with the necessary time and facilities to undertake the research incorporated in this book. I also feel indebted to Professors Ely Devons and H. D. Dickinson, dr Ivan Maksimović and dr Kurt Martin, who patiently read the entire manuscript, discussed it with me and made many valuable comments. In addition, some more controversial parts of the manuscript were circulated among a number of my friends as well and quite a few of their comments found their way in the final draft. But, of course, I bear sole responsibility for the content of the book.

I am grateful to the editors of Ekonomist, Economic Journal, Ekonomski pregled, The Manchester School *and* Income & Wealth: Series IX *for the permission to use, partly or wholly, my articles published in these journals and in the last mentioned book.*

This book was essentially completed in 1958 and published in Yugoslav in 1961 under the title Ekonomska teorija planske privrede. *The English version now published has been slightly modified here and there in order to make the text more readily understandable to a non-Yugoslav reader.*

The Index for the English edition has been prepared by my collaborators Božo Marendić, Miodrag Ostraćanin, and Pavle Sicherl, while many language improvements are due to Mrs. Olga Tomić. I wish to thank them all.

Beograd, April 1964

Branko HORVAT

CONTENTS

Book Two: The Working of the Economic System

INTRODUCTION

1. The purpose of this study is to discuss the possibility of designing an efficient economic system, i.e., a system which would generate maximum product, potentially achievable in the historically given social-economic conditions. As it is not proposed to describe the working of any particular existing institutional system, the theory expounded might be labeled "normative". However, one should be careful in interpreting this ambiguous term. The term usually implies value judgements, and value judgements have no place in economics, or for that matter, in any science. "Normative" in the present study is used in the same sense in which economics *as such* is normative; it simply implies the principle of maximization, which is a logical derivative of the fundamental economic concept of valuation. We choose something rather than something else because we value it more. Then, "rational" choice implies that means are efficiently used to achieve the professed ends. If in this context we say that something "ought to be done" we simply mean that it is "rational" to do it, which in turn is reduced to the tautological statement that valuations, whatever they are, "ought" to be valued i.e. maximized. "Normative economics", in the sense in which I propose to use the term here, generalizes the application of the maximization criterion even to the choice of institutional systems. It follows that the alternative — and rather traditional — approach is either arbitrary — and thus *sensu stricto* not economic — or implies value judgements — and thus violates fundamental requirements of a science.

2. "Maximum product" implies a concept of a common denominator, namely the traditional economic concept of value. The relative values (prices) of the economic goods are derived from the valuations of consumers (individual and institutional) who choose goods and services and workers who choose occupations. Therefore free choices of consumption and occupation are necessary conditions of the postulated maximum. Closely related to this is the choice between work and leisure which, within certain limits, may be exercised individually, but basically, in industrial societies, is a social choice. As a social choice it is reflected in the institutionally given length of the working day. Like the other two, the choice between work and leisure represents a datum for the economist.

Goods appropriated by and services rendered to individual consumers are evaluated by consumers and as such constitute their economic welfare. It follows that only the product which directly or indirectly contributes to the economic welfare of consumers is product

1

in an economic sense. Thus we may say that economic science is about maximization of economic welfare. Or, the same expressed more loosely, economics is about production for the satisfaction of human needs. Or, again, economics is about maximization of consumption.

Whether maximization of consumption is a good or a bad thing, ethically commendable or not — is no concern of ours. The definition — like any other definition — can neither be proved nor disproved. But it can be found meaningful or meaningless, the criterion being whether, or not the science in question explains a part of reality or helps us to solve the actually existing practical problems. A glance at the history of the human race suffices to convince us that the definition is meaningful.

3. As a measure of the economic efficiency of a particular social-economic system I propose the rate of growth of social product. I argue that private capitalism was so universally successful because it immensely expanded productive forces as compared with all other previous systems. But the institutional set-up of this system is far from being rational from the economist's point of view. First of all, unco-ordinated economic decisions result in business fluctuations with a tremendous waste of resources. Monopolies lead to a maldistribution of resources. The long-run rate of growth is still relatively modest — 1 to 4 per cent per annum in the case of thirteen advanced capitalist countries in the period 1860—1950 (1, 115). The obvious potential improvement in efficiency lies in co-ordinating economic activities by way of planning[1].

Secondly, privately owned economy generates an irrational distribution of income. It is irrational because a more equal distribution of income — possible in a different institutional set-up — would increase economic welfare. But it is irrational for yet another reason; it lowers the potential productive efficiency of the economy. The volume of production — and for that matter of consumption — depends on an efficient use of all resources, including labour resources. Now, labour resources *are not given*, they have to be built up and they can be built up in various ways. The most efficient solution is achieved when *health, education* and *creative will to work* of the population are maximally enhanced. Adequate shelter, proper diet and medical attendance produce not only healthy bodies — an asset in itself — but, as psychological investiga-

---

[1] Many naïve misconceptions are connected with the institution of planning. The following argument advanced by L. Robbins may be considered characteristic for the "theoretical" refutation of planning: "The alleged advantage of economic 'planning' — namely, that it offers greater certainty with regard to the future — depends upon the assumption that under 'planning' the present controlling forces, the choices of individual spenders and savers, are themselves brought under the control of the planners. Therefore a paradox presents itself: either the planner is destitute of the instruments of calculating the ends of the community he intends to serve, or, if he restores the instrument, he removes the *raison d'être* of the 'plan'" (2, 113). The paradox arises only because in the good neoclassical tradition Professor Robbins makes an implicit assumption that "choices of individual spenders and savers" are made in a physical and social vacuum. In other words, he overlooks the fact that economic process occurs in time and space and makes a value judgement by implying that the distortions of choices due to social relations and economic institutions do not matter. Strangely enough, the quoted passage was written in the middle of the worst economic depression ever experienced (1931).

tions have beyond any doubt established, they also foster the development of intellectual capacities. More equal distribution of income being likely to increase the standard of health, it is desirable, on economic grounds. The same applies to education. If the market system is left to operate uncontrolled, it will cause a waste of talents, because not the most promising children but children of parents able to pay would get educated[1]. The problem of education is not exhausted by school attendance. It has a much broader aspect in sharing the total cultural tradition of a given society. Again, greater equality of income is conducive to building up more efficient labour force and, conversely, inequality reduces social mobility which, from the economic viewpoint, is undesirable like any other reduced mobility of resources.

The question arises whether all these distortions are significant enough to be worth bothering about? Empirical investigations suggest that they are. As potential abilities appear to be distributed in a random fashion — or, at least, there is no conclusive evidence that they are not (cf. 4) — any other significantly different distribution of individuals in, for instance, skilled and unskilled jobs, is indicative of a malallocation of labour resources. And this is just what happens. As D. V. Glass and associates have established, in Britain children of unskilled workers find it very difficult to move upwards to more responsible and more skilled occupations. People born into upper strata find it even much more difficult to move downwards to occupations requiring technically less abilities[2]. A recent study on American business leaders by Warner and

---

[1] An interesting study by Gray and Moshinsky in the interwar England may be mentioned as a quantitative illustration. The authors established that a pupil, whose parents were able to pay for his education, had about 6 times greater chance to receive secondary school education, than an *equally able* (index of brightness of 130 and over taken as a criterion) pupil whose parents were not rich enough. And conversely, a sub-standard child of freepaying parents had a 60 times greater opportunity of receiving secondary education than a similar child of less rich parents (3, 372—3). If one thinks in terms of potential abilities, these differences are seriously underestimated because intelligence tests do not measure "innate ability" as such but ability shaped by material (diet, etc.) and cultural environment. It should also be noted that the chances for obtaining *higher* education would necessarily be much more unequal and that the English community was relatively wealthy.

[2] To construct a measuring device, Glass postulates a society where every member has an equal chance of entering any occupation. The ratio of the actual to expected number of sons in the occupational groups of their fathers is termed index of association. In the case of a hypothetical perfect mobility, there would be no association between parental and filial status, expected and actual numbers would coincide and, consequently, the index of association would be equal to 1. Perfect mobility is not likely to be attained because "there will probably always be some premium (if only in the sense of encouragement or stimulus) on a given parental background" (5, 196); therefore, we must compare different indices directly with each other. Nevertheless, occupational category 5 (skilled manual and routine grades of non-manual) with its index 1.16 comes very closely to the hypothetical standard. The higher the degree of self-recruitment, i.e., of inheritance of parental status, the higher the index of association. Glass finds that starting from category 5 social-occupational rigidity increases downwards and upwards. The respective indices for categories 6 (semi-skilled manual) and 7 (unskilled manual) are 1.84 and 2.26; for categories 2 (managerial and executive) and 1 (professional and high administrative) they are as high as 5.87 and 13.16 (5, 199). If the index of category 5 can be taken as a measure of attainable mobility, then the sons of unskilled workers become unskilled workers themselves in numbers twice as

3

Abegglen also calls for our attention. It is in fact of particular interest for us because it deals with the mobility within the business sector. The authors find that families of major business executives produce as many business leaders as the entire labour population, and the families of business owners produce nearly twice as many (6, 38). The chance of the son of a business executive or owner of a large business, of becoming a successful businessman himself, is about 1,100 per cent greater than that of the son of a skilled worker, about 50 times greater than that of the son of an unskilled or semi-skilled worker, and hundreds of times greater than that of the farm labourer's son for whom it is virtually impossible to penetrate into the business elite (p. 41).

The waste of talent is not a mechanical consequence of an irrational distribution of income. In fact, both are determined by a more fundamental cause. If we can accept the Marxian explanation — which, in my judgement, is still the best we have — the fundamental cause is to be found in the institution of private property, an institution which also implies private control of the production process. This institution being given the rest follows, though with modifications due to historical circumstances. The "rest" includes capitalist market and formidable barriers to social mobility. Thus, in addition to planning, it would seem desirable, *on economic grounds*, to have the system of private property replaced by a more efficient system.

Indeed, the economies which practice planning and in which the means of production are appropriated by the state[1], expand at a much higher rate than privately owned economies — at about 7—9 per cent per annum, if Soviet economy in its Stalinist period and M. C. Kaser's estimate of its rate of growth may be taken as representative (7, 101). Is this the maximum efficiency we can hope to achieve? There is as yet no possibility of answering the question by producing empirical evidence, but general theoretical analysis will lead to a negative answer. State-owned economy implies bureaucratic economic organization which, in turn, is based on hierarchical principle. It will be shown that the institution of state ownership (with bureaucracy as its derivative) reduces potential efficiency of the economic machine in a manner similar to that of the institution of private ownership. Co-ordination is less than optimal. Social mobility is less than potentially possible because the sons of those holding offices — like the sons of those owning wealth — are necessarily privileged in a hierarchical society. And, fundamentally, the operation of the hierarchical principle produces social polarization, social polarization generates conflict and conflict is not conducive to efficiency.

The efficiency of a state capitalist system is imperfect. But if so, is there any other *feasible* (i.e. realizable in practice) socio-economic system which is more desirable on economic grounds? It is exactly the discussion of this question that the present study undertakes.

---

great as is potentially necessary and the sons of men in the top social-occupational category remain in the same category 11 times more frequently than do the sons of skilled and white collar workers in the professions of their fathers.

[1] The influence of planning is self-evident. As to the use of human resources, there is some evidence that bureaucratization increases social mobility (cf. Warner and Abegglen, 6, 164-9).

4. The presentation of the problem in the preceding section has a slightly utopian flavour, because it is not pure rationality which governs the economic affairs of humanity. But such an assumption was not implied, as the actual *analysis* of the problem will presently show. My intention was only to indicate as clearly and simply as possible that we can generalize the application of rational choice and, so, see the consequences that are likely to follow.

One consequence is particularly important for the understanding of the nature of economic theorizing. If economic institutions change, economic theories must change as well. But not only theories; basic analytical concepts will have to be reshaped too. It is a great illusion to believe that these concepts are given once for all. And it is, indeed, amusing to watch those innocent attempts which begin by applying the old tools of analysis, representing rationalizations of private capitalist institutions, and end by reaching the "surprising" result that socialism, in order to be rational, must work like ideal capitalism.

Unfortunately, the world is more complex and every subsequent step in the analysis will help to convince us in that. Wage, interest, profit, national income — all these fundamental concepts will have to be reshaped. And once we start the business of reshaping, we are on a very slippery ground. For we are never sure that we have grasped all the ramifications of the new concepts in a new frame of reference. It is this fact that provides the practical justification for the present study.

Watching for a decade or so a planned economy that struggles to realize the efficiency potential in the system, I have been struck over and again by the impossibility of using the available theoretic apparatus for a meaningful analysis of the most outstanding problems of this economy[1]. Even a careful study of a particular problem would end in an unsatisfactory improvisation. Eventually, it became clear to me that no amount of sectional work would do; the inherited tools were designed to tackle different kinds of problems. So, not refinements in sectional analysis, but a general conceptual framework particularly designed to suit the task, a *simultaneous* study of fundamental analytical concepts which make them consistent with each other — this seemed to be the thing needed first. In other words, to make the analysis meaningful, an adequate theory was required. In trying to solve this task I simplified my problem to the utmost by considering only closed economy and by neglecting monetary and fiscal questions. Even so, I have no illusions to have escaped the pitfalls which so densely cover the ground to be explored. What follows is intended to be no more than prolegomena to a future general theory of planned economy.

---

[1] For this reason I could only agree with Mrs. Robinson when, teaching a lesson to a simple-minded Oxonian economist, she concludes: "In short, I fear we must sadly admit, whatever mistakes the planners have made, they have not lost much by failing to read our text-books" (8, 273).

References:

1. R. W. Goldsmith, "Financial Structure and Economic Growth in Advanced Countries," in *Capital Formation and Economic Growth*, National Bureau of Economic Research, New York, 1955.

2. L. Robbins, *An Essay on the Nature and Significance of Economic Science*, London, Macmillan, 1932.

3. J. L. Gray, P. Moshinsky, "Ability and Opportunity in English Education," in L. Hogben (ed.), *Political Arithmetic*, London, Allen and Unwin, 1938.

4. K. W. Eells and others, *Intelligence and Cultural Differences*, The University of Chicago Press, 1951.

5. D. V. Glass and others, *Social Mobility in Britain*, London, Routledge and Kegan, 1954.

6. W. L. Warner, J. C. Abegglen, *Occupational Mobility in American Business and Industry 1928—1952*, Minneapolis, University of Minnesota Press, 1955.

7. M. C. Kaser, "Estimating the Soviet National Income", *Economic Journal*, 1957, 83—104.

8. J. Robinson, "Mr. Wiles' Rationality: A Comment," *Soviet Studies*, 1955—56. 269—73.

Book One

ECONOMIC CATEGORIES

I. THE THEORY OF PRICE

Price mechanism is of fundamental importance for the economic organization. That is a mechanism by which economic valuations are being transformed into market categories. As value is the most general and so the most elementary economic category, the theory of price will provide a convenient starting point for our enquiry. As we progress, we shall be considering ever more concrete and complex categories and, subsequently, structures, until we reach the stage of dealing with all aspects of economic organization simultaneously.

The theory of price has its historical origin in the classical labour theory of value. For this reason, a brief discussion of the classical theory might serve as a useful introduction to the theory of price with which we shall be concerned. Besides, there is also more compelling reason for adopting this course. The labour theory of value has come to be used as a battleground between two schools of thought, each of them speaking a different language. It has been discussed, both by socialist and anti-socialist economists, to such an extent and with so frequent a misunderstanding of what it was about, that it is important to define one's own position in this respect. We have, therefore, to attempt to establish the meaning of the theory when Marx conceived it and developed to its ultimate social consequences, and define its relation to the theory of price. These two points determine the scope of the discussion which follows. The discussion will, consequently, be extremely condensed and so in many respects necessarily simplified. But simplification is the "price" we have to pay on this occasion in order to avoid more dangerous potential misunderstanding on another.

1. ON THE LABOUR THEORY OF VALUE

(a) The Relation between Labour and Utility Theory of Value

1. The original and elementary economic situation may be reduced to the situation of a human group in natural environment. Human labour appears to be the only relevant dynamic factor in this situation. In order to live, people have to work and by their work, the members of the community transform *natural* resources into something which has *economic* value. The more labour is expended on a certain product wanted by the community, the greater value is attached to this product. Thus labour is in a sense proportional to the value of the product it

9

creates. Consequently, it may be used as a measure of value. Moreover, as it follows directly from the underlying axiomatic system, labour is the only creator of value. If a useful object embodies no expenditure of labour, it will have no *economic* value. The doctrine is simple and perfectly logical.

2. It also gives a valuable insight into the essentially social character of the production process. Compare, for instance, the propositions: "scarcity creates value" or "the commodity has value because it is scarce". As it stands, the proposition is *necessarily* true and as such a tautology. The concept of scarcity is a mere derivative of the concept of valuation. This being so, the statement that scarcity determines value means that value is determined by value; instead of saying that the price of the commodity is now lower than it used to be, we would say that the commodity has become less scarce. By changing the words we get no new information about the economic process and the phenomenon of the lower price still lacks an *explanation*. If the good is a reproducible good and the price an equilibrium price (just covering costs of production), the explanation of its change in terms of labour time is straightforward: productivity of labour has risen — less labour time is expended on the production of that particular commodity and therefore costs of production are lowered. Or, to make use of the famous example of Smith, if one beaver exchanges for one deer, and not for two deers as before, for some reason or other the productivity of beaver-hunting in relation to that of deer-hunting has increased. If the productive forces of a society are developed to such a small degree that more work than the members of the society would willingly supply is required and this state of affairs is characteristic for all historically known societies — then a proposition which explains economic valuations by the amount of labour expended has an obvious sociological connotation and provides a fruitful conceptual scheme for a comprehensive analysis of the social process of production, i.e., of the economic relations of men.

The main objection advanced against the labour explanation of value is that it is unable to explain the value of objects which are not products of work such as old postage stamps or old pictures. On the other hand, the value of such things should be easily explained by the scarcity theory. But this is an illusion, as far as an *explanation* is concerned. Imagine an economy where the supply of all goods is absolutely fixed or where reproducible goods are in plentiful supply so that there is no need to economize on labour. Prices in both situations will be pure scarcity prices. By definition they cannot be explained by the amount of labour time expended. However, they can neither be explained by the scarcity principle if this principle is to mean more than a truism. For, scarcity is absolute in both situations, while prices obviously change with the distribution of income and with preference schedules of consumers. If we reinterpret the scarcity principle to fit this situation also, we shall get a concept which explains everything and which is therefore devoid of any concrete meaning, in other words, we encounter the familiar phenomenon of an empty tautology. Thus, when we are faced with the choice between labour explanation, which is invalid for some economically irrelevant cases like objects of art and scarcity explanation, which is formally correct but empty, the choice of the alternative seems to be obvious if we are interested in an *explanation*[1].

3. Connected with the problem just discussed is the problem of the relation between the labour theory and the utility theory of value. There is a widespread opinion, shared by both socialist and non-socialist economists, that the two theories are contradictory in the sense that if one is true, the other must by false. But this is in general not so, and as to the concrete theories, not every labour theory is necessarily correct and not every utility theory is necessarily false. Classical economists, including Marx, had in fact both theories. Marxian double character of labour — an abstract human labour creating exchange value and a concrete labour creating use value, the latter being *conditio sine qua non* for the former — shows this straightforwardly. Historically the difference was primarily in emphasis (and, connected with this, in the sociopolitical connotation).[2] For Marx the use value was a concern of the consumers and, perhaps, of the advertisers and psychologists, while the problem of the exchange value he reserved for economists. For, obviously, the slumps and big fortunes were not the results of the working of the utility calculus — the world could do with all the bread produced and no amount of personal sacrifice involved in saving could create Rothschild's capital — but rather the results of an erratic and irrational functioning of an atomistic economic system characterized by the alienation of the labour of producers. Granting this, or thinking of a planned economy, there is nothing contradictory in itself in having a labour theory of value and a theory of consumers behaviour. However, the latter needs a few additional words of explanation.

4. The older utility theory implied — as it is nowadays generally considered — a pseudo-psychological[3] assumption based on an identification of the hedonist with the rational. The more respectable modern theory involves no assumptions about the causes of utility, rationality is identified with consistency, and the theory is generalized. The price for this has been the usual one: an *economic* theory — leaving aside

---

[1] Nevertheless, the concept of "scarcity" will be useful when it makes possible an economy in thinking or in words. The term "scarce" shall occasionally be used as short for "economically relevant". For instance the phrase "scarce factor" will be used to denote a factor which is relevant for economizing on the social labour time and which therefore must be adequately priced.

[2] This point is, I think, adequately expressed by R. Meek when he says that "the theory of value, with which an economist begins, usually embodies some sort of *general principle of causation* which he believes will be useful in the explanation of economic reality. And the principle of causation embodied in the marginal utility theory is radically different from that embodied in the labour theory ... What we must start with, the marginal utility theory says in effect, is not the social relations between men and men in production, as the labour theory implied, but rather the mental relation between individuals and finished goods" (1, 14).

[3] Cf. Schumpeter: "If we ask how consumers come to behave as they do in all those wider problems of human behaviour for which particular psychological propositions become relevant, we must in fact appeal to all that modern professional psychology ... might have to give us. As a rule, however, the necessity of such an appeal does not arise in technical economics — it is different, of course, in economic sociology" (2, 1059).

11

the question of its adequacy — has been transformed into a *logical*[1] system. There is in fact no theory of consumers' behaviour, there is only a theory of rational choice valid for all societies in all situations which conform to the initial assumptions, necessarily true and therefore a truism like all pure logical deduction. This conclusion should not be interpreted to mean that the modern theory of consumers' behaviour is useless. On the contrary, it has proved to be useful, for instance, in designing economic research of demand functions, and as such it should be considered even more useful to planned economy. The statement is only intended to clear up the potential misunderstanding about the nature of economic theory. The use of the logical system (called also "pure theory") in economics is similar to the use of mathematical systems in physics: they provide tools of analysis. These tools may be more or less useful, but in the nature of things they cannot be wrong *as such*. In this sense the popular contention, that the labour theory and the theory of choice are incompatible with each other, is a logical contradiction and as such unsustainable.

(b) The Rationale of the Marxian Labour Theory of Value

1. After the digression we return to our main theme. In the preceding section we established that in the general nature-man situation the amount of economic wealth created is related to the amount of labour expended and that changes in relative values of particular goods may be meaningfully related to changes in the productivity of labour engaged in their production. The next step is to explain the act of exchange of commodities in an atomistic society based on division of labour. We again observe a social act in which two individuals exchange their products on the basis of labour embodied in them. This is roughly what happens in the situation of so called simple commodity production, e.g., when handicraft products are bought and sold in a mediaeval town. When money is introduced into the system, the value of the product is expressed as a *price* of the *commodity* on the *market*. Value and price phenomena are integrated into a single system. In the sphere of reproducible goods labour is a single explanatory principle of the pricing mechanism; outside this sphere ("free gifts of nature") it is modified by the principle of rent. This was the state of the theory when Marx took it over from Smith and Ricardo[2].

---

[1] Cf. Schumpeter: "... the utility theory of value has much better claim to being called a logic than a psychology of values" (2, 1058). Also Little: "... the orthodox theory of economic behaviour is not a study of human behaviour at all. It is in fact incorrect to call it a *theory* for it does not seek to explain behaviour. It should rather be called a *system* of behaviour; the sole purpose of this system being the provision of a criterion for being 'economically better off' " (3, 52).

[2] The strict proportionality between value and labour time was obtained by Ricardo — or, at least, this is the analytical implication of his system in its pure form — by means of the following assumptions: (1) marginal land pays no rent and determines the price, therefore rent does not enter into price; (2) capital is proportional to the amount of labour employed by it; (3) there is a fixed scale of transformation of different individual labours into a single homogeneous social labour. Granting all this, products are exchanged in proportion to the amount of labour expended on them. Cf. G. Cassel, 4, 289. For an interesting recent view on what Ricardo actually meant see G. J. Stigler, 5.

2. Integrating sociology and economics into a single political economy, Marx gave a sociological interpretation to the economic categories he had inherited. In a collective economy, production is organized with the direct purpose of satisfying the needs of the community. In an atomistic society producers produce for the market, products become commodities. It is not enough that a product has use value, it also must have exchange value. The latter is established in the market, which, determining in this way socially necessary labour embodied in the particular commodities, regulates the allocation of labour among various lines of production. In the capitalist economy value and price diverge. Capital is also a sociological category and represents a definite social relation: the relation between the class of owners of means of production and the proletarians who own only their labour power. The owning class owns capital, not labour, and so in organizing production it is not concerned with the amount of labour expended but with the amount of capital invested. Therefore, prices are determined with respect to the capital used in production of commodities. The second consequence of the capitalist mode of production consists in the exploitation-through-trading relation between two classes. There is no "cheating" in the process (in its pure form). Proletarians own only labour power and sell this "commodity" on the market in the same way as all other sellers trade their commodities. But the value of labour power — as measured by the amount of labour necessary for the production of the wage goods the labourers consume — is smaller than the value created by the labour of its owners. Indeed, it is smaller not only in capitalism, but also in all class societies, the difference representing the income of the ruling class. This difference between the value of the commodity after deducting the transferred parts and the value of the labour power used in its production, Marx calls surplus value and uses it as a measure of the degree of exploitation[1]. In the capitalist system, the surplus value is on the market transformed into profit to satisfy the principle of distribution on the basis of capital invested. Tracing the transformations of value, Marx describes the functioning of a particular social system.

---

[1] To analyze exploitation relations in the capitalist society one may, of course, design a theoretical framework different from that of the Marxian labour theory of value. The theory of monopolistic pricing has often been suggested as a more efficient modern equivalent. To my knowledge, the best work in this field is H. D. Dickinson's book on what he calls, *institutional revenue*. Dickinson starts from the observation that any cause that restricts the supply of a factor raises its return relative to that of other factors. This happens in two ways: the factor in question is rendered more scarce and so its marginal net product rises; other factors, being forced into sub-optimal uses, have their marginal products lowered. Social institutions generate non-competing groups and secure for the more favoured of these groups, institutional restriction of certain factors of production. The part of an individual's income that is due to an institutional restriction of some factor of production supplied by him, is institutional revenue which thus appears to be monopoly revenue. Only a system, embodying complete equality of opportunity, would give rise to no institutional revenue (6). Significantly enough, Dickinson's book seems to be completely forgotten today.

Value is conceived as a "materialization of relations of production" (7, 358)[1].

And what about socialism?

On those rare occasions when he was induced to consider the subject, Marx envisaged socialism as a system characterized by free labour, social ownership and planning of economic activities to satisfy the properly understood needs of the community. In such circumstances, no contradiction between value in use and exchange value can exist since labour is no more alienated. The whole conceptual apparatus, developed to cope with an essentially different situation, becomes inapplicable. If the socialist economy is to have a theory of value, it should be a different theory. An attempt to use Marxian categories outside the context of the capitalist political economy would show a complete misunderstanding of his theory[2].

(c) The Theory of Price in a Socialist Economy

The adequacy of the Marxian theory of value for the capitalist system is not our concern here and, as we have just seen, it is neither meant for nor applicable to a socialist economy. Therefore, we may safely neglect the controversy which is being drawn from these two positions. But it will be useful to consider briefly the lessons one can draw for a subsequent discussion on prices.

1. If all productive agents were homogeneous, labour time might serve perfectly well as a measure of value and as a direct determinant of prices. But, of course, they are not. First of all, labour itself is heter-

---

[1] Thus the Japanese economist Tsuru is right in stressing that "the major contribution by Marx in the field of value theory was in pursuing the implications of the *specific form* of value which labour takes under the system of commodity production" (review article in the *Economic Journal*, 1957, p. 702). Tsuru's assertion that it would be better to call Marx's theory "the value theory of labour" rather than "the labour theory of value" (*ibid.*) might perhaps clear much of the confusion with respect to this issue. The "value theory of labour" was not meant to describe the *technique* of pricing, let alone normative pricing, but to analyze the underlying social relations in the production process. As Sweezy, an American Marxist, put it: "The entire social output is the product of human labour. Under capitalist conditions, a part of this social output is appropriated by that group in the community which owns the means of production. This is not an ethical judgement, but a method of describing the really basic economic relation between social groups. It finds its most clearcut theoretical formulation in the theory of surplus value. As long as we retain value calculation, there can be no obscuring of the origin and nature of profits as a deduction from the product of total social labour" (8, 129).

[2] All this should be obvious. Nevertheless, I find it necessary to follow the custom and provide a quotation from Marx. To avoid any possible controversy, I choose to quote from his *last* theoretical writing, a critique of a book by A. Wagner. Marx leaves no doubts about his general theorizing and its relation to a possible political economy of socialism: "In the opinion of Mr. Wagner, the value theory of Marx constitutes a *'foundation stone of his socialist system'* ... As I have never built a *'socialist system'*, this is just an imagination of Wagner ... and *tutti quanti*" (9, 456). Later he is more specific in ridiculing the idea that his value theory is applicable to socialist society: "... all this reduces just to ... the presumption that in the 'socialist state of Marx' his value theory *has* validity (though) it was developed for *bourgeois* society ..." (9, 476). For a survey of other relevant passages of Marx and Engels see R. L. Meek, 10, 256—62.

ogeneous. Economists have tried to circumvent this difficulty by assuming that labour of higher quality, i.e. more productive labour, can be expressed as a multiple of the simple homogeneous labour. Next, natural resources are notoriously heterogeneous, and this has an obvious impact on the productivity of otherwise homogeneous labour. Therefore, it will be necessary to construct extensive maps of various productivities of labour resulting from the differences in natural resources in order to get the necessary data for the most efficient allocation of available labour force. Further, capital goods may be expressed as stored up labour with familiar difficulties of reducing past labour to something comparable with present labour. Finally, even with the summation of the homogeneous simple labour time one cannot arrive at the price, because the price is determined by the interaction of demand and supply, and the socially necessary labour[1] is established only on the market. The system is conceptually complete. But it is unsuitable for a *normative* theory of prices. Between the first link — labour time — and the last link — price — so many interacting processes take place that we cannot hope to derive price technically in an efficient way *directly* from labour time. Such an attempt would destroy its own purpose, the goal of economizing social labour. This goal, however, may well be achieved in an indirect way; we can simply reverse the direction of our calculation and start from the other end.

2. In any economy at any given time there are certain natural resources in existence and there is also a certain amount of stored up (capital) and living labour. This available quantity of labour has to be economized, i.e., it has to be used in the most productive way. Now, the most productive use is certainly the one which satisfies the needs of the community most fully. Here we get our starting point: the dictate of demand. In satisfying demand, labour will be applied to heterogeneous units of the factors of production, and therefore their heterogeneity has to be measured. *Varying* productivity of the *same*-quantity labour applied to natural resources (or generally: to non-reproducible factors) will be levelled out by rent. The relative productivity of living labour working with capital will be measured by interest. And the relative productivity of the living labour itself will be measured by wages and profits. Thus instead of pricing one single factor of production, we price four different classes, and within them each unit of factor separately. By means of this procedure we eventually achieve the necessary homogeneity: it suffices to compare the prices of individual units of factors of production to be able to choose the most efficient combination, and it suffices to add the prices of factors (per unit of output) to arrive at the price of the product.

3. The labour theory of value was first conceived as a price theory; prices were considered proportional to values of commodities exchanged

---

[1] Socially necessary in two senses: as input in technological sense, to produce certain output under average production conditions, and as the proportion of the total available labour time allocated to the particular line of production.

For an attempt to construct a theory of price along similar lines as described above see the recent book of I. Vrančić, *The Problem of the Law of Value in the Transitional Period* (11).

and their values were determined by the labour embodied in them. Marx brought a sociological element into this scheme by pointing out that the exchange value expresses the equality of two private labours of free individuals in the simple commodity production, and of two private capitals in a capitalist system. If the labour theory of value is to be applied in the socialist system, it can only mean either equality at the level of social economy — which amounts to a tautology — or economy in the use of the available labour resources of the community. The latter interpretation we may safely accept. To achieve this economy in the use of labour resources, it is necessary to have planning. And the calculation elements for planning are to be provided by a theory of *price*.

The outline of such a theory is attempted in the chapters which follow. There the categories like value (equals price times quantity), capital, profit, etc., are used, as much as this is possible, in a technical sense, i.e., without a direct sociological connotation. This is done not because I consider such an approach scientifically superior — in fact no economic category is free from sociological connotations — but because my task is much more modest than that of describing the fullness of economic relations in a socialist economy. It is primarily technical, that of designing an economic mechanism which will perform certain specified functions.

4. However, although the intention is to use the economic categories in a technical sense, it will become apparent that almost all categories I shall have to use will have different meanings from those devised for the analysis of a privately owned economy, and a considerable amount of redefining will be necessary. Thus an important terminological point arises: should one coin new terms to emphasize these differences in meaning? Economists in planned economies have in fact partly chosen this way. Terms like capital and profit have become so closely associated with the institutions of the capitalist economy that socialist economists as a rule use different terms to denote corresponding categories in the planned economy[1]. On the other hand, terms like rent and interest have

---

[1] Capital etymologically originates from Latin *caput*, head, adjective: *capitalis*, then *capital*, meaning livestock (presumably counted in "heads") and also property and wealth in general. In the former meaning the word has survived as *cattle* (Skeat's *Etymological Dictionary*). In the latter meaning the word has remained unchanged and has become an economic term.

As examples of terminological substitutes I quote Soviet and Yugoslav usage. Fixed and circulating capital is called *basic* and *circulating means* (Russian: *osnovnye i oborotnye sredstva;* Yugoslav: *osnovna i obrtna sredstva*). However, in this respect Soviet terminology is not quite consistent and so capital formation is called *capital construction (kapitaljnoe stroiteljstvo,* or *kapitaljnoe vloženie* for productive investment). Money capital is usually called *financial means*. Financial counterpart for real capital is known as *basic* and *circulating funds*.

Profit in Russian usage implies profiteering. In the economic analysis of either capitalist or socialist economics the domestic equivalent *pribylj* is used. In the Yugoslav terminology *profit* has also a strong connotation of an unearned income derived from exploitation and in the case of socialist political economy it is as a rule substituted by the term *dobit* (gain), a word of similar technical meaning but of an uncompromised Slavonic origin. In the same sense *wages* imply a definite social relation, that of hiring labour by the owner of productive means; therefore in the Yugoslav terminology this term is usually substituted by *personal income* (*lični dohodak*).

been accepted by socialist economists also. As there undoubtedly exists an aversion to the introduction of new technical terms, I chose to use terms which have become traditional in the Anglo-Saxon economic literature. But neither this choice is quite harmless and we have to be constantly on the guard not to carry over the old meaning with the old terms. As we proceed the differences in meaning will be carefully analyzed. In general, it might be helpful to make use of the Soviet economic parlance and think or speak in terms of *transformed* profit, capital, etc. This would emphasize the common technical origin of the categories used, attributing the differences in economic meaning to the differences in the institutional set-up of respective economies.

2. THE THEORY OF PRICE

(a) The Statement of the Problem and the Survey of the Main Contributions

1. Prices are instruments which register the preferences of economic agents. At the same time they also indicate the alternatives to be chosen in the present and future production of goods and services. As far as the latter, normative characteristic of prices is concerned, the economist is free to choose, among the innumerable conceivable price patterns, a price pattern which will best facilitate the achievement of a certain accepted social goal. Economists and non-economists seem pretty much in agreement that the satisfaction of human needs is the purpose of production. Hence prices should reflect individual and social valuations of the relative importance of economic goods and services in so far as they can satisfy human needs. At this stage the definition is left vague on purpose in order not to prejudge the subsequent enquiry.

2. It has been maintained for a long time that the best price system in the sense just defined is the one resulting in prices covering properly defined total costs of production. This principle will be referred to as the *full cost principle*. But then, with the development of welfare economics, the principle has been challenged and the following proposition has been put forward: Prices should be devised in such a way that no commodity is produced unless its importance is greater than that of the alternative sacrificed[1]. Now, as the costs of production are not homogeneous, the introduction of the new principle will affect

---

[1] It has also been proposed to abolish prices altogether and to apply measurement characteristic for natural sciences. Thus in the Soviet Union Preobraženskij argued that what a socialist economy needed was not market categories but a *social technology* (cf. 12, 155). Similarly in Britain L. Hogben suggested that market be replaced by a planned survey of human needs, because basic needs of humanity can be ascertained better by scientific study than by free choice. Thermodynamics, not social product accounting, should be used in evaluating alternatives: "When there is a science of *social technology* it will give us a balance sheet of human effort, materials and natural resources expressed in the established equivalence between the various physical units of heat, kinetic energy and potential energy" (13, 45). National wealth ("plenty") may be expressed as "the excess of free energy over the collective caloric debt of human effort applied to securing the needs which all human beings share" (p. 42).

different cost items differently. Normally the production of an additional unit of a commodity will require an increase in perfectly divisible and timeless variable costs, but will not affect the lumpy cost of durable fixed assets. Accordingly, the new principle, which we shall refer to as the *marginal cost principle*, requires that price is equated with marginal cost regardless of whether or not it covers total cost. And if a collection of commodities is produced such that the marginal units of all components are of equal "importance", then there is no conceivable better allocation of resources and the economy has achieved an optimum result. The marginal cost principle[1] appears to be theoretically superior to the former full cost principle.

3. The idea has had an obvious appeal to economists and since that principle has been discovered, an extensive literature has been written on it[2]. The marginal cost principle implies a radical reorganization of the economy and so it is natural to find that socialist economists have been first to take it up[3]. The first to discuss the matter was H. D. Dickinson in 1933 in an article on price formation in a socialist community (20). In a later book on socialist economics (21) Dickinson accepts the marginalist rule only with qualifications[4]. The subsequent discussion of socialist pricing was linked up with the refutation of von Mises's contention, advocated by von Hayek and others[5], that rational

---

[1] Note that here we are not concerned with the controversy whether the actual business behaviour of firms in privately owned economies is better described in marginal cost or in average cost terms. Cf. Hitch and Hall (14), Andrews (14), Wilson (15), Wiles (16; 17). Our problem lies in finding out the particular price-output control which, in a planned economy, *ought* to be applied. Besides, the empirical controversy centres on observability of the equation *marginal cost equals marginal revenue*, while for the purpose of the present discussion the marginal cost principle has been defined by the equation *marginal cost equals price*.

[2] See the bibliography of 106 items compiled by Beckwith (18).

[3] As A. Lerner put it emphatically: "Price must be equal to marginal cost. This is the contribution that pure economic theory has to make to the building of a socialist economy" (19, 270).

[4] Beckwith quotes a letter from Dickinson saying: "I still think (as I did when I wrote the *Economics of Socialism*) that price should be based on marginal or average cost, whichever is higher" (18, 78).

[5] Von Mises's thesis has provoked an extensive discussion, although his own reasoning was extremely shallow and could be reduced to the following chain of propositions (22): Economic prices are possible only where free market exists. Free market exists only where there is private ownership of means of production. In socialism there is no private ownership and therefore no free market and therefore no possibility for rational economic calculation! Having thus proved the impossibility of rational pricing, von Mises goes on to make a prophecy which deserves to be immortalized in the history of economic thought: "If the intellectual dominance of Socialism remains unshaken, then in a short time the whole co-operative system of culture which Europe has built up during thousands of years will be shattered. For a socialist order of society is unrealizable. All efforts to realize Socialism lead to the destruction of society. Factories, mines, and railways will come to a standstill, towns will be deserted. The population of the industrial territories will die out or migrate elsewhere. The farmer will return to the self-sufficiency of the closed, domestic economy. Without private ownership in the means of production there is, in the long run, no production other than a hand-to-mouth production for one's own needs" (22, 511). Essentially the same type of learned analysis, although less sensational, one finds in the recently translated book by the Norwegian economist Hoff (24).

economic calculation was impossible under socialism. Attacking this contention, Durbin also criticized the marginal cost proposition (1936) and later (1946) restated his criticism (26). At the same time Lange produced a devastating criticism of von Mises—von Hayek ideas in his celebrated essay "On the Economic Theory of Socialism". In the first version of the essay Lange used the average cost principle, but after a critical note by Lerner, he accepted the marginalist rule (27). Durbin's first article also provoked a reply by Lerner (19), who, a few years later, elaborated the marginal cost theory in his well known *Economics of Control* (28). After the war the theory received mathematical treatment by Krishnamurti (29) and an attempt was made to devise a realistic economic theory of socialism on marginalist principle in a book (written in fact before the war) by Beckwith (30). A brief history of the theory was produced by Bergson in 1948 (31), and another review by Dobb in 1953 (32).

4. In the meantime, other economists interested in welfare economics, in economics of public utilities and public enterprises, joined the discussion. The real impetus to the discussion was given by the article by Hotelling "The General Welfare in Relation to Problems of Taxation and Railway and Utility Rates" (33). What Hotelling suggested was in fact a more sophisticated version of the old Dupuit approach in an analysis of the implication of consumer and producer surpluses. The article appeared in 1938 and was followed by a number of sympathetic and critical reactions. Among the more important later contributions are those of R. H. Coase (in 1946) who was equally sceptical of both pricing principles taken separately and tied to marry them by proposing a multipart pricing[1] (34); A. M. Henderson (1947) who comes to the conclusion that there is "no unique right method of finance for public utilities" (35, 241); and of C. A. R. Crosland (in 1950) who tries to show that marginalist pricing is inapplicable in the nationalized industries and that in multi-plant industries the marginal unit of resources is frequently the entire new plant, hence it should be made the centre of analysis[2] (36). In 1950 Nancy Ruggles wrote the first

---

Among others of the anti-socialist guard, von Hayek was sensible enough not to accept von Mises's thesis as it stands, but modified it by emphasizing the impracticability of rational pricing in socialism (23). After the appearance of the books of Lange and Dickinson he retreated further to say that pricing in socialism is practicable, but is not so efficient as under capitalism. This mainly because "the rates at which commodities will be exchanged by the parties in the market will have to be decreed by the authority" (25, 129). The contention is, of course, arbitrary, and so the conclusion based on it is invalid. One should add, however, that although von Hayek, and similarly Robbins, were demonstrably wrong in attacking socialist economics for an immanent irrationality, they were often right in criticizing the shortcomings of the theories put forward by socialist economists. I shall occasionally make use of these criticisms.

[1] To demonstrate his principle, Coase designed an example of customers being located at various distances from a centrally located store so that all costs are directly assignable to specific customers who pay the store cost plus the cost of each delivery. Needless to say such a situation is far from being representative.

[2] In fact the idea was not new. As Wiles reminds us (17, 3) already in 1919 and 1920, respectively, Taussig (*Quarterly Journal of Economics*) and Birck (*The Theory of Marginal Value*, pp. 189—91) treated the average cost of the marginal firm as marginal cost of an industry.

history of the theory (37); it was related to the development of new welfare economics. An extensive history with a restatement of the theory written by Beckwith in 1955 (18) conveniently concludes this brief survey of more important contributions.

Parallel with the marginal cost discussion a discussion on the distribution of income was taking place among welfare economists. As any change in pricing leads to a redistribution of income, it was natural to ask what valid statements might be made concerning the effects of this redistribution on general economic welfare.

5. Finally, being interested in pricing in planned economy, we should take into account price theories developed in the Soviet Union, which until recently was the only country where normative pricing was of much more than academic interest. Surprisingly, no general price theory has been developed. The by now traditional *hozraščët* (economic calculus) is not a theory but a technical description of the existing practice and as such it does not provide a criterion on which to base efficient pricing. After the war an extensive discussion on the theory of price was initiated by S. G. Strumilin in 1946 (38)[1]. The discussion stated with the problem of evaluation of alternative investment projects and was later continued to include general problems of pricing. The main question debated was: how to distribute "accumulation" (the difference between price and cost of production) among individual commodities? Eventually, three solutions emerged. Those who, like Strumilin, advocated "value" approach tried to derive price from the amount of labour time expended and, as a technical solution, suggested that accumulation be spread proportionally to the wage bill. The other group advocated the "price of production" approach, and this in two variants: some were in favour of using costs of production as a basis for calculating the rate of accumulation, others denoted fixed and circulating capital as such a basis. In evaluating these three proposals we can rather quickly dispose of the first two. It was shown in the preceding chapter that building up prices from the labour time, though conceptually possible, is not technically feasible. Mechanical spreading of accumulation in the proportion of wages — is manifestly arbitrary. The second solution advanced is also arbitrary, because it neglects rent, and even if it did not, it would still be arbitrary because it neglects differences in the capital turnover periods. The third solution — the traditional market solution needs further examination, and we shall not be able to pass judgement on its rationality before we reach the last chapter.

Another country with instructive pricing practices is Yugoslavia. However, here the discussion on pricing in the conditions of planning has only started (12; 40) and no distinct price theory has emerged so far.

---

[1] Since 1948 the main contributions have been published in *Voprosy Ekonomiki*. In English the discussion has been closely followed in the *Soviet Studies*. See also Kondrašev, 39.

(b) The Theory of the Optimum Allocation of Resources

1. If instead of analyzing the vast and conspicuous structure of details and refinements, created by the voluminous literature on the marginal cost principle and on welfare economics, we proceed straightforwardly to examine the fundamentals of these theories, we shall find that they are composed of a relatively simple set of propositions. One may conveniently start with a definition of optimum conditions. A variety of definitions have been suggested. Perhaps the simplest and the most useful approach to the problem will consist in defining the basic two optimum conditions in the following way (cf. Dobb, 41, 9):

(1) *The marginal rates of substitution for every pair of consumer goods are equal for all consumers and equal to the price ratios of these goods.* If this condition were not satisfied, an exchange of goods might bring about a preferable distribution of them.

Having defined the production program by (1), we have to state the condition for the optimum combination of factors of production which are to help carry this program out.

(2) *Factors of production (resources) are combined in such a way that their marginal value productivities* (marginal physical product times price) *are equal in all uses.* Otherwise a shift in factors might produce an increase in total product.

The conditions will be fulfilled if the following two technical rules are obeyed:

(1) *The price is set so that demand is equalized with supply.* This rule assures that more important needs (in money terms) will be satisfied first.

(2) *The production of every commodity is then pushed to the point where the marginal cost* (the marginal quantity of factor for the last unit of product times the price of the factor) *is equal to the price of the product.*

The two rules have been formulated so as to show that the marginal cost principle is primarily a principle of fixing output, not price; the phrase "marginal cost pricing" should therefore be understood in this sense (cf. Fleming, 42, 1—2, and Dobb, 41, 4).

2. The conditions just described were not left unchallenged. First of all, the decreasing cost industries will operate at a loss and the increasing cost industries at profit, but these profits and losses do not necessarily cancel. It has, therefore, been suggested, that in order to make provisions, price should be proportional and not equal to marginal cost. In this case, it has been said, the proper balance between work and leisure would be destroyed because the reward for an additional unit of work (the utility of additional income) would be different from the real cost of labour (the marginal disutility of work). In addition, there would be a pyramiding effect of cost (18, 89) because commodities are not consumed immediately after they have been priced for the first time and so they may be repriced several times (raw material, various stages of semi-finished goods) before they reach the consumer. To avoid these difficulties, various sorts of taxes have been proposed (on income, on inheritance, on rent, poll taxes), but no solution has as yet been uni-

versally accepted as satisfactory. Price discrimination has been found impracticable, and even if not so, it would not help[1].

Further, each change in pricing changes distribution of income, consequently, the change has to be evaluated in terms of general welfare. Even if there were no changes, one would have to ask what is the optimum distribution of income. The discussion started with the assumption of the so called Pareto optimum, which is defined as a situation in which it is impossible to increase the welfare of any individual (or household) without reducing that of the others. Naturally, this was a too restrictive condition; it petrified the existing income distribution which in the society in question was evidently bad. In search for an absolute optimum, Kaldor (43) and Hicks (44) suggested two compensation tests: Kaldor that the change will increase general welfare if potential gainers can compensate potential losers and still remain better off; Hicks that the same will be true if losers cannot bribe gainers into rejecting the change. Before long Scitovszky pointed out that, in order to arrive at correct result, both criteria have to be applied at the same time (45). In other words, the same criterion, when applied *after* the change, i.e. on the basis of the new distribution of income, must again show that the second situation is preferable. Even with this improvement, the proposition was soon criticized for its implicit introduction of the old Marshall-Pigou assumption of the equal marginal utility of income for everybody. Marginal utility of income not being equal, compensation must be paid to enable the economist say anything about the change in welfare.

Thus, after a quarter-of-a-century of theorizing, economists have arrived at a somewhat pessimistic conclusion that there is no possibility to build up an internally consistent theory on this assumption. As a matter of fact, the same conclusion might have been reached at the very beginning of the discussion. In an interdependent system, based on one axiomatic principle, all corrective devices are necessarily arbitrary. If production has to follow a rule and if its natural substratum has a definite structure (e. g., asymmetry in the cost-increasing and cost-decreasing industries), it is only by chance that these two facts can be made consistent with each other. If economists cannot make interpersonal comparisons of utility, while at the same time every change in pricing results in a redistribution of income, they will also be unable to say anything about the optimum price system.[2]

3. Having got so far, we may safely conclude that in this case, inconsistency objections are trivial and irrelevant for a sound economic

---

[1] Suppose certain commodities are found suitable for the application of price discrimination. In this case, the individuals consuming relatively more of these commodities will find the part of their income available for expenditure on other, "free market" commodities, reduced. Consequently, their economic welfare as compared to that of other individuals, will be lower. The changes in the absolute amount of money income also imply a rearrangement of consumption choices; as a result the total consumption pattern will change in an arbitrary manner.

[2] It may appear that the existence of the so-called Pareto-optimum contradicts the conclusion in the text. But the contradiction is specious because Pareto-optimum is a misnomer. It is not an optimum at all, there are as many such "optima" as there are income distributions.

theory.[1] If strict marginal cost pricing is impossible, the best approximation may be made, in the way as say Lerner[2] attempted it, or possibly in some other way. The real test for theoretical validity of marginal cost pricing does not lie in its logical perfection but in its applicability to the phenomena of the real world.

(c) The Applicability of Marginal-Cost-Equals-Price Principle

1. If the marginal cost principle is to be tested for its applicability, it will be necessary to attempt an operational definition of marginal cost. Here we encounter the surprising fact that the most competent writers in the field, rarely ask themselves the obvious question: what in fact is "marginal cost"? The concept has been defined as a logical category the definition being: marginal cost is an increment in total cost, due to the production of an additional unit of output, or, in a more refined form, marginal cost is equal to the value of additional factor or factors (additional quantities of factors times their prices) used to increase output by one unit. Apart from Beckwith, hardly anybody attempted to define the concept as an accounting category.

Among the three writers of more extensive studies on marginal cost as a normative guide, Lerner is quite obscure about what sort of marginal cost he has in mind (28, pp. 187, 197, 214), while Krishnamurti (29, pp. 73, 83, 89, 131) and Beckwith (30, p. 13 and passim) have arrived at the conclusion that the marginal cost principle alone is insufficient as a criterion for the economic allocation of resources in all circumstances. They have therefore suggested a double criterion: the marginal cost principle for cases with divisible inputs where marginal analysis is applicable and another one for cases with indivisible inputs. The latter, called total analysis by Beckwith, and the Dupuit-Hotelling principle by Krishnamurti, rest on the familiar Marshall-Pigou analysis of surpluses represented by the area between supply and demand curves, these surpluses being now called total net social benefit. It is said that a new plant will be installed if the cost of fixed assets is less than the social net benefit. The double criterion leads to a number of logical difficulties,

---

[1] On this point the following dialogue may be constructed. Beckwith, irritated by Mrs. Ruggles's theoretical nihilism (37), writes: "Like other new welfare economists, Mrs. Ruggles seems unaware that in the real world one must choose among price-output policies and that a critique which invalidates all of them is useless" (18, 162). In defence of the profession, I imagine, E. J. Mishan would reply that the attitude adopted should be considered "as an attempt to construct a logical scaffolding as free as possible from value judgements, but so fashioned that it can accommodate itself to various systems of values" (47, 446). Both appear to be right.

[2] Lerner tried to improve the old Pigovian proposition that the equalization of incomes maximizes social welfare by saying that it leads to a maximum of *probable* total satisfactions, assuming, of course, that we are not solipsists and that therefore it is meaningful to say that the satisfaction one person gets is greater or smaller than the satisfaction enjoyed by another person (28, 25—32). However, M. Friedman rightly objects that one of the crucial assumptions used — the assumption that the total amount of income is unrelated to its distribution — is invalid and so must be the conclusion (48, 308—9). See Ch. 6 -d-6.

well known from the analysis of consumer's surplus, and to certain economic difficulties. Our interest will be centred on the latter.

2. Beckwith defines marginal costs as variable current costs and equates them with the prices of products. Production should be carried to the point where this equality is achieved. The procedure takes into account the difference between marginal product and marginal revenue, and its importance depends on whether this difference is significant or not. This difference appears in monopolistic situations (falling demand curve) and may be considerable in uncontrolled economies. However, a planned economy is equipped to cope with the monopoly. For instance, by means of imports or exports, prices can be manipulated so as to induce firms to operate at full capacity. In this case, the difference between marginal product (value of the last unit of output) and marginal revenue (the addition to total revenue resulting from the sale of the last unit of output) disappears. However, the question of the *right* kind and size of the capacity is left open.

But suppose we use marginalist pricing. Empirical investigations appear to show that a major portion of a marginal cost curve is horizontal. If the equalization rule is proclaimed compulsory it might lead to serious consequences. Even in the best planned economy there will always be small fluctuations in demand relative to supply. Thus, whenever demand contracts relatively, some firms (with higher variable costs) will cease to produce altogether, while other firms will continue to produce almost at capacity. For a variety of rather obvious reasons all firms will try to avoid recurrent stoppings of production and, consequently, they will try to minimize their variable costs. By doing so they will tend to overcapitalize the factor input which will lead to a considerable economic waste.[1]

According to the variations of demand-supply relations, the industries or firms will have to be classified not into decreasing-cost and increasing-cost industries, but into those that work at capacity and cover (or almost cover) average cost[2] and those which do not do so.

3. Passing to the second criterion — the principle of net social benefit — we may first note that it is not entirely consistent with the first one. Situations may appear where price has already become higher than marginal cost, but the potential net social benefit does not warrant the expansion of the productive capacity. In such a case the marginal cost principle will be violated in order to comply with the superior net benefit principle. Of course, formally, the equality of marginal cost and price is preserved by calculating the risk of the breakdown as a cost

---

[1] The following example may in sense be interpreted as a practical illustration of this possibility. After the war, in Yugoslavia there was a great shortage of raw material and labour, while (once installed) fixed capital, due to inflation and accounting rules, was treated almost as a free good. As a result, the firms have found innumerable ways to acquire additional equipment, while there was no inducement to get rid of unnecessary equipment. The great waste in fixed capital became apparent when, after 1951, the economic system was radically changed.

[2] Wiles's (16) "marginal cost (partial adaptation)", i. e., marginal cost which includes the ultimate disadvantages of overworking the machinery, seems to describe fairly well the actual process. In the vicinity of "full capacity", the marginal cost curve steeply rises, cuts the average cost curve and, with increasing production, continues to rise.

item. But who is to determine objectively the magnitude of this cost item?

Next, once we leave marginalist analysis, we are in the world of the Walrasian general equilibrium. It is impossible to draw the demand and supply curves for one commodity — in order to find net benefit — without taking into account what is happening in the rest of the system. However, the most important question is again the question of application: in which way is social net benefit to be measured? We may attempt an estimate of demand and supply curves — after all, the application of full cost principle requires a similar estimate — but there is no possibility to check the *correctness of the estimate against the facts*. There is, consequently, no possibility to correct mistakes while the plant is in operation. No fixed investment is absolutely fixed. Small changes, adaptations and additions to capacity are constantly being made, so that, if the full cost principle is applied, possible initial mistakes may largely be corrected. Finally, if the estimates are not open to check, there is no possibility of improving the estimating procedures. All this seriously reduces economic superiority of marginalist pricing over full cost pricing.[1]

Consequently the first part of the double criterion has turned out to be almost unnecessary and the second part operationally unsatisfactory. Is it possible to save the principle by redefining the basic concept, marginal cost?

4. Some economists will disagree with Beckwith's definition of marginal cost and will be prepared to follow Wiles (17, 12 and 49) and among relevant cost include not only current variable cost, but also some other items and notably user cost (wear and tear of equipment and buildings due to production). Thus the gap between marginal and average cost would be filled up to a considerable extent, and so the malallocation of resources, resulting from the full cost rule, would not appear so great after all. However, this procedure would liquidate the smallest chance of defining marginal cost as an accounting category, i.e., something capable of *objective* measurement. Besides, Beckwith would argue that by accepting this view we have in fact accepted the concept of long-run marginal cost, and that this concept is logically contradictory. If the capacity of a plant is not fully utilized, its marginal cost reduces to its current variable cost. If capacity is fully utilized, and the question of building a new plant arises, the lumpiness of the cost prevents the application of the marginalist rule. In the first case — timeless costs — the marginalist principle is to be used. In the second case, — costs with time dimension — the principle of net social benefit applies. These two principles logically exhaust all possibilities. If on the basis of the second criterion the plant is found worth building, we cannot include user cost in the marginal cost as well because this would involve double counting.

---

[1] But it is still possible to say with W. Vickrey: "Either we accept marginal cost pricing, with attendant subsidies and necessity for making an over-all decision as to whether to undertake a given service, without any positive check (even retrospectively) on whether the decision was right or wrong; or we accept a more or less substantial misallocation of resources" (49, 225).

The problem may also be approached in another way by using a single criterion instead of two. In the long run, all, or nearly all, costs are divisible. Thus marginal cost is represented by that increment in total cost which is necessary to produce the last addition to output (e.g., the increment in cost of a 101 ton oil refinery over total cost of a refinery with the hourly input of 100 tons of crude oil), and this marginal cost has to be equated with price.[1] With such a pricing rule possible mistakes are smaller, but it does not lead to an ideal output as defined above. However, the decisive argument lies again elsewhere.

5. It lies in, what one might call, the sociological aspect of the marginalist principle. The problem is not so simple as Lerner has put it,[2] and it has been too frequently implicitly assumed that the behaviour of economic subjects remains unaffected by changes in economic organization. In what way is the economic success or failure of an enterprise (i.e., of its management or of its entire working kolektiv) to be assessed? Beckwith suggested that the degree of success should be measured by the sum of deviations of marginal costs from prices (30, ch. VIII; 18, 128). Other writers are mysteriously silent on this point. Beckwith's suggestion presupposes that variable costs are (a) identifiable with a practical degree of precision, (b) that the price-output mechanism works smoothly, and (c) that costs are technologically determined. But neither assumption is warranted. A large item of costs is represented by semifixed non-depreciation overhead costs. There usually exist many ways of distributing these costs among specific products; thus, there are always many possibilities of adjusting marginal costs to prices. As to (b), it is certainly dangerous to confuse an economy with a machine. The machine works according to a prescribed and relatively stable pattern, the economy has to be continually adjusted. This means that there will be continual changes in output programs in order to meet continually

---

[1] It seems that this was the line of argument suggested by Schumpeter. He requires that *all* costs, and not only prime costs, be reckoned when calculating marginal costs and says that marginal cost rule "should prevail over the rule of equating prices to total cost per unit whenever it conflicts with it". But then he becomes quite obscure by proclaiming the need for "equating prices to total cost per unit of product as long as things develop according to plans" and by concluding that it is "never part of that logic (rational choice) to operate an industry at a deficit" (50, 176). If marginal cost of 101 ton refinery is equated with the price, the refinery will operate at a loss. The loss may be avoided only in one of the following two cases: (a) refinery faces a large export market and therefore behaves as under conditions of perfect competition (price of the product stable), while the marginal cost curve of its inputs will eventually cross the demand curve from below; (b) refinery considers the price of the inputs and the price of the products to be stable, but capturing a larger share of market leads to an increase in total costs (transport cost, discount and various facilities to consumers), the additional distribution cost will turn upwards marginal cost curve. If in either case the lowest point of the average cost curve happens to coincide with the price, both requirements are happily fulfilled. If average cost curve cuts demand curve, profits will arise. If it is above demand curve, loss is inescapable; only by applying the rule *current marginal cost equals price* loss will be made greater.

[2] "Anyone brought up in a capitalistic society feels 'instinctively' that something is wrong when outlay exceeds income... All that can be said here is that this feeling is nothing but an illogical... transference from the capitalist economy, where it is in perfect order, to the controlled economy, where it is simply irrelevant" (28, 199).

changing demand pattern *directly,* and not *via* marginal cost-price equalization. As to the (c), the equality of marginal cost with price does not necessarily imply that cost is the lowest possible. A glance at the conditions of ideal output will suffice to make it clear that in such an economy no force is working in the direction of lowering all costs or towards an overall increase in output. The whole conceptual scheme depicts a curious — though historically understandable world in which distribution, and not production, is what is needed for an increase in economic welfare. In order to cure this deficiency to a certain extent, we could compare the cost patterns of several enterprises, as it was suggested by Meade and others (cf. 18, 128). But this involves troublesome and endless administrative interventions, with all the dubious effects on efficiency following. On the other hand, the social net benefit criterion in investment, implies an administrative intervention in every act of investment. It is hard to believe that, in this way, all the investment opportunities will be utilized as soon as they arise and in the manner they deserve, let alone that the usual bureaucratic lags and the pressure of political and other vested interests would not interfere.

One is, therefore, justified in concluding that, regarding the economic organization, the application of the marginal cost principle would be far from neutral. Inducement to substitute cost accounting manipulations for real improvement in efficiency, impossibility of checking the efficacy of investment decisions, administrative interventions in assessing the economic success or failure and obligatory administrative interventions in every act of fixed investment — all this spells arbitrariness and bureaucratization. The *productive* efficiency of an economic system varies in an inverse proportion with the degree of arbitrariness and bureaucratization it involves.

Accordingly, our final conclusion is definitely negative: the marginal cost principle is not desirable as a general pricing principle in planned economy. This does not mean that it is inapplicable in every single instance. For some specified cases, and in some special instances, it may provide a useful pricing or costing guide either in its pure form (e.g., toll-free bridges) or combined with the full cost principle as in two-part (51) and multi-part (34) pricing and price discrimination. But the examination of these cases, as well as of all concrete pricing procedures, lies outside the scope of the present study.

6. We are, therefore, left with the choice of the second alternative, i.e., with the full cost principle. The analysis has shown that it is logically an imperfect principle but that, when applied, it is likely to lead to a better approximation to ideal output than the rival principle. This contention is based on the findings that, in the short run, the full cost principle leads to approximately the same results as the marginal cost principle: with regard to investment it is open to check and so immensely less arbitrary, and with respect to overall efficiency[1] of the eco-

---

[1] The term "efficiency", as used in this study, refers to growth, and as such has a dynamic connotation. Consequently and contrary to the common usage, it is inapplicable to the problem of resource allocation taken in isolation, i.e., when other effects of the change are neglected. An "efficient" allocation in terms of welfare economics may prove to be very inefficient indeed.

nomic organization it is superior. Even if *given* resources were better allocated on the marginal cost principle, the full cost principle would still be preferable. For, when the *efficiency of allocation* — which is a static principle — *is compared with the efficiency of production* — which, in the sense of the growing social product, is a dynamic principle — *the latter is preferable, for it ultimately leads to better satisfaction of human needs*[1].

This conclusion needs a small elaboration in order to make its implications perfectly clear. It is generally valid only if the community is assumed to have no time preference. The growth curve of the full cost economy is steeper than that of the marginal cost economy; therefore, starting from a certain point of time, economic welfare provided by the former will become greater, and from then on the difference in welfare between the two economies will be continuously increasing. *A priori* we only know that there is such a point of time. If now we allow for time preferences, we must also know something about the length of the intervening period. On this point we can organize our thinking in the following way.

Consider two economies which are in every respect equal; both operate at full capacity and both have been using full cost pricing. We shall also assume that output is uniquely determined by the existing output capacity, which means that there can be no change in the current product mix. Full cost pricing will be retained by economy A, while economy B will introduce and use marginal cost pricing. The transition cannot be carried out instantaneously because of the existing structure of economy B. For the same reason, the bulk of the current investment is already earmarked and only a small portion of investment can be used for correction of the existing economic structure in accordance with the marginalist principle. This part of investment is by definition more productive than the same amount of investment in economy A. But in A people work more efficiently, because, as we have seen, they possess objective criteria of success and failure, they are free from bureaucratic interventions and they are motivated to increase production and not to manipulate book-keeping. Assume continuous and uniform changes. If the advantage of B over A is greater than that of A over B, the first year social product (after the change) of B will be greater than that of A. If this happens, the social product of B will also be greater in all future years, because the share of "more productive" investment in B can only increase until the total investment quota is exhausted. As this result contradicts our earlier conclusions, the advantage of B's marginalist investment in the first year must be less than the advantage of A's full cost economic system. The procedure yields the same results when applied to all subsequent years. The efficiency theo-

---

[1] Cf. an ingeniously simply formulated similar dilemma of allocation versus growth in a different context by P. Wiles: "... in the Soviet economy there are, as it were, always too few hair brushes and too many nail brushes in view of the resources available, while in a 'capitalist' economy this proportion is always more nearly right. But the production of both these articles is growing at about 10% per annum in the U.S.S.R. and about 2% per annum in 'capitalist' countries. In the end the Soviet citizen will be supplied better even with hair brushes" (52, 251).

rem may now be formulated in perfectly general terms· If the choice is to be made between the relative efficiency of production and the relative efficiency of allocation, the former is preferable. Under certain simplifying assumptions, welfare gains of more efficient production appear not only ultimately greater, they are greater all the time. If the assumptions are relaxed, this or, for that matter, any other conclusion cannot be derived on a priori grounds and it becomes a matter of fact. But the nature of restrictive assumptions is such that, from all we know about the actual economic process, we have every ground to believe that the effect of relaxing the assumptions is negligible. It follows that the institution of full cost pricing is economically more efficient than that of marginal cost pricing even if time preference is taken into account.

(d) Full Cost Pricing

1. Although marginal cost pricing has been found inapplicable to the real world, the whole discussion of this logically superior scheme is far from being useless once it is put in its proper setting. "The 'welfare' conditions — says Wiles with some justification — are not a categorical imperative, but an important desideratum of the second rank. If they conflict with technical progress or sound administration they must be abandoned or only partially satisfied" (17, 289). Once established, this scheme may serve as a sort of standard with which the over-all more efficient — but less efficient with respect to the problem of allocation taken in isolation — full cost scheme can be compared in order to determine differences and, perhaps, to assess the magnitude of deviations. In that sense there may be some truth in Wiles's dictum that "it is not laughable to maintain that these equations (Lerner's welfare equations) are, taken normatively, perfectly realistic and a suitable guide to policy. They are an enormous intellectual achievement of which economics has every reason to be proud" (17, 277).

Now, similarly as for an *ideal optimum* of allocation of resources in section (b), a set of conditions and rules may be laid down for an *attainable optimum* based on full cost pricing.

(1) The first condition is again the same and reads as follows: *The marginal rate of substitution for every pair of consumer goods is equal for all consumers and is equal to the price ratio of the goods*. The presumption is that in a reasonably well organized market with consumers exercising their choices the condition is likely to be fulfilled and the available consumer goods will satisfy the needs of the community most fully.

(2) The second condition, the one concerning the combination of factors of production (resources), is now less restrictive and, consequently, no more self-sufficient. It reads: *The value of marginal product per unit of outlay must be equal for all factors employed by the firm, and every firm should endeavour to minimize the total input of factors (total cost)*. The second part of the condition ensures that, out of many possible combinations of input, output being given, the firm will choose the combination which minimizes cost. This optimum choice will not

be made automatically, it requires an appropriate institutional system which will generate such an effort to use the best possible combination of factors. The merit of the presentation of the second optimum condition in the manner done here consists in this explicit emphasis on the dynamic factor of the economic process. The first part of the condition is concerned with optimum allocation of factors from the point of view of an individual firm which is not necessarily the same as the optimum allocation from the point of view of the economy as a whole. In other words, marginal value productivities of factors are now *not* equal in all their uses and, compared with the ideal output, there will be a certain amount of economic waste. The amount of this "waste" is determined by the relation between the program in (1) and the execution in (2), which is now not given implicitly by (2) as earlier. The relation is now determined by the institutional set-up expressed in two additional rules about the technical fulfilment of the optimum conditions. These rules are:

(1) The first rule remains the same and says that *the price should be set so as to equalize demand with supply.*

(2) The second rule expresses the whole difference: *The production of every commodity has to be pushed to the point where it entails maximum profit,* profit being defined as difference between the price and the rewards to factors other than entrepreneurship. Thus the formula *marginal cost equals price* has been transformed into the formula *marginal cost equals marginal revenue.* The profit maximization rule ensures that the condition (2) be fulfilled and that, in a competitive economy, price tends to be equal to full cost of the unit of product.

A few more words about marginalist formulation of full cost principle of pricing will appear necessary. It goes without saying that the formula does not pretend at describing of the behaviour of the firms in the real world. In this respect the recent anti-marginalist rebellion (14; 15; 16; 17) has also some relevance to the theory of the firm in planned economy. This, however, is a matter of empirical studies and generalization of the actual behaviour of firms in an already established economic system, and as such not my immediate concern. For the present purpose we only assume that the firm, when evaluating various production possibilities open to it, chooses that production program which maximizes the difference between the revenue and the cost, both defined from the point of view of the firm. The marginalist formulation of the rule is just a neat mathematical description of this assumption. Marginal cost is primarily an *ex ante* concept. It becomes *ex post*, and thus objectively measurable, if the anticipation of the firm proves to be correct. If the firm makes a mistake in its anticipations, this will have a negative effect on profit. Profit will be reduced either below the anticipated level or below the level which might have been attained. Provided that the institutional set-up ensures an identity of interests of the firm and the community, profit becomes a device for a continual correcting of productive choices in the direction of achieving maximum economic efficiency. And this is all we need.

2. If the two rules are obeyed, the working of the price-output mechanism is theoretically fairly simple. At any given time on the market

consumers find a certain amount of consumer goods valued at certain prices. Taking prices as given (Lange's "parametric function of prices", 27, 70), they exercise their free choices within the restraints of their income and their scales of preferences. This suffices to determine the price system, because "consumers in evaluating ('demanding') consumers' goods *ipso facto* also evaluate the means of production which enter into the production of those goods" (50, 175). Following the profit maximization rule, consumer goods industries combine their input in the most economic way and so transmit consumers' choices to producer goods industries; the latter transmit them further to each other and back to consumer goods industries. In this way, the total price-output structure of the economy is being continually determined. In these adjustments rule (1) acts as an equilibrating force. Prices are varied in an inverse proportion to the movements of stocks, which indicate the supply-demand situation. Continual demand-supply equalization may be conducted by pure market forces or by a deliberate action of a central planning body or by both. The last solution is clearly preferable because it excludes the possibility of exploding cobwebs (inherent in the first solution) and may always be adjusted in such a way as to have the most stabilizing effect. In planned economy, much of the market play will be anticipated by the firm because the firm (a) will have access to the best available information about the future trends of demand, (b) will be informed about the plans of other firms, and (c) will be informed about Planning Board's activity and intentions. If the price-output mechanism still refuses to work properly, the Planning Authority may intervene directly by using market instruments (e.g., buying or selling reserve stocks) or instruments of physical control (e.g., rationing).

3. However, all this is a grossly oversimplified picture of the real economic process and already at this stage of discussion some further comments are in order.

(1) First of all, prices of consumer goods reflect only approximately the objective relative importance of consumers' wants, i.e., of their true needs. Consumers' choices are often irrational, shaped by habit, custom and lack of knowledge. Use of narcotic drugs and liquors, conspicuous consumption and purchasing foods of little nutritive value in proportion to the money paid out by the housewives of the poor, are examples frequently quoted (53, 55). The phrase "consumers exercise free choice" used above should also be interpreted in a broad sense since there is no possibility for consumers to be absolutely sovereign. As Dobb points out: "... the consumer and his wants are a social product, moulded both by the commodities which enter into his experience and by the social standards and customs among which he has been reared. Thus, in shaping the course of development economic policy inevitably shapes the changing pattern of consumers' wants ..." (32, 79).

(2) Next, prices are *money* indices of alternatives. As all valuations cannot possibly be expressed in money, occasionally considerable differences arise between real social cost and money cost and between real social benefit and price. Air pollution, professional diseases and

destruction of aesthetic values may appear on the cost side. Whereas, enjoyment of economic and social equality, security from disease and employment security (26, 130) will appear on the benefit side.

It follows that *individual valuations* are an insufficient basis for a price system in a planned economy and that market prices alone are an insufficient instrument for guiding production. Both have to be supplemented by *social valuations* resulting either in a new set of market prices directly or in administrative interventions in the production process. The examination of how social valuations are arrived at falls outside the field of economics. For the purpose of this study it will be considered (a) that the need for social valuations arises when the choices to be made would lead to a diminution of the potential welfare of the community if they were made on a strictly individualist basis, (b) that social valuations somehow reflect the preference scale of the community and (c) representing the preferences of more than one individual, consumer communal preferences are superior to isolated individual preferences. Prohibition of liquors, subsidies for publishing books, compulsory education and free health services, all of these are instances where social valuations have been imposed upon individual valuations.

In this connection it would seem necessary to call the attention to a dangerously misleading practice, common to many economists, of treating all non-individualist choices as *arbitrary*, the implication being that economic theory (and policy) ought to be based on individual choices exclusively[1]. This conception implicitly attributes a quality of absoluteness to the choices of the individual, while they are doubly relative: they are socially shaped and their fulfilment depends on the interaction with all other individual choices in the system; in other words, it is socially determined (e.g., slump as a result of such an undesirable interaction of individual choices). Thus, if social valuations were arbitrary, individual valuations would be even more so. As a result, it would be impossible to rationalize the conduct of the economic affairs of mankind. This simple common-sense conclusion has been so generally ignored that I cannot emphasize too strongly the importance its implications have for economic theorizing.

(3) The third comment refers to cases where prices are in principle applicable, but production does not react so that price-output mechanism breaks down, or, simply, that uncontrolled price system leads to uneconomic production solutions. In all such cases, adjustment has to be brought about directly by the Planning Authority. The examples to be mentioned are the case of external economies and diseconomies which the profit maximizing firm does not take into account; new industrial locations; establishment of a monopoly; great or sudden

---

[1] This is the basic assumption of new welfare economics. It underlies the type of reasoning illustrated earlier by quotations from L. Robbins, von Mises and others. The assumption seems to be one instance of *rationalizing* institutions of an individualist society. Rationalization in this context means the "habit of our minds that ... consists in comforting ourselves and impressing others by drawing a picture of ourselves, our motives, our friends, our enemies, our vocation, our church, our country, which may have more to do with what we like them to be than with what they are" (Schumpeter, 2, 35).

economic changes like acute shortage of certain commodities, or the state of war, when the supply does not react even to enormously increased prices.

(4) Finally, there remain two vitally important decisions which ought to be made in every economy and which in a planned economy cannot be left to a free play of market forces. Every price system will also produce *a certain* distribution of income among the members of the community and *a certain* division of the social product as between the investment and consumption part. However, in planned economy the *optimum* is required in both cases. So far, the distribution of income and division of social product have been considered arbitrary. One of the purposes of this study is to attempt an economic determination of both optima.

4. Concluding the discussion of this chapter, we may note that a definition of planning has been gradually emerging. In a non-planned free market economy — which, however, in a pure text-book form has never existed — production and distribution, including human relations in production, are determined automatically by haphazard market forces, i.e., by a more or less uncontrolled price mechanism. In other words, the "Market" is the Planning Authority. Now, if the market is left to operate as an automatic choice-mechanism, but at the same time its choices are constantly being corrected in the four respects described above, the economy will be transformed into a planned economy. Planning means perfection of market choices in order to increase the economic welfare of the community. Consequently — this will appear to be the only economically meaningful criterion of efficiency — an ideal planning will lead to a maximum *rate of growth* of economic welfare.

References:

1. R. L. Meek, "Is Economics Biased?", *Scottish Journal of Political Economy*, 1957, 1—17.
2. J. A. Schumpeter, *History of Economic Analysis*, New York, Oxford University Press, 1955.
3. M. D. Little, *A Critique of Welfare Economics*, Oxford, Clarendon Press, 1950.
4. G. Cassel, *The Theory of Social Economy*, Vol. I, London, Fisher Unwin, 1923.
5. G. J. Stigler, "Ricardo and the 93% Labour Theory of Value", *American Economic Review*, 1958, 357—67.
6. H. D. Dickinson, *Institutional Revenue*, London, Williams and Norgate, 1932.
7. A. Bajt, *Marxov zakon vrijednosti* (The Marxian Law of Value), English summary, Ljubljana, Ekonomska fakulteta, 1953.
8. P. M. Sweezy, *The Theory of Capitalist Development*, London, Dobson, 1946.
9. K. Marx, "Zamečanija na knigu Adoljfa Vagnera" (Remarks on the Book of Adolf Wagner), *Sočinenija*, Tom XV, Moskva, Partizdat, 1935.
10. R. L. Meek, *Studies in the Labour Theory of Value*, London, Lawrence and Wishart, 1956.
11. I. Vrančić, "Problem zakona vrijednosti u prelaznom periodu" (The Problem of the Law of Value in the Transitional Period), *Ekonomski pregled*, Zagreb, 1956.
12. F. Černe, "Alokacija proizvodnih faktora u narodnoj privredi" (The Allocation of the Factors of Production in the National Economy), *Ekonomski pregled*, Zagreb, 1956, 145—75.

13. L. Hogben (ed.), *Political Arithmetic*, London, Allen and Unwin, 1938.
14. T. Wilson, P. W. S. Andrews (ed), *Oxford Studies in the Price Mechanism*, Oxford, Clarendon Press, 1951.
15. T. Wilson, "The Inadequacy of the Theory of the Firm as a Branch of Welfare Economics", *Oxford Economic Papers*, 1952, 18—44.
16. P. Wiles, "Empirical Research and the Marginal Analysis", *Economic Journal*, 1950, 515—30.
17. P. Wiles, *Price, Cost and Output*, Oxford, Basil Blackwell, 1956.
18. B. P. Beckwith, *Marginal-Cost Price-Output Control. A Critical History and Restatement of the Theory*, New York, Columbia University Press, 1955.
19. A. P. Lerner, "Statics and Dynamics in Socialist Economics", *Economic Journal*, 1937, 255—70.
20. H. D. Dickinson, "Price Formation in a Socialist Community", *Economic Journal*, 1935, 237—50.
21. H. D. Dickinson, *Economics of Socialism*, London, Oxford University Press, 1939.
22. L. von Mises, *Socialism*, London, J. Cape, 1936; originally published in German in 1922.
23. F. A. von Hayek (ed.), *Collectivist Economic Planning*, London, Routledge, 1935; the book contains two essays of von Hayek and translations of articles of N. G. Pierson, L. von Mises, G. Halm and E. Barone.
24. T. J. B. Hoff, *Economic Calculation in the Socialist Society*, London, W. Hodge, 1949; translated from the Norwegian edition of 1938.
25. F. A. von Hayek, "Socialist Calculation: The Competitive 'Solution' ", *Economica*, 1940, 125—49.
26. E. F. Durbin, "Economic Calculus in a Planned Economy" (1936), "The Problems of the Socialized Sector" (1946); both papers are reprinted in *Problems of Economic Planning*, London, Routledge, 1949.
27. E. B. Lippincott, F. M. Taylor and O. Lange, *On the Economic Theory of Socialism*, Minneapolis, University of Minnesota Press, 1938.
28. A. P. Lerner, *The Economics of Control*, New York, Macmillan, 1944.
29. B. V. Krishnamurti, *Pricing in Planned Economy*, Bombay, Oxford University Press, 1949.
30. B. P. Beckwith, *The Economic Theory of a Socialist Economy*, Palo Alto, Stanford University Press, 1949.
31. A. Bergson, "Socialist Economics", in H. S. Ellies (ed.), *A Survey of Contemporary Economics*, Philadelphia, Blakiston, 1948.
32. M. Dobb, "A Review of the Discussion Concerning Economic Calculation in a Socialist Economy", in *On Economic Theory and Socialism*, London, Routledge and Kegan, 1955.
33. H. Hotelling, "The General Welfare in Relation to Problems of Taxation and of Railway and Utility Rates", *Econometrica*, 1938, 242—69.
34. R. H. Coase, "The Marginal Cost Controversy", *Economica*, 1946, 168—82.
35. A. M. Henderson, "The Pricing of Public Utility Undertakings", *Manchester School*, 1947, 223—50.
36. C. A. R. Crosland, "Prices and Costs in Nationalised Undertakings", *Oxford Economic Papers*, 1950, 51—68.
37. Nancy Ruggles, "The Welfare basis of the Marginal Cost Pricing Principle", *Review of Economic Studies*, 1949—50, 29—46; "Recent Developments in the Theory of Marginal Cost Pricing", *Ibid.*, 107—26.
38. S. G. Strumilin, "Faktor vremeni v proektirovkah kapitaljnyh vložęnij" (The Time Factor in Investment Projects), *Izvestija Akademiji Nauk SSSR, Otdelenie ekonomiki i prava*, No. 3, 1946, 195—215; for an extensive English review see J. Miller in *Soviet Studies*, 1949, 119—27.
39. D. D. Kondrašev, "Voprosy cenoobrazovanija v SSSR" (Questions of Price Formation in the U.S.S.R.), in *Voprosy socialističeskoj ekonomiki*, Moskva, GOSPOLITIZDAT, 1956.

34

40. I. Maksimović, "Teoretični problemi cen v socijalizmu" (The Theoretical Problems of Prices in Socialism), *Ekonomska revija*, 1956, 55—66.

41. M. Dobb, "The Problem of Marginal Cost Pricing Reconsidered", *Indian Economic Review*, 1952, 1—13.

42. J. M. Fleming, "Production and Price Policy in Public Enterprise", *Economica*, 1950, 1—22.

43. N. Kaldor, "Welfare Propositions of Economics and Interpersonal Comparisons of Utility", *Economic Journal*, 1939, 549—52.

44. J. R. Hicks, "The Foundations of Welfare Economics", *Economic Journal*, 1939, 696—712.

45. T. de Scitovszky, "A Note on Welfare Propositions in Economics", *Review of Economic Studies*, 1941—42, 77—88.

46. E. J. Mishan, "A Re-appraisal of the Principles of Resource Allocation", *Economica*, 1957, 324—42.

47. E. J. Mishan, "An Investigation into Some Alleged Contradictions in Welfare Economics", *Economic Journal*, 1957, 445—54.

48. M. Friedman, *Essays in Positive Economics*, University of Chicago Press, 1953.

49. W. Vickrey, "Some Objections to Marginal-Cost Pricing", *Journal of Political Economy*, 1948, 218—36.

50. J. A. Schumpeter, *Capitalism, Socialism and Democracy*, New York, Harper and Brothers, 1950.

51. W. A. Lewis, "The Two-Part Tariff", *Economica*, 1941, 249—70, 399—408; reprinted with some changes in *Overhead Costs*, London, Allen and Unwin, 1949.

52. P. Wiles, "Growth versus Choice", *Economic Journal*, 1956, 244—55.

53. R. T. Bye, *Social Economy and the Price System*, New York, Macmillan, 1950.

II. THE PRICING OF THE FACTORS OF PRODUCTION

The moving force in the economic process is Man. In this sense, Labour is the only factor of production. But variations in productivity of labour cannot be determined or analyzed in any simple way; labour productivity is a function of a complex set of conditions. These conditions, according to their economic characteristics, may be classified in four broad categories which, using partly the traditional terminology, we shall call *Monopoly, Capital, Labour* and *Entrepreneurship*. As the economic process can be conveniently analyzed in terms of these four categories, we shall call them *Factors of Production*. The prices of Factors of Production we shall call, using again the traditional terminology, *Rent, Interest, Wages* and *Profit*.

A few more words by way of introduction. *Monopoly* replaces what has traditionally been called *Land*. The reason for the change in terminology is rather obvious: we need a perfectly general *rent earning factor* and *Land* does not exhaust this species[1]. Monopoly will mean a non-reproducible factor (condition) of production like a unique advantage in production, ownership of mineral deposits or ownership of land. As to land, it is often said that unlike capital (which is a product of labour) land has productivity of its own. But this is not so. If we compare two economies alike in every respect except in the endowments of natural resources, the economy with more fertile soil and richer mineral deposits will generate a larger social product (measured, say, in terms of consumption goods). This is obvious, but the distinction is irrelevant for our purpose. The economy with *more* natural resources is quite likely to generate *less* rent[2]. Or take another example. Imagine a closed economy whose agriculturalists have just applied a costless innovation, say rotation of crops. As a result the "productivity" of land

---

[1] Monopoly is the best term I could find for this purpose. It is, clearly, not very satisfactory. Nevertheless, it seemed to me preferable to a highly artificial remoulding of the concept of land as for instance that of D. A. Worcester who defines land as "that group of the productive agents whose fitness *for a particular use* is not likely to change as a result of a change or even the elimination of the remuneration of its owners" (1, 259).

[2] Richer mines and better soil require less capital intensive technique to produce the same output. Therefore, Differential Rent II will be lower. A larger proportion of richer mines and superior soil in the total available resources will, if the output is to remain the same as in the economy with poorer endowment, render unnecessary the exploitation of certain number of poorest mines and soils. Thus Differential Rent I also is likely to be lower. For the meaning of the concepts Differential Rent I and II see next chapter, section (a), para. 2 and 3.

will *rise* while rent is likely to *fall* (because demand for food is very inelastic and so fall in prices will reduce output in value terms).

The last observation helps also to explain the difference in meaning of the concept *Factors of Production* in my and in the more traditional usage. This difference in approach will turn out to have far-reaching consequences. Here we are not concerned with factors productive in any *absolute* sense. When we speak of *Factors of Production*, we only assume that they somehow influence the volume of production — the productivity of social labour — and that there are four analytically meaningful types of these influences. Apart from this fundamental meaning, in a number of instances the term "factors of production" will be used to mean *resources*, or *units* of resources, in other words it will be used in the traditional sense. Terminologically it would be more correct to distinguish these uses by two terms. However, it is usually quite obvious from the context which meaning should be attributed to the term and so we may stick to our rule of minimizing terminological changes.

Finally, there is a strong tendency in the modern economic analysis to treat *Factors of Production* as in every respect symmetrical. In so far as this aim is achieved, the distinctions between the four classes disappear and we consider only the marginal productivity of a unit of an amorphous productive factor, whatever it is. In some circumstances this approach may have its advantages; in addition, pure marginal productivity theory undoubtedly represents an appealing logical system and is a historically significant achievement in the development of economic analysis. However, in so far as we are interested in *economics*, the usefulness of the generalized approach is relatively modest; for whenever we try to think in terms of potential economic policy, this approach is bound to become misleading. Factors of production are not symmetrical, the four classes enumerated differ widely in their functioning in the economic process, and in what follows our main business will consist in an examination of these differences within the framework of planned economy.

3. RENT

(a) Agricultural Rent

The same amount of labour, combined with natural resources of different "quality" will produce different results. The differences in the productivity of labour that are due to the inelastic supply of co-operant factors, are measured by rent. In this context, historically and institutionally agricultural rent plays the leading role. Several cases of the increasing degree of complexity may be envisaged.

1. Suppose, first, that there is an unlimited supply of land of homogeneous quality. In that case factor of production not being scarce, land has no price and, there is no rent. If, however, the whole land available has gradually been taken into cultivation, and demand for agricultural goods continues to rise, prices will begin to rise above costs of production (including profit and interest). As a consequence, rent

will appear. This is the Marxian *Monopoly* or Marshallian *Scarcity Rent*, called also Absolute Rent (2, 31), and is obviously a result of the natural scarcity of land. But rent may also arise from an institutionally caused scarcity. If the agricultural area we are concerned with is owned by a single family, and if these people try to maximize their net return, they will utilize the notorious inelasticity of demand for agricultural products by limiting supply of land, driving prices up *more than proportionally to the decrease in demand* and reaping the increased amount of rent from their competitive tenants. This form of rent, which arises from the private ownership of land, corresponds[1] to Marxian Absolute Rent. Finally, being monopolists, our landowners may try to exploit not only consumers, but producers as well. They will succeed in this whenever their tenants are not capitalist farmers (as in Marx's model), but peasants who till the land for a living and not for profit, i.e., when in the given institutional set-up no other choice of occupation exists for them. Historically, this sort of monopolistic exploitation has been very frequent[2]. Being paid out of profits and wages, this part of rent may be conveniently termed negative absolute rent. The common characteristic of all three forms of rent is that they exist independently of any assumption about the *differential* fertility (or locational advantage) of soil. In this sense they represent three varieties of an *Absolute* Rent.

2. Assume, next, that the technique of cultivation does not change, but that land varies in quality of soil and in situation, so that the best situated best quality land becomes scarce and has to be priced. Price is determined by the difference in productivity between this land and the poorest land which must be taken into cultivation to satisfy demand. Following Marx, we may call this difference Differential Rent I.

3. Finally, drop all particular assumptions except that, for analytical convenience, innovations occur at disparate points of time, and observe what is happening between such two points. When the area under cultivation ceases to satisfy growing demand for agricultural produce, farmers face the following choice: either to apply more capital and labour on the already cultivated land or to start cultivating the next inferior grade of land. Rational solution implies, of course, equalization of marginal productivities in both alternatives. Or, more precisely, of marginal cost on the superior land and lowest average cost or marginal cost — whichever is higher — on the inferior land. As in our case the

---

[1] It corresponds to but is not identical with the Marxian concept and for two reasons. First, Marx was concerned only with the pure capitalist system — no peasantry in existence — while this restriction is not necessary here. Secondly, Marx tied the existence of Absolute Rent with the surplus of value over price of production, which cannot be sustained, and which he would have probably corrected had he lived to publish the respective manuscripts *(Capital III* and *Theories)* himself. See also Bortkiewicz who describes Marxian Absolute Rent as a *Prohibition Rent* (3, 430).

[2] For instance in the pre-war Yugoslav and Indian agricultures. As B. Narain describes it: "When prices are high the peasant (tenant) earns his subsistence, not more. When prices fall, he may not only earn nothing but work for a whole year entirely for the benefit of his landlord. It is not rent but wages and normal profits which do not seem to enter as an element in cost of production in the Punjab!" (4, 81).

law of diminishing returns must be operative, the intramarginal units of capital and labour, before additional land becomes worth while cultivating, will earn surplus over most[1]. Under conditions of competition this surplus will accrue to the landowner as the familiar Differential Rent II. When the population continues to grow, the absolute amount of this surplus will change, but nothing can be said *a priori* about the path or even about the direction of this change. Thus premarxian classical economists were obviously mistaken in believing that the amount of rent must *necessarily* increase with the growth of the population. In fact all depends on the rate and kind of innovations.

4. The concept of Differential Rent II, being free from any particular assumption, is the most general concept of rent. This fact may mislead one to proclaim all other rent concepts analytically useless[2]. It is certainly true that in all cases of rational choice one has only to compare marginal productivities. But this does not exhaust the *economic* problem. We are also interested in finding out the forces and processes behind marginal productivities, in knowing how they are determined. Precisely for this purpose, i.e. for the purpose of describing in full all the essential characteristics of an economic situation, we need the notions of quality and situation of land, of natural and institutional monopolies, in short, we need the other two rent concepts as well. In this context let us consider once more the problem of Absolute Rent.

The question whether the poorest land bears rent or not used to be a very controversial one. However, if it is put in its proper setting, the question is relatively easy to answer. If we may assume that in a country, in a district, or, generally, in an area whose boundaries are defined in terms of decreased mobility of capital and labour, the whole land is not appropriated and the cultivated area is equal to the appropriated one, then, disregarding discontinuities, the poorest cultivated land will bear no rent. If we cannot assume these conditions, we are obliged to accept the existence of absolute rent. Apart from natural scarcity of land, two possibilities exist. For rent to arise on the poorest cultivated land it is necessary that the next worse land be appropriated and withheld from cultivation. For the existence of an absolute rent in general it is sufficient that any class of land be withheld from cultivation, or that farming is less efficient than possible and that therefore prices of agricultural products are higher than necessary. At this point an interesting theoretical problem arises: Is there any difference between planned and non-planned economy in that respect? As far as

---

[1] The way in which rent is generated may vary according to circumstances. Take, for instance, Marx's observation that it is not necessarily the poorest land which determines the price (on the supply side). If discontinuities exist, the last portion of capital applied to superior land may be less productive than the last but one portion applied to inferior land. In this case it is the latter and not the former which earns Differential Rent II (5, Ch. XLIV).

[2] P. Samuelson would take this view: "...all land rents can be measured as a differential between what non-land factors produce on the land in question and what those same factors would produce if working out on no-rent marginal land. This theory of differential rent is not untrue. But it is rendered unnecessary by the analysis of the last section (referring to the marginal productivity principle)" (6, 574).

natural absolute rent is concerned there can be no difference. But institutional absolute rent makes for an obvious difference which affects the allocation of resources. Under conditions of private ownership a considerable amount of land — agricultural and non-agricultural — is left idle, mainly for speculative reasons[1]. Farming, as well is often inefficient because of the uneconomic size of holdings[1]. This waste can be escaped in a planned economy. On the other hand, the exploitation of peasant tenants, resulting in an irrational distribution of income, may be avoided as well. Thus the fact that planned economy is able to dispense with institutional absolute rent means that such an economy provides better scope for the rational use of land resources than the privately owned non-planned economy.

(b) Nationalization of Land

1. Planned economy requires social control. To many earlier socialist economists social control in agriculture meant nationalization of land analogous to nationalization of industry and other sectors of the economy. But no political régime can afford to undertake a nationalization of millions of peasant small holdings. Even the spectacular Soviet nationalization of land in 1917 was only an agrarian reform by which large private estates were broken up and transformed into state farms or, more frequently, distributed among poor peasants with little or no land. From the economic point of view the mere legal act of nationalization mattered neither then nor a decade later when the collectivization drive was initiated. And not only is it impossible to carry out an agricultural nationalization according to the industrial pattern, but it is also unnecessary to do so.

2. Suppose that the agrarian taxation is devised in such a way as to syphon off from agriculture the whole amount of rent generated there. Moreover, suppose that the landowners have to pay an adequate amount of rent-tax irrespectively of how they use their land[2]. By this fiscal measure we create exactly the same situation as if the land were nationalized and then leased to highest bidders. The land tax prevents landowners from leaving their land idle. And if we assume that the prices of agricultural products measure correctly their economic importance, the land tax becomes also an instrument of planning. For if prices of products are given, and costs of production with an average technique in use are known, then the rent determination reduces to a simple output maximization problem. Having established the optimum combination of crops in particular circumstances — which serves as a basis for

---

[1] For examples from British agriculture see J. Mackie, 7, pp. 2, 6, 7.

[2] Taxation according to "cadastral revenue", as a similar system is called in Yugoslavia. In fact the idea is a very old one and is connected with the name of Henry George and the Single Tax movement. It is important to note that this scheme corresponds closely to peasant's idea of "just taxation" (provided some adjustments for the size of the family and similar other conditions are made) and so it is likely to be very *popular* in countries with large peasant population — countries which are usually thought as extremely difficult to plan and socialize.

the rent-tax assessment — agricultural service of the Planning Authority undertakes to instruct farmers in this respect. And everyone is free to follow or not to follow the advice. Moreover, not only the kind of the crop, but also the intensity of cultivation, i.e., agricultural investment, may be planned through rent-tax: increase in rent necessitates capital investment if the farm is to avoid going bankrupt. In both cases also the question of choice of state farms *versus* kolektiv-farms *versus* co-operative farms *versus* private farms[1] will not be prejudged; successful organizations will flourish, those unable to meet rent payments will get bankrupt and disappear[2]. And all this smoothly and without social tensions.

3. The introduction of the land tax must lead to an immediate decline in the price of land. Many financially marginal lands, i.e., those not cultivated and only partly cultivated, will be offered for sale thus increasing supply of land. And many would-be buyers, now obliged to pay rent in addition to the price for land, will become reluctant, thus reducing the pressure of demand. But the price of land will not immediately fall to zero. Traditional preconceptions are too strong to be abandoned at once. And land may be regarded, quite rationally, as an insurance against inflation, against food shortage due to bad administration, against all other possible contingencies. However, parallel with the stabilization of the economy and with the "traditionalization" of the new order of things, economic agents are bound to move towards a rational solution and the price of land will be gradually falling towards zero. Another pair of old market categories will disintegrate: land will earn rent but will have no price. The falling price of land will immensely increase the mobility of factors of production in agriculture and will enable co-operatives and government agencies to speed up the reorganization of the agriculture by buying land from the less efficient producers.

It is hardly necessary to stress that the foregoing analysis is applicable to the case of urban land also. Agricultural and urban rents are different in appearance but not in essence; they represent one and the same economic category[3]. The tax on housing and commercial sites breaks monopoly and equalizes conditions of economic competition.

---

[1] State and co-operative farms can be broadly identified with Soviet *sovhozi* and *kolhozi*, while kolektiv-farm is an agricultural analogue for the kolektiv-enterprise in Yugoslavia. For the meaning of the term *kolektiv* see Ch. 6-c.

[2] This applies to organizations, of course, and not to people who will simply join a more successful organization for their own benefit. The Planning Authority is to arrange for painless transfers.

[3] Not in the opinion of E. H. Chamberlin: "Urban rent for retailing purposes is a different sort of income from agricultural rent... the *only* resemblance between them appears to be that they are both paid for the use of land" (8, 242; my italics). The former is a purely monopolistic return, while the latter is a purely competitive one. "The rent of urban land is explained wholly, that of agricultural land partly, by the factor of location. Yet the locational advantage adhering to a business site is not the same as that which forms a part of the explanation of agricultural rent. Agricultural land bears a higher or lower rent according as it is near or far from the market where its product is sold. It is always *at a distance* from the market. Urban land carries its market with it — those buyers who find it most convenient to trade at the location in question — and its rent is high or low depending upon the size and nature of this market" (p. 242). "The

(c) Mining Rent

While land is generally owned privately, there is a long tradition of state ownership of mineral resources in many countries all over the world. And even when mines are privately owned their nationalization, particularly the nationalization of yet undiscovered mineral deposits, will cause no greater problems than the nationalization of industry, which is taken for granted in this study.

1. Mining rent has its peculiarities but is also in many respects similar to land rent. Mines working under most unfavourable conditions may or may not earn rent, depending on whether they are operating after or at the point of minimum average cost, i.e., whether continuity does not or does exist. In the case of mines, similarly as in the case of land, private ownership (which means that would-be operators do not have free access to mineral deposits) entails an absolute rent and so prevents rational allocation of resources. Non-marginal mines will earn differential rent. There is a slight difference in the morphology of the mining rent which is usually composed of three parts. The first

---

retail market... contains monopoly elements, for the factor of convenience differentiates the product spatially. The movements of buyers being impeded, the 'product' of each site contains an element of convenience to a certain group, and the seller locating on the site has a monopoly of its product... If the buyers moved freely over the entire area, as they would if the market were a purely competitive one, the differences in urban rent and in land values would entirely disappear" (p. 243). Comparing urban sites with agricultural land, Chamberlin finds that urban rent "is not paid in order to save transportation charges. It is paid in order to secure a larger volume of sales. Buyers and sellers alike are scattered over a wide area. Movement among them is so impeded that one place within the area gives advantages in securing the custom of a portion of the buyers. It affords a market which is, to a degree, distinct from the whole. The amount of product each seller can dispose of is not indefinitely large at the prevailing price. It is very definitely limited by location... If we regard the whole area as one market, it is clear that rent is paid because it contains elements of monopoly. Spatial differentiation results in demand curves for the goods of individual sellers which have a negative slope instead of being perfectly horizontal. Since urban site rent would disappear if they were horizontal, we must conclude that it is due to the monopoly elements and it is a pure monopoly return" (p. 243).

The last generalization is not true: for rent to disappear not only demand curve but also supply curve must be horizontal. In other words, land must cease to be scarce. But this is a minor point. The fact of the matter is that all these lengthy quotations deal with irrelevant differences between two industries, agriculture and retail trade. As far as rent is concerned the only relevant fact is that it is in *both* cases a monopoly income — that of the landlord. In retail trading as well as in agriculture the same inputs on the geometrically same land area produce different outputs and these differences are equalized by rent. The differential advantages in production may be of various kinds, but they are never reproducible at will and therefore represent sources of monopoly income for their owners. In fact, Chamberlin could not help reaching the same conclusion himself: "To sum up the theory simply: each site tends to be put to the use where it will yield the maximum total return over the costs involved in utilizing it... the differential remaining, which is due to the profit-making opportunities afforded by one site as compared to another, is rent, and it is put into the hands of the landlords by the competition of entrepreneurs for the best opportunities" (p. 245). Thus once summed up Chamberlin's new theory of urban rent reveals itself — in the full contradiction to the opening statement — as the familiar and time-honoured theory of land rent. Cf. also J. J. Spengler, 9.

43

part is a rent paid for the right to explore a certain area. When the ore deposits are found, rent is considerably increased to induce the operator to open the deposits. Once the regular exploitation has started, rent is paid in the form of royalty proportional to the amount of the ore produced. Here, then, another difference appears. In so far as royalty is proportional to output, it is variable and not fixed as agricultural rent. Therefore royalty enters as an element of cost of the marginal unit of output, which is normally not the case with land (though it may be the case as, for instance, in those land-rent systems where rent is determined as a share in gross product). Thus output of all rent-paying mines will be unnecessarily restricted. As royalty is only an imputational cost, the actual (opportunity) cost of natural resources being zero, marginal cost of operating the mine must be calculated free of royalty charges and output must be pushed to the point where so calculated marginal cost is equal to marginal revenue.

2. Apart from minor differences mentioned in the preceding paragraph, mining rent seems to be essentially the same economic category as land rent. But one characteristic of mining rent calls for a brief analysis. A number of economists felt that there was a significant difference between mining and land rent due to the fact that land is eternal while mineral deposits are exhaustible. Thus Marshall thought that royalty was not rent because, unlike the latter, it was included in the marginal supply price of minerals[1]. Hall suggests that in a socialist economy royalties should be charged to restrain the use of the product and should be accumulated to provide the source of additional capital which will offset the loss of depleted deposits.[2] Cassel distinguishes be-

---

[1] "A royalty is not a rent... For except when mines, quarries, etc., are practically inexhaustible, the excess of their income over their direct outgoings has to be regarded, in part at least as the price got by the sale of stored-up goods — stored up by nature indeed, but now treated as private property; and therefore the marginal supply price of minerals includes a royalty in addition to the marginal expenses of working the mine... But the royalty itself on a ton of coal... represents that diminution in the value of the mine, regarded as a source of wealth in the future, which is caused by taking the ton out of nature's storehouse" (10, 364). Cassel criticizes this statement on the ground that if the poorest and rentless land determines the price of agricultural products, then the poorest royalty-less mine also determines the price of the minerals. Rent and royalty equally enter or equally do not enter into the marginal cost (11, 286). Schumpeter raises the same objection adding that Marshall has violated his own definition of rent as an income derived from the ownership of land and other free gifts of nature (12, 935).

[2] "... if only rent as so far calculated is charged, the community will gradually impoverish itself. It must also charge something for royalties, and these should be charged on the product even of the marginal deposits. This additional charge has the twofold purpose of restraining the use of the product and providing a source of additional capital the possession of which will offset the loss of the deposits when they are exhausted. The exact amount to charge for this purpose is somewhat difficult to decide. The reduction in national income when the deposits are exhausted is the difference between the cost of producing a similar annual quantity of the next available substitute: so that the maximum amount to add is a sum which, accumulated at compound interest over the period of exhaustion, will produce this difference". Hall then advises to charge less than that because cheaper substitutes may be discovered and reserves at the beginning are usually underestimated (13, 96).

tween "pricing of the use of land" and "pricing of the natural materials"; the latter not being durable goods cannot, in his opinion, have a special price for the use different from the price of the goods (11, 279). He also postulates the indeterminateness of mining rent in a socialist economy[1]. Wicksell sees the difference between royalty and rent in that "the former is a monopoly rent, the latter a pure scarcity rent" (14, 245)[2].

The value of these distinctions is very unequal. Some of them seem to be based more on instinctive feelings that something is "wrong" with mining rent — than on the logical analysis of the problem. Consequently, I find it difficult to penetrate the minds of the authors of these ideas. In so far as Marshall's point implies the already discussed possible distortion of marginal cost, it may be easily remedied; it is a matter of technique, not of principle. If it should imply a matter of principle, there is no need to supplement criticisms of Cassel and Schumpeter quoted in the footnote. Wicksell is quite obscure. I suspect that he had in mind some sort of absolute rent.

As to Hall's proposal that royalties be accumulated to provide a source of capital, it is clearly based on a confusion between an individual business and the economy as a whole. No financial arrangements can create *real* capital by which to offset the loss of exhausted mineral deposits. But the other element in his scheme, that of reducing present output for the sake of the future use, deserves to be considered. Imagine a stationary economy with the zero rate of interest. Rational allocation of resources would imply an absolute maximization of output up to infinity. Assuming continuities, there is no reason why output of minerals should vary from year to year. Thus all known minerals from all known deposits will be used every year in the same proportion (and in infinitesimal quantities). Next, allow for a positive time preference. Then better mines and more useful minerals will be exploited faster than poorer mines and less valuable minerals, the speed of exploitation being a function of the rate of time preference. Similar is the effect of the interest rate in the capitalist growing economy as shown by Cassel and discussed in the next paragraph. Finally, consider a growing economy with zero rate of time preference (to be explained later). Maximization

---

[1] "Just as a Socialist State has, in a sense, to choose the rate of economic progress, and thus fixes the conditions which determine the rate of interest, so the distribution in time of the available natural materials is for the isolated community which controls these materials an indeterminate factor which the community must settle in its own way. Prices are not a definite problem before this decision has been made" (11, 284).

[2] "If on this assumption (mining rent determined in the same way as land rent) the better mines were released for free exploitation, labour and capital would flow from the worse to the better mines, the annual output would rise and the price of ore fall. We maintain on the contrary that there would be no such change in the price of agricultural products when the rent of land is confiscated or remitted by the State. The owners of the better mines can therefore only procure incomes by an artificial lowering of the gross product, and even in this case there would be an essential difference between "royalty" and "rent". The former is a monopoly rent, the latter a pure scarcity rent. When we take an imminent exhaustion of the mines into account, the difference is naturally accentuated, but it tends to disappear to the extent that relatively increased costs are involved by increasing the annual product of either mines or agriculture in general" (14, 245).

of welfare requires that the rate of growth be maximized. If it can be shown that by varying the rate of exploitation of a particular mineral the growth curve of the economy can be shifted to various positions, then the highest attainable growth curve ought to be used to determine the adequate price of the mineral. It is, however, impossible to devise any simple computational formula — like the one suggested by Hall — for dealing with this case. But, fortunately enough, this case is likely to occur extremely rarely, if at all, within the economic sphere. Because, by using the mineral, productive forces of the economy are expanding and by the time original deposits are exhausted technological knowledge, the stock of productive capital and, perhaps, newly discovered deposits are all available on a larger scale than before. Outside the economic sphere, as for instance when a particular mineral is considered "strategically important", this case may be more frequent. But economics proper has nothing to say about it.

3. Cassel's concept of rent as a price for the use of a durable good (11, 256) is a definitional matter, and as such irrelevant. For the purpose of this study rent is determined as the surplus over the minimum supply price of a factor which, in the case of socially owned land and other resources, is zero. But Cassel's contention about indeterminateness raises a very important question. Take first Cassel's calculation for capitalist conditions (11, 280—82).

The working of a mine takes time. The period of working is not settled in advance by technical considerations; it may be shortened if the costs of the necessary extensions of equipment, means of transport, sources of power, etc., can be borne. Additional costs for working the mine more rapidly must be spread over the same quantity of ore. On the other hand, assuming constant selling price, shortening of the period of working will have the advantage of securing the price of sale earlier. To arrive at the correct solution the mine-owner who works the mine himself must reduce all income and expenditure during the period of working for the entire concern to their present value and on this basis maximize his net return. In other words, it pays to speed up the working of the mine until gradually rising marginal cost becomes equal to marginal revenue from saving of interest due to earlier sales. If cost of production remains unchanged while price of the mineral is expected to rise (due to exhaustion, for instance), the same calculation leads obviously to a redistribution of production in favour of later years: mine-owners will restrict output and so raise present prices, while in the future a relatively more abundant supply will relatively lower prices.

Returning to the problem of planned economy, let us first enquire into the alleged indeterminacy of the rate of economic progress. In a planned economy people are obviously free to choose the rate of economic growth and thus determine the rate of interest. In this respect, their choice cannot be less rational than the same aggregate of choices in an individualist economy. But the solution in question is in fact much more determinate. The characteristics of the economic process are such that no rate of growth higher than a certain maximum rate of growth can be chosen, and, on certain plausible assumptions, the rational behaviour requires that the lower limit of the rate of growth cannot be more than just a shade lower than the maximum rate of growth (see Ch. 10). Thus, there is an extremely narrow range of indeterminateness which for practical purposes may be taken as non-existent. To simplify the analysis theoretically, we may assume that exactly maximum rate of growth has been chosen. Given this rate of growth, the rate of interest is determined and is equal to zero (see Ch. 4-c). The rent of a particular mine will in these circumstances be determined in the following way.

First, engineers have to find out what are the *minimum average costs* for working the mine. If the price of the mineral is lower than so established cost of exploitation, it does not pay to open the mine; if it is just equal to the cost, the mine will bear no rent but its operation is clearly justified. If the price is higher than the minimum average cost of the mineral, one can proceed to calculate the second approximation and add subsequent doses of capital and labour in order to utilize poorer quality ore or to achieve a more complete exploitation of the deposits and watch the possible changes in the demand curve for the mineral. When marginal cost becomes equal to marginal revenue, the absolute net output of the mine is maximized. A further modification of the exploitation program is necessary if it is to be established that by speeding up the working of the mine — and taking into account additional costs — the marginal economic efficiency of the project does not fall below that of alternative projects. In other words, the working of the mine is intensified up to the point where marginal net productivity of investment becomes equal to marginal net productivity of investment of all other investment projects undertaken in the economy. This modification rests on the presumption that, in order to have the entire economy expanding at a maximum rate, the output of constituent units must be organized so as to take the time element into account, which means that marginal rate of net return must be equalized. The final result may be modified once more according to the Hall's principle, discussed in the preceding section, if it is relevant for the case in point.

(d) Rent Generalized

Rent theory used to be, and perhaps still is, a controversial part of the general body of the economic theory. The debate over the relation of rent to prices represents one of the longest controversies recorded in the history of economic thought. Put in its simplest form the question reads as follows: Does rent enter the price or not? One group of economists answered the question with *no*, the other with *yes* — and both groups were right[1]. This indicated that something was wrong with the

[1] D. H. Buchanan quotes Taussig as one of the *no*-men and Jevons as a representative of *yes*-men. Explaining the difference in approach, Buchanan remarks: "The Ricardian writers reached their conclusion because they considered the relation of rent payment to the value not of particular products, but to the value of raw produce as a whole" (15, 622). On the other hand, quotations from Mill, e.g., show "that there is a *competing use for land* and that because it is valuable for one use that rental becomes a necessary expense for whatever commodity it furnishes" (p. 626). In other words: "The essential difference in the two questions is that in

generality of the rent theory. Moving towards a general theory of rent, modern writers deprived land of the privilege of being the only factor of production bearing rent and applied the same treatment to all units of all factors. Rent then becomes a surplus over the *transfer price*, i.e., over the price necessary to retain a given unit of a factor in an industry (J. Robinson, 16, 104) or, which comes to the same, a surplus over opportunity cost (therefore *opportunity rent*, Brockie, 17, 248). Let us briefly enquire what are the consequences of this generalization for our four classes of factors of production. To avoid circular reasoning I shall for the moment substitute traditional *land* for my first factor *monopoly*.

1. Rent, as just defined, changes with the extent of the economic activity considered: it is a rent from the point of view of an industry. Thus, e.g., opportunity rent of the corn growing industry is the surplus which corn producers earn over potential proceeds of the next most profitable crop. The producers of this second best crop earn also an opportunity rent with respect to another, third alternative. And so right down to the last crop and the last unit of land which have no other alternative. In this last case the transfer price of the factor "land" is zero. The *total* amount of rent generated by land is therefore given by the surplus over the *minimum* supply price (Brockie), and for land this price is zero. Or it is given as a surplus over the transfer price of the factor land when economic activity is defined so widely — the economy as a whole — as to include all possible uses of the factor land. Consequently the transfer price of land becomes zero.

2. Brockie tries to apply the same conceptual scheme to the factor *Labour* (17, 250). But as the factors of production are not symmetrical, the success of this attempt is dubious. Brockie defines opportunity rent again as surplus receipts over opportunity cost, which is not untrue, but neither is particularly enlightening and means that a certain occupation will be chosen because, for variety of reasons, it is preferred to another one. He next defines the total rent of labour ("quasi rent") as any surplus revenue over minimum supply price, the latter being given by the cost of subsistence. This definition implies that the performance of a worker and his wage — as long as the latter is above subsistence level — are two independent variables, while they are obviously mutually dependent. Therefore, unlike by land, the minimum supply price in terms of potential performance will vary from individual to individual and will normally be greater than the subsistence cost (in so far as this concept can be attributed a precise quantitative meaning at all). Anticipating the analysis of pricing of labour in Chapter 6, let us assume that the minimum supply price of labour — i.e., the earnings which will induce workers to produce maximum attainable output — is socially determined and that it is known. Then the surplus of product over so defined minimum supply price is the rent generated by labour.

---

one the land was supposed to have an alternative use, while in the other it had none. In the one case a number of uses were sharply competing for the land and whatever use secured it was compelled to pay the competitive rent; in the other case the land had only one annual use and could only accept whatever rental the one use offered, or return to nature and receive nothing. The conclusion therefore followed that in the one case rent was a necessary payment, which in the other it was not" (15, 600).

In this connection another issue requires to be cleared up. It is frequently argued that, if marginal worker determines the wage rate, all intramarginal workers earn rent because their wages rise with the arrival of the marginal worker or, putting it differently, they would stay in the industry even if their wages were lower (cf. Boulding, 18, 211—13). The question arises whether this apparent surplus can be attributed any economic meaning. Suppose all workers are equally productive. If analogy is drawn with land, in this case there is no place for rent. But workers will remain "marginal" and "intramarginal". Clearly, "rent" can arise only from the psychological heterogeneity of workers. Now, if some workers have their houses, relatives and friends, happen to be born in a particular locality or into a particular profession (coal-miners, for instance), and, generally, are socially (and, perhaps, institutionally) tied up with the place of work, while others are not, then the first group is relatively immobile. Even if wages in another industry are higher and they would prefer to move, the social obstacles would prevent them from doing so[1]. It follows that these obstacles should be properly defined as "costs"[2]. Thus when wages rise in their own industry, this increase may simply compensate for costs, leaving no surplus. It may be argued that apart from social obstacles there is also a positive preference of an individual for a particular job and that, to the degree that his preference is stronger than that of another individual, he earns psychic rent. But, how should we measure this rent? And in which sense is it relevant for *economic* analysis? Suppose we try to extract this rent by means of wage discrimination, similarly as we discriminated between various parcels of land. However, workers, being human beings, would strongly object if one or more of their colleagues got paid more for doing the same job. This would adversely affect both their physical performance and their "psychic income". The equalization of wages is price for these costs and so again no room is left for rent. It is idle to speculate whether the maxim "equal pay for equal work" is rational or not, the fact is that workers behave in the way as if it is. Economics has to take this fact into account. The final conclusion to be drawn is not that all people enjoy work equally, because they do not, but that differences in enjoyment of work are immeasurable — and irrelevant. Also, that it would be manifestly absurd to argue that, e.g., British miners, who, for similar reasons as Punjab tenants of Mr. Narain, were underpaid for generations, now earn rent because, after the last war, miners' wages were relatively increased and the vast majority of miners would not leave their jobs even if their wages were lower. Thus calling the area above the rising text-book supply curve of labour "economic surplus" or "rent" proves to be meaningless.

3. *Capital* as a factor of production has its own peculiarities. Capital *ex ante* is nothing else than the social permit to use resources of the

[1] Unless, of course, we make a definite value judgement and proclaim this world the best of all possible.

[2] Cf. also L. G. Reynolds's saying: "The view that workers can be redistributed only by changes in wage differentials seems to be mistaken. They are redistributed much more directly and forcefully by differentials in the availability of jobs" (19, 224).

4

community productively. Thus *per definitionem* all "inputs" of capital are homogeneous and their marginal net productivity is equal. The minimum supply price is equal to the cost of administering loans (including risk premiums) to firms. The difference between the productivity of capital and its minimum supply price is economic rent which accrues to the owner of capital. Capital, like land, being monopolized, yields to its owner the same sort of income: rent. However, as we shall see presently, on a lower level of abstraction some differences arise. It is, therefore, justifiable to classify capital as a separate factor of production, characterized by homogeneity and (in planned economy) by fixed supply. The particular form of rent earned by capital will be called *Interest*. It may be added that we shall normally think in terms of Gross Interest because there is usually no necessity to separate and analyze banking costs.

4. We have next to distinguish between capital *ex ante* and capital *ex post* (capital sunk into concrete buildings and machinery) or, what comes to the same thing, between capital in money form and capital goods. The latter are heterogeneous and as such will earn rent in addition to interest. However, this rent is not a consequence of capital *qua* capital but of the economic opportunities open to entrepreneurs and — this is the last important element — of the entrepreneurial abilities which are heterogeneous. Once again, anticipating later analysis, let us postulate that the minimum supply price for the factor Entrepreneurship is Profit. If productivity of entrepreneurship is greater than profit necessary to induce it, the resulting surplus is again rent.

5. The foregoing discussion leads to a perfectly general definition of rent: *Rent is that part of the price of factors of production which represents surplus over their minimum supply price*. From this definition the general rule of distribution in the planned economy follows straightforwardly: *Rent, bearing no influence on the supply of factors of production, should not accrue to suppliers of factors but to the general fund of the economy administered by the Planning Authority*. One part of this fund consists of rent proper while the other part consists of interest charges to the analysis of which we now proceed.

4. INTEREST

(a) Time Preference

1. The phenomenon of interest poses more difficult problems than the phenomenon of rent. It is also much more tied up with the institutional set-up of a particular economy. For both reasons there is much less agreement about interest than about rent which represents a comparatively simple technical problem. For the same reason it would seem necessary to review briefly the theoretical heritage in this field in order to find out those elements which may be used for building up an interest theory applicable to a planned economy. The relevant theories for this purpose are obviously only those which try to discuss the problem of interest in a general way, regardless of any particular institutional system.

50

For a start let us apply the same formula as with rent — without enquiring into its proper meaning for the moment — and say: labour equipped with capital will be more productive than labour alone. This difference is measured by the rate of interest which is therefore the price for the use of capital goods. Thus the way seems to be opened to the currently most popular interest theory which in its modern textbook form, inescapably inspired by that great genius Robinson Crusoe, runs as follows:

"Let us assume that Crusoe knows that he will only be shipwrecked for six days, during which time he can catch 30 fish by using his hands alone. He can, however, choose to spend one day making a net and five days using it to catch fish. If the net is to be made, it must catch at least 30 fish, or Crusoe will be worse off. But, in order to make the net, Crusoe will have to go without food for one day, and since we may reasonably assume that Crusoe prefers present to future satisfactions[1], he will need to be offered more than 30 fish to make the postponement of satisfactions worth while. If he catches 33 fish with the net, the interest on it will be 3 fish. If these fish are just sufficient to induce Crusoe to make the net, his rate of time preference is such that one day's hunger must be repaid by 3 extra fish — representing interest — within the next five days. Crusoe calculates whether the net is worth while by comparing the interest earned from it with his rate of time preference[2]. If these are just equal, the net is just worth making" (20, 304).

Now, if instead of Robinson Crusoe we imagine a centrally planned economy[3], the planning authority will have to make basically the same choice between current and future satisfaction, and the decision made will reflect the rate of interest.

This Robinson model is in fact an exact replica of the old Roscher-Böhm-Bawerkian fishermen model (21, 271) and the theory it purports to explain is, as Schumpeter calls it (12, 930), the simplified Böhm-Bawerkian system: interest arises from the interaction of psychological time preference (present goods are more valuable than future goods)

---

[1] The assumption is not necessarily the most reasonable one. Crusoe knows that fish cannot be stored and for some reason he may expect that his hunger will rise with the lapse of time while his alternative production functions may be (a) a steady decline in catching fish with bare hands from 6 pieces first day to 1 piece last day, and (b) a steady increase in catching fish with the net — allowing also for the time spent on the construction and improvements of the net — from 1 piece first day to 6 pieces last day. In this situation his time preference will be negative while the productivity of capital is zero.

[2] Again the reasoning is not necessarily correct. If Crusoe has the knowledge of the future productivity of his net, the length of his stay on the island, etc., then all risks are excluded. If in these circumstances his normal diet requires 6.6 fish a day (33:5), and with the bare hands he can catch only 5 fish a day, then the relevant question is as follows: what affects his health more adversely, one day of full hunger or six days of 24% hunger? If his "consumption function" is such that every extra fish he can catch improves his physical health, then the rate of interest may vary from zero to any positive value, depending on the maximum point on the production function, and has nothing to do with his psychological rate of time preference. However, it would be unfair to criticize a simplified text-book model and we shall therefore consider it only as a point of departure.

[3] Stonier and Hague speak of the Soviet Union (25, 305—6).

with the physical productivity of investment. The latter is the source of interest and so determines the upper limit for the quantity of investment. If the rate of interest were zero, there would be an infinite demand for capital goods.

In what follows we shall be first concerned with the supply side of the capital market taken in isolation. In this connection note that Böhm-Bawerk and his successors use the concept of *time preference* to mean two different things. There is a pure time preference — considered "irrational" — which means relatively greater valuation of present goods as such. And there is also "rational" time preference, resulting from the law of diminishing marginal utility. It means that if we expect to become richer at some future date, the marginal unit consumed now has greater utility than the marginal unit consumed in the future.

2. The origin of the concept of the psychological time discount is attributed to the writings of Senior who is known as the inventor of the *Abstinence* theory of interest. According to Senior the owner of capital abstains from consuming it and for this sacrifice he has to be paid; the price is interest[1]. Thus not saving itself but the psychic cost of saving is what one would call a factor of production[2]. The abstinence theory bears a strong apologetic implication and has often been put to this use[3]: owners of wealth appear to be useful members of society merely because they continue to be rich and have to be paid for this

---

[1] Quoting Senior's definition of abstinence ("the conduct of a person who either abstains from the unproductive use of what he can command, or designedly prefers the production of remote to that of immediate results") Schumpeter remarks that the first part refers to abstinence *sensu stricto*, while the second part refers to what should be called 'waiting' and objects to Marshall for the interchange of the terms (12, pp. 639, 926).

[2] Logical difficulties inherent in this approach, i.e., of considering abstinence (or waiting) to be an independent item of real cost, have been stressed particularly by Böhm-Bawerk (22, 281) and Fisher (24, Ch. 20, para. 7). If *abstinence* is a factor of production different and independent from *labour*, then the cost of abstinence has to be added to labour cost to arrive at the value of the commodity. If then, Böhm-Bawerk remarks, a man works one day planting fruit trees which will bear fruits in ten years and in the following night the storm destroys the whole plantation, what are the costs incurred? Obviously only one day of labour, because "an unfruitful piece of work cannot be represented by a limited quantity of labour sacrifice and an unlimited quantity of sacrifice composed of waiting to all eternity" (23, 38). Fisher points out that if abstinence were a cost, it would be different from all other costs: it cannot be discounted like other costs because it is discounting itself; it leads to absurdity in economic calculation because it will be found, for instance, that a perpetual annuity yields no income (since interest is equal to the cost of abstinence) which is contrary to common sense. Note the naïveté of Fisher's criticism. The absurd conclusion that capital yields no net income was the virtue, not the shortcoming of the theory; it was its *social* justification. See next note.

[3] Compare, for instance, the restrained and cautious evaluation of Böhm-Bawerk: "It seems to me... that this popularity (of Senior's Abstinence Theory) has been due, not so much to its superiority as a theory, as that it came in the nick of time to support interest against the severe attacks that had been made on it... the vast majority of its later advocates do not profess it exclusively, but only add elements of the Abstinence Theory in an eclectic way to other theories favourable to interest... this... points to a preference for that practical and political standpoint which is satisfied if only a sufficient number of reasons are brought forward to prove the legitimacy of interest..." (22, 286).

peculiar productive service. It is, of course, easy to reject this interpretation of *technical* grounds: interest, like every other price, is a marginalist phenomenon, it represents the reward for the sacrifice of the last pound saved which may be the one of the poor working man. Nevertheless, the uneasy feeling remains. In order to soften the unpleasant connotation of the theory, Marshall (following the suggestion of Macvane, cf. 10, 193) introduced a more colourless term *waiting*, and his example was widely followed. But even with the changed term and not contradicting the canons of technical economics one is entitled to say with Mrs. Robinson that "since saving is mainly out of profit, and real wages tend to be lower the higher the rate of profit, the abstinence associated with saving is mainly done by workers who do not receive any share in 'reward'" (25, 393). Is it then that in a socialist economy the concept of abstinence or waiting might become theoretically meaningful? Let us leave this question unanswered for the moment.

3. Waiting may be interpreted not merely as a substitute for abstinence but also as a concept reflecting the fact that capital goods are scarce and that their services must be priced. That was Cassel's interpretation: "Interest must, in relation to the supply, be regarded as the price that has to be paid for 'waiting'. Like every other price, it must be such that it will attract an adequate supply, yet sufficiently restrict demand ... The 'waiting' means that a man forgoes for a time the disposal of a sum of value" (11, 184). This notion of waiting contains a valuable element but is also not free from contradictions. Even a stationary economy will require a certain amount of 'waiting' because the depreciation quota has to be regularly reinvested and must not be consumed. But there is no productive interest in a stationary economy and so this amount of 'waiting' has to be supplied free[1]. One may try to help Cassel out of the mess by postulating positive consumption rate of interest and a perfect money market by which the production rate of interest would be kept positive even in a stationary economy[2]. The artificiality of this construction is of course enormous as it becomes clear the moment we try to apply it to any historically known economy. But for the time being we are confined to our imaginary world of logical structures and we must proceed exploring it. The next step consists in asking the following question: Can one assume anything at all about the value of the consumption rate of interest in the absence of investment opportunities, say in a stationary state?

---

[1] The following explanation of Cassel certainly cannot be taken seriously: "... the ultimate reason why prices must be raised is the fact that the community requires more waiting than it can afford for nothing, as it does in the stationary state. Hence it follows that the Socialist community will have to put a price on waiting; that is to say: so long as the community already possesses the whole capital that it wishes to use, it can afford to supply waiting for nothing; but as soon as it enters upon an increase of its capital, fresh waiting is needed, and this cannot be supplied without a sacrifice on the part of the present labourers ..." (26, 176—7). On another occasion Cassel writes: "In view of the actual possibilities of the profitable use of capital-disposal for the better satisfaction of wants, a stationary economy is only possible at the rate of interest which living humanity would regard as extraordinary high" (11, 242).

[2] We shall consider this idea a little later, in section (b). Compare also Hayek, 27, 58.

4. Here, as in any other economy, mistakes, windfalls and accidents are possible and, generally, people may have various scales of time preferences. If two individuals with different marginal rates of time preference meet, then it pays to the individual with the lower value of the "psychological time discount" to lend his purchasing power and it pays to the other individual[1], for whom the present purchasing power has a relatively greater value, to borrow it. The size of this transfer of purchasing power will be determined by the marginal equality of the rates of time preferences of two individuals, from which equality one may derive the rate of interest. The meaning of the whole transaction is as follows: initially the lender refrains from consumption in favour of the borrower, in compensation for this the borrower refrains from more consumption in favour of the lender at some later date. The additional consumption (above the amount lent) enjoyed by the lender at later time is interest. Consumption interest has its source in the differences of time preference schedules and has nothing to do with capital productivity.

It is a fairly popular view, particularly among text-book writers, that the psychological time discount has necessarily a positive value. Human beings are said to possess an irrational faculty of discounting future enjoyment — the deficiency of the telescopic faculty in individuals, as Pigou would say, leads to a myopic underestimation of the future — therefore present goods are always more valuable than future goods and the difference in value represents the source of income. However, this difference is not necessarily positive and depends primarily on the institutional system of the economy. There are many reasons why in this connection the interest rate may assume negative or zero values. Individuals may expect smaller income in the future (for instance in the time when they retire) and may therefore wish to save from the present income to make their consumption more evenly distributed over their lifetime. Or, they save from current income to accumulate resources for larger expenses which occur at discrete intervals like holiday travelling or buying a house. Or, they may wish to leave consuming power to their heirs. They may collect money as philatelists collect postage stamps and as bibliophiles collect books without being less rational than the collectors in these two fields. For, in a money-centred economy money means prestige and power. People may also enjoy productive work for its own sake and go on investing until there is any possibility for an increase in production.

It becomes apparent that a great many individuals will be eager to save and, far from regarding this as a sacrifice to be paid for, will be prepared to pay for a safe transfer of the present purchasing power to the future. It is, therefore, "impossible to say what price would rule if there were a market for present *versus* future purchasing power, unaffected by any other influence except the desires of individuals about the time-pattern of their consumption" (J. Robinson, 25, 395). To establish that a zero or a negative interest rate is not only a mere possibility

---

[1] For instance a student who is the sole heir of a wealthy aunt with delicate health — to use Schumpeter's example.

but also a real world phenomenon, it suffices to observe the post-war economies of those European countries where the rate of inflation was higher than the rate of interest on savings deposits[1].

(b) Productivity of Capital

We now pass on to the demand side of our initial Robinson-economy model, assuming for the time being that the consumption rate of interest is zero.

1. That human labour is more productive when equipped with capital goods is an everyday observation and as such self-evident. However, this observation does not exhaust the problem. Since the days of Böhm-Bawerk, economists have come to realize — and, as we shall see, to forget over and over again — that although *physical* productivity of capital is self-evident, the same is by no means true for its value productivity (surplus over cost). The interest rate is exactly a value phenomenon. Perhaps, the easiest way to tackle the problem — at any rate, this is the way in which the interest theory has historically been developed — is to start with an analysis of a stationary situation. One must, however, be cautious enough to bear always in mind that a stationary state with constant tastes, resources, and technique, with risk premium excluded from interest (or simply non-existent) and with a developed money market (production and consumption lending at a uniform interest rate) is a non-existent rational construction. The possible conclusions must therefore be interpreted by taking into account these qualifications.

2. Suppose the production function of a primitive stationary economy undergoes an once-for-all progressive change, say the iron axe has been invented. Something of the sort can be found described in an illuminating model constructed by O. Lange (28). After this shift in the production function it pays to draw some resources from production for current consumption to production for future consumption (=investment) because the latter, aided by iron axes, yields larger output. The present loss of consumption may be considered as cost of investment, the permanent future addition to the output stream as its net yield, and the ratio between the latter and the former as the rate of interest. Now, if net output is to be maximized, this transfer of resources must be continued as long as a net addition to net output can possibly be obtained. Obviously, maximum is attained when the rate of interest reduces to zero. In *such* circumstances the rate of interest is an index of the discrepancy between actual and optimum allocation of

---

[1] Yugoslav experience suggests that in a planned economy, after a certain moderate level of development has been achieved, consumption interest rate is likely to be zero or negative. See footnote to Ch. 4-d-3. But no generalization is possible as yet and much seems to depend on what is sometimes called "national temperament". The communities of Jews, Scots, Slovenes or Macedonians, as we know them — or as they are reputed to be — are likely to save from small incomes and even at a negative interest rate. Not so a community of Bosnians.

resources[1]. Optimum allocation means that the economy is saturated with capital and that therefore the price for its use is zero[2]. All this seems more or less obvious. But it is in fact not quite so, and it may be worth while considering possible complications. Let us do it by means of a brief analysis of the argument advanced by F. Knight, who attacked Lange's conclusion as fallacious.

Knight maintains that time is cost exactly as labour is cost and that they must continue to be cost unless all their products are free goods (29, 199); from the moment when first capital goods were created, capital co-operates in the production of further capital on the same terms as do other factors (30, 454). If only axes existed in the system, the state of capital saturation would be feasible, but as a general proposition it is untenable. For it would require a definite "limit to the possibility of producing new capital goods (desirable things of every sort) which require no maintenance or replacement". To Knight it seems "self-evident that there is literally no limit to the amount which might be invested at some rate of yield in practically every single investment". The examples mentioned are furniture, polishing diamonds and permanent improvements on land (30, 625; 31, 224).

Knight's argument is based on several unwarranted implicit assumptions[3]. Define, as Knight does, diamonds and other consumer durables as capital goods which render services representing interest. If we assume that diamonds are owned and "consumed" by the same people, then there is no market for their services. Consequently, interest cannot be ascertained and the proposition is analytically useless. If owners and consumers are different people and hiring diamonds is organized like hiring cars, with the increase in the quantity offered, the price of diamonds services will fall. The limit and the final equilibrium are reached when the price just covers expenses (depreciation, labour cost, risk) of the diamond-letting firm, leaving no surplus whatever for inter-

---

[1] As it stands this is true only under restrictive assumptions of stationariness. "The real rate of interest ... may thus serve as an index of the distance of the actual allocation of the labour resources from the allocation producing maximum net output" (28, 170). After having introduced money capital, Lange writes: "The rate of interest, being an index of the shortage of capital, is also an index of the distance of the actual state from a long period equilibrium" (p. 190). But the concept of the "long period equilibrium" is ambiguous and requires a careful treatment. See section (c).

[2] Under the conditions stated Lange is right to say: "These considerations expose the fallacy of the superstitious belief current among many economists, that there would be an infinite demand for money capital if the rate of interest were zero, or that a saturation with capital could be attained only when all commodities were to become free goods. It follows clearly from the theory of production that a saturation with capital is attained when the marginal productivity of indirect labour becomes equal to the marginal productivity of direct labour" (28, 190). The phrase "superstitious belief" provoked a violent reaction on the part of F. Knight (31). Knight's argument is discussed in the text together with his earlier views.

[3] For this reason there was no need for Lange to concede: "I do not state that capital accumulation must lead *necessarily* to a zero marginal net productivity of capital. I quite agree that there may be cases where saturation with capital can never be attained. But I am inclined to be more sceptical about frequency of their occurrence" (32, 234). In a stationary economy, accumulation must *necessarily* lead to capital saturation. See Appendix.

est. (Note that here we are not concerned, as Knight was not[1], with consumption interest which is assumed to be non-existent.) Take next the general case of permanent improvements. Unless the number of "permanent improvements", for which there will be a demand at a zero rate of interest, is infinite, there must be a limit for the investment of new capital. In a stationary economy, the number of possibilities is less than infinite by definition, and so durables will be produced until demand is saturated; in other words, only this special category of goods becomes free, not *all* goods. But even so, the statement is not correct. In the *human* economy no good is absolutely durable and so no improvement is permanent. An irrigation scheme or a tunnel require maintenance, and as with every new irrigation scheme the maintenance cost rises and the increment of product falls (because more productive schemes are chosen first), sooner or later the equilibrium position must be reached. Similarly, every year a certain amount of diamonds is simply lost and must be replaced; and the yearly waste is likely to increase with the increased stock which causes the prices of diamonds to fall. All this imposes a definite limit to the productive investment of capital[2]. Capital productivity reduces to zero while productivity of labour remains positive. It follows that capital and labour do not co-operate on equal terms, which invalidates Knight's starting assertion. Consequently, they cannot be treated on a par simply because the one is the product of the other. The last point requires an elaboration. And also the general proposition of a zero productive rate of interest in a stationary economy deserves to be discussed more fully, for the problem seems to have been often misunderstood[3].

3. Suppose in a stationary economy an entrepreneur has bought a machine that earns more than its amortization quota. If this is a property of the machine itself, nothing will stop other entrepreneurs from buying the same machine. The increase in the demand will temporary drive up the price of the machine enabling its producers to collect unexpected profits. They will also gradually increase production in order to meet the demand. For this they will need more labour and more raw material the prices of which will therefore also rise absorbing a part of producers' profits. In this way the initial disturbance caused by an appearance of unexpected profits will be gradually transmitted backwards to all original factors of Production. A parallel forward process will likewise be going on. The increased supply of machines will lead to gradual cheapening of their products reducing thus the profits at the other end in favour of consumers. When this twodirectional pro-

---

[1] However, in a later article dealing with the same problem, Knight adds the following explanation: "I do propose to treat as literally self-evident the proposition that the rate of interest on loans could never be zero unless all goods were free. One who could borrow "money" without interest could certainly secure the use, indefinitely and without cost, of any useful agent purchasable with money. No reservation is necessary for the terms of the loan or necessity of repayment, since one loan could be repaid with the proceeds of a new one" (33, 26n). The statement is meaningless since the borrower must repay all the loans within his lifetime which is finite.

[2] For a slightly different argument see Appendix.

[3] In this connection the *locus classicus* is, of course, Schumpeter's Chapter 5 in the *Theory of Economic Development*.

cess comes to an end and a new equilibrium position is attained, nothing will be left from the initial profit, it will be completely absorbed by rents and wages. The machine is physically as productive as it was before, social product is permanently larger than it was and yet it is completely exhausted by the shares of wages and rent leaving nothing for a separate share of interest. Competition destroys every possible surplus which may be attributed to the physical productivity of a good.

If the equilibrating process encounters some obstacle so that, for instance, there is a strict limit for the additional supply of our exceptional machines, the permanent net income they generate will not disappear. But this is then due to some monopoly, either natural or institutional, and has been accounted for by the concept of rent. Monopoly gains are thus by definition something different from interest.

Unlike the physical productivity of a machine, which is a man-made product the services of which may be resolved into the services of labour (and monopoly), the productivity of some natural processes seemed often much more difficult to reconcile with the concept of competition and caused much confusion in the theory of interest. Böhm-Bawerk's oak samplings planted in a socialist forest (21, Book VI, Ch. X) and Wicksell's wine which matures in capitalist cellars (34, pp. 172—7), are much quoted and equally misleading examples. In both cases, the value of the product increases with the mere passing of time. Is not this an obvious proof that time is somehow productive and that the interest rate is simply a price for "waiting"? Take Wicksell's example.

4. The entire capital of community in a closed (with respect to capital) economy consists of stored wine and is assumed to be fixed: it just suffices for each year's vintage to be stored for four years. The cost of storing is negligible. Our community sells the wine to neighbouring countries in exchange for commodities. If the size of the vintage and the prices of the wine of various ages are given, the equilibrium rate of interest is determined. It must be such that it pays to increase the storage period from three to four years but not to increase it from four to five years[1], and in Wicksell's example it is about $10\frac{1}{2}$ per cent.

If storage period were extended to five years, a *smaller amount of money* would be available for the purchase of grape juice whose price would, consequently, fall. But the lower price of the new wine makes a shorter storage period more profitable[2]. The argument also applies, *mutatis mutandis*, to the case of shortening the storage period to under four years. Thus the four-year period is really the equilibrium storage period. As the total supply of labour and land is given, the example is

---

[1] If 3-year wine commands a price of 90 s. per hl., 4-year wine 100 s. and 5-year wine 110 s., then the rate of interest must be less than 11.11% (=10/90) and more than 10% (=10/100). For a simple graphical representation of Wicksell's case see Lutz, 35, 32.

[2] Normally, subsequent increments in price, due to increase in age, are diminishing and so are the corresponding rates of interest. The 3-year equilibrium interest rate is higher than the 4-year one and therefore the price of grape juice (derived by discounting for the time of storing) is lower in the former than in the latter case. It follows that a lower price of grape juice will make a shorter storage period more profitable.

so designed as to make the length of time the only variable dimension of capital. Leaving the 3-year wine to mature in cellar for another year, its value will increase by $10\frac{1}{2}$ per cent. "The rate of interest here appears clearly in its simplest form as *the marginal productivity* of 'waiting'" (34, 177).

However, much as Wicksell's reasoning seems convincing at first glance, it is really a *quid pro quo*: it was not time but the arbitrary limitation of the (money) capital[1] which caused interest to appear. Every year entrepreneurs in this Bacchus celebrating community earn an amount of profit (interest) equal to $1.105^4 - 1 = 49\%$ of the value of one-year vintage. Wicksell fails to discuss the question: What do they do with this profit? The implicit assumption of the model is that they *consume* it. Now, if entrepreneurs' consumption is in line with the consumption of other members of the community — if it is a reward for the work done — it will represent *wages* and an additional year of storing the wine will require more labour than entrepreneurs are willing to supply at the lowered wage rate. If entrepreneurs' consumption is greater, the difference will consist of *monopoly gains*[2]. If our wine-growing entrepreneurs are not monopolists, they will have to behave in the same way as their competitive brethren do elsewhere and invest their profits. As soon as they do, the well known chain reaction develops: the amount of capital begins to increase, with it the profitable storage period is prolonged and therefore the equilibrium rate of interest is reduced; in the absence of innovations the process develops towards the point of capital saturation where interest rate assumes zero value because all possibilities of additional increments in product are exhausted.

Let us now bring a few additional complications into our story in order to emphasize some important points more strongly. If during the process of prolongation of the storage period, the *consumption* rate of interest has been negative or zero, the *production* rate of interest will vanish in the way described. But what happens if the consumption rate of interest remains positive? Clearly, entrepreneurs will find it more profitable to lend money than to keep on investing in stored up wine. Would this indicate that waiting is productive after all? It would not, as the production rate of interest owes its existence to another factor.

---

[1] Cf. Lange: "Not the introduction of time as a variable into the equations of the theory of production, but a *shortage of capital*, which affects the distribution of original resources... between their direct and indirect uses, is at the basis of the theory of interest... When the shortage of capital disappears... interest vanished, however much time the production process may take" (28, 189).

[2] It may be of some interest to recall that in historically stationary economies the ruling classes did in fact enjoy monopoly income. Capitalist entrepreneurs have largely destroyed this monopoly, but with it they have destroyed the stationariness as well. It follows that from a historical point of view it is nonsensical even to pose the question of production interest in a stationary economy; such a thing simply did not exist. Interest which was known was something else and the disgust and indignation it was causing for centuries were not so irrational after all. Interest in the ancient world and in the Middle-Ages, similarly as prostitution today, was a robbery of the poor and distressed and as such an illegal, or at least socially unapproved, economic activity.

If everybody can earn profit (interest) simply by lending money, our representative wine-grower ceases to exist as an entrepreneur and becomes either a worker or a monopolist. Suppose, however, that his entrepreneurial mentality suddenly reappears and he finds himself mixing his wine with a certain powder which speeds up the maturation process for one year. Capital invested in one-year vintage will thus be set free and brought to the lending market. Suppose that the ultimate effect of the additional lending capital is to drive the consumption rate of interest to zero (community is now wealthier and all anticipations of future incomes happen to be just matched by current savings of the respective group of individuals). As a consequence, the storage period will be expanded to the limit of its maximum productivity; wages (or wages and rent) will now exhaust the whole product. The innovation, once applied, will deprive the innovator of his earlier net income stream as expressed in interest. This result is due to the fact that the innovation has as it were been applied in a wrong sector. In the stationary economy time is not a genuine cost factor and therefore saving of time does not become a source of permanent income. (With consumption interest rate zero, further saving in time does not increase net product.) The innovation has only created an abundance of capital which annihilated the rate of interest, showing so that in the stationary economy, the real cause of the production rate of interest is to be sought in shortage of (money) capital. In order to create a permanent source of net income our innovator should have saved labour expenses in the cultivation of his vineyard and, when others followed the suit, he should have remained in the forefront of further improvements.

5. Let us now summarize. The *consumption* rate of interest may conceivably be negative, zero or positive. The fact that it is not *necessarily* positive has important consequences. If interest is to be considered a *permanent* value phenomenon, the mere possibility of its disappearance in the stationary state, suffices to invalidate any attempt to derive interest from stationary conditions. This conclusion is sufficient for our present purpose. However, if it pleases us, we can easily postulate conditions under which consumption interest rate *must* be *exactly* equal to zero. Schumpeter shows the way.

A consumer, if he is to be rational, must maximize his consumption not in this or that year but within his lifetime. Schumpeter defines the pure rational type of a stationary state consumer as a person with approximately constant needs and with a life-rent sufficiently safe and also allowing the creation of a reserve fund for contingencies. If the stream of income is given, if utility is the function of income, and if marginal utility is diminishing, the optimum solution consists in an even distribution of income through time. The individual cannot estimate his future annuities less than his present ones, because in the course of time he would experience less satisfaction than he could have attained with zero time preference[1] (36, 55). It follows that maximization of consumption implies zero interest rate.

---

[1] This is the formal part of the argument as developed in Chapter I. In Chapter IV Schumpeter is concerned with proving the same thing by historical considerations. He admits that accidents, windfalls, etc., cause value agios to appear even

If in a stationary economy the consumption rate of interest is zero, the *production* rate of interest also vanishes, which means that the economy is saturated with capital. Occasional progressive changes in the production function may cause a certain net yield of capital to appear. But this net yield is only temporary and owing to competition it will sooner or later be absorbed into wages and rent. The new stationary level of output is higher, physical productivity of capital goods has been permanently preserved, but their value productivity has been destroyed.

The analysis of a stationary state has helped us to provide unequivocal answers to three Schumpeterian questions about the source, the cause and the permanence of interest. The answers are also essentially Schumpeterian.[1] The source of interest is surely to be found in those temporary profits which appear during the transition from a lower to a higher stationary output. The cause of these profits is to be found in the progressive shifting of the production function, in innovations. The permanence of the net yield of capital is to be attributed to the permanent flow of innovations, in other words — to economic growth. Interest, as a value phenomenon, independent from wages and rent, and in the form of a permanent net income due to use of capital, is to be found in a growing economy only.

(c) Production Interest in Planned Economy

None of the interest theories discussed so far is satisfactory for our purpose. Nevertheless, the foregoing discussion was useful because it revealed a number of essential characteristics of the rate of interest as well as a number of pitfalls of this intricate subject. We are now well equipped to tackle our main problem.

1. In one of his five postulates Schumpeter contends that in a communist or, generally, in an exchange-less economy, there will be no interest as an independent value (it would, perhaps, be better to say: market) phenomenon (36, 348). And this is obvious. If the state owns capital goods and *directly* organizes the production process, interest as an instrument is superfluous. And in the country which comes nearest

in a stationary state, but argues that this interest would be utterly unimportant, only a couple of usurers could live on it, payment of interest would be considered as an anomaly and therefore it cannot be an essential part of the economic process (pp. 341, 375).

Essentially the same as the second Schumpeterian version is the argument of Max Weber who makes a sharp *sociological* distinction between budgetary units oriented to provision for needs, characteristic for historically stationary societies, and capitalist profit-oriented enterprises. "The purchase of securities on the part of a private investor who wishes to consume the proceeds, is not an investment of capital but of personal resources ... On the other hand, a loan made to a consumer and one to an entrepreneur for business purposes, are quite different from the point of view of the borrower" (37, 184—5; see also Ch. II, sections 11 and 15). One may add that also Marx would subscribe to this view.

For some evaluations of Schumpeter's interest theory see G. Haberler (38), Clemence and Doody (39, 28—30) and F. Lutz (35, 117—9).

[1] His three basic postulates are: interest is a product of development; it flows from the profit of the entrepreneur; it does not stick to concrete goods (36, 347).

to this form of economic organization, in the Soviet Union, it is indeed so. Investment projects need only be arranged according to their profitability and then adjusted in such a way as to equalize marginal profitability of all chosen projects.

If, however, the central planning authority does not directly organize the entire economic process, but the initiative, responsibility and risk are shared among several links in the planning chain with, say, an emphasis on the firm as the basic decision making unit, then the interest rate becomes a useful economic instrument again. Why this type of economic organization is preferable will be discussed later (Part III). For the moment it will suffice to realize that interest as a regular cost item in the accounts of firms automatically checks the efficiency of the use of capital goods and so prevents waste of this scarce factor of production.

In principle, the problem is then relatively easy to solve. The Planning Authority determines the size of the investment fund and invites applications for investment credits. The firms apply offering various rates of return. Applications are accepted following the order of magnitudes of the rate of return offered until the investment fund is exhausted and the rate of interest is set so as to be equal to the marginal net productivity of all investment projects considered. Of course, this pricing process, like all other pricing processes, is not smooth and free from outside interventions. To take an obvious example: new industry requires that the generation of power is increased and a well made investment plan has to provide means for this regardless of the height of the interest rate offered by power stations. But the basic principle is clear enough.

2. The interest rate is therefore the price a firm has to pay for the social permit to use social capital, i.e., for the use of factors of production owned by society.[1] Note the double meaning of capital[2] in this pricing process. The permit to dispose of a part of the social investment fund means the disposal of *ex ante* capital (i.e., of a potential combination of capital goods) which is by definition everywhere equally productive at the margin. Ideally, the applying firm prepares several alternatives of its investment project corresponding to several possible interest rates. The rate of interest which the Planning Authority eventually adopts is equal to the marginal productivity of each of all those

---

[1] Compare the following definition by Schumpeter: "Interest — more correctly, the capital sum plus interest — is ... the price paid by borrowers for a social permit to acquire commodities and services without having previously fulfilled the condition which in the institutional pattern of capitalism is normally set on the issue of such a social permit, i.e., without having previously contributed other commodities to the social stream" (40, 123). In the "institutional pattern" of socialism this definition must be slightly broadened to include also investment financed from the internal resources of the firm (from profits, for instance), for interest rate has to be paid for the use of all capital goods irrespective of the source of their finance because "means of production" are socially owned and should be put to the best possible use.

[2] Cf. Schumpeter: "Capital in this sense is not goods but balances, not a factor of production but a distinct agent which stands between the entrepreneur and the factors" (40, 129). Capital in my interpretation is both, goods and balances, and is in any case factor of production because the latter concept is in this study used to mean "factor influencing the organization of production in the sense of being conducive or not to an optimum allocation of resources".

investment projects which in their sum total just exhaust the available investment fund. However, once incorporated in concrete equipment and buildings, *ex ante* capital is transformed into capital goods which by themselves do not have the extraordinary faculty of net value productivity and even less that of equal marginal net productivity. For this reason, pricing consists of two separate procedures: first, the firm pays interest rate for the permit to use capital goods, and second, these goods are bought from other firms in the same way as any other commodity and then their value is gradually reproduced, in the same way as the value of raw materials, in the output of finished product. The value of this output is higher than the value of the corresponding input because it is a result of a "new combination" of factors of production, it is a non-stationary output. The resulting surplus is a source of interest, and if this surplus (after the rent, resulting from the diminishing marginal productivity of investment, has been deducted) is greater or smaller than interest, the firm will earn net profit or suffer losses respectively.

3. The rate of interest is determined by the marginal productivity of investment projects and the size of investment fund. It remains to enquire how the "available investment fund" is determined. Until now it has been the *communis opinio doctorum* that the amount of investment in a planned economy is a result of a widely arbitrary decision.[1] But, as we have already noted (see Section c-3), it is not. Neither does it result from aiming at reducing marginal net productivity of capital to zero (42, 85). This (i.e., any addition to capital leaving output unchanged) would be impossible to achieve in a progressive economy, and there is no justification for assuming that the flow of innovations will eventually peter out. In fact it is primarily with respect to the problem of the optimum rate of investment that the traditional interest theories have singularly failed to provide a satisfactory solution. And the reason is a simple one. Considering the changes in the productivity of capital, economists — misled by their vision of a private capitalist personified in Robinson Crusoe — were always thinking of a single marginalist process, while in reality two processes occur simultaneously. Anticipating fuller analysis in Part V, the basic characteristics of these two processes may be described as follows.

---

[1] Cf. Lerner: "The determination of the rate of investment is unavoidably political ... There is no certain way, in a collectivist economy, of permitting the consumers, *as consumers,* to make this decision *via* the price mechanism" (41, 263). And Lange: "But the rate, i.e., the speed, at which accumulation progresses is arbitrary" (42, 85). Next Dickinson: "... the marginal productivity of capital goods will establish ... a definite relation between the quantity of resources so available and the rate of interest that just allocates them without deficit or excess. But in absence of a free market for savers there is no means of deciding, on individualistic principles, what quantity of resources should be saved. This decision will have to be taken by the planning authority on behalf of the community as a whole and will be, from the liberal individualistic point of view, arbitrary" (43, 80). Also G. D. H. Cole: "There is no way of determining in principle how much a society ought to set aside for these (investment) purposes; ... What is clear is that this choice ought not to be left to the chance of individuals' willingness to spend less than their income: it ought to be made socially and democratically ..." (44, 64). All quoted writers are socialists. As non-socialist economists could only agree with the same view, there is no need to quote them separately.

Suppose a long term investment plan is drafted for a given economy with an aim of maximizing total output within a period of, say, ten years. If various total amounts of potential investment are considered, it will be found, at least after a certain critical point, that successive additions to investment, *within the same period,* yield decreasing increments in output. All new factories that will be built are more efficient than the already existing ones. It follows that marginal productivity of investment, *ergo* the rate of interest, is always greater than zero. But each additional factory means additional strains on material and human resources of the economy lowering thus the general efficiency of the economy. Clearly, marginal productivity of investment is declining, may become zero, even negative, and the same applies to the rate of interest. It follows that, in order to describe what is happening, we have to use two different concepts of the rate of interest. Interest Rate I, call it the *allocation rate of interest,* is always positive and is used to allocate resources from the investment fund to the most productive uses. Interest Rate II, call it *investment determination rate of interest,* provides an "index of the distance between the actual position and the point of capital saturation" and in the limiting case, when output is maximized, becomes equal to zero. Optimum optimorum is achieved when, given IR II, the corresponding IR I is at its maximum. These conditions determine the point of equilibrium we are searching for.[1]

4. It may be useful to attempt building a bridge between this conceptual scheme and the traditional reasoning. Assume that (1) all firms are "perfectly competitive" in the sense that at the margin investment opportunities are the same for all of them; (2) that the effects of the marginal doses of investment can be observed while these doses are defined as infinitesimal variations of investment expenditures and (3) that all firms move simultaneously towards, along or beyond the frontier of maximum output. In such a hypothetical world IR I and II would coincide. No firm would find it advantageous to increase investment for an infinitesimal quantity because the output, being at the maximum point, would not react. It would also not pay to increase investment for a finite quantity because, by definition, all other firms would do the

---

[1] Compare Dobb's analysis of a Lange-type model of direct *versus* indirect labour applied to a socialist economy. "When the position of 'capital saturation' has been attained (which alone can be spoken of as a position of 'equilibrium' in a socialist economy), different technical conditions in different industries and their resulting differences of 'organic composition', will cease to exert any influence on relative prices. In other words, an economic plan which distributes capital resources in the most productive manner will necessarily, owing to the limited development of the productive forces at any one time, produce a system of prices analogous to Marx's 'prices of production'. But this will not be a position of equilibrium. In the degree that capital accumulation proceeds, and the productive equipment of society is extended, the dispersion of prices away from their labour values will tend to disappear. In this final position prices will conform to labour values, and all industries will attain equilibrium when their receipts cover their current wage costs..." Footnote: "The occurrence of new technical inventions... would, of course, continually be jerking the economy away from this final position, so that it might never be actually attained, or never long maintained" (45, 328). The inadequacies of the analysis are obvious: like others, Dobb is unaware of the possibility of a *dynamic equilibrium,* of a state of *capital saturation in a progressive economy.*

same and so total output and output of each of the firms would be reduced simultaneously.

In the real world none of the assumptions applies. Investment opportunities are grossly unequal, investments are finite quantities usually in big lumps and individual firms are far from knowing anything about each other's action, let alone synchronizing them. It follows that it pays to firms with superior investment opportunities to invest at the expense of other firms. No firm need go bankrupt as a result. Only the total output of all of them will be lower than otherwise. This is a simple consequence of the diminishing productivity of investment. The properties of investment just described help to explain the meaning of IR I and II.

The whole problem reduces to the difference between the marginal productivity of investment to particular firms and to the economy as a whole. The marginal productivity (to the firms) of investment projects included in the investment plan must not be less than zero, for otherwise the projects would not be considered. It can only by chance be equal to zero, because that would mean that marginal productivity curves of all firms considered coincide at this point with the marginal productivity curve of the economy, and there is no necessity for this to happen. Hence, normally, marginal productivity of investment to the firms included in the plan will be still positive, while marginal productivity of investment to the economy will already have been driven to zero. Thus, IR I will normally be positive. In addition, IR I will be positive for practical reasons, because it is calculated on a finite amount of investment and we have assumed a continuously diminishing marginal productivity of investment. Experience suggests that the values of the IR I are likely to be of the same order of magnitude as those of the ordinary market rate of interest. IR II determines the total volume of investment and hence must not be less than zero.

(d) Consumption Interest in Planned Economy

1. In planned economy, consumption and production rates of interest are clearly unrelated to each other: consumption is a matter of the individuals while production is a matter of the community as a whole. Moreover, the amount of personal saving in a socialist economy is economically negligible because the institutional set-up of such an economy eliminates some of the strongest motives for saving which exist in capitalist societies. Free medical care eliminates illness and accident exigencies. The right to work eliminates fear of unemployment. Pensions as great as the highest wages and salaries earned, make saving for retirement age unnecessary. Social care for children and for those unable to work renders life insurance superfluous. As money loses its quality as a means for acquiring power and higher social status for the person who possesses it, the rationality of saving on this account is destroyed. For the same reason and also because education is free and

accessible to everybody, the incentive to save for heirs is undermined as well.[1]

2. The motives for saving, still existent, are those concerning the provision of funds for occasional lumpy expenditures like travelling during holidays, buying furniture, or acquiring a car. How much will in fact be saved for all these purposes and to what extent will they be financed by instalment credits, depends mainly on the character of the saver and on the characteristics of goods (usually a function of real income). Persons highly appreciating independence will try to avoid financial commitments and to save all the funds they will need. Others, who care less for this, will easily plunge into hire-purchase schemes. On the other hand, primary necessities like furniture, are more likely to be bought in instalments than cars which still represent luxuries and therefore, at least a part of the sum will be saved.

3. As the volume of investment is completely independent of the amount of personal saving, there exists, theoretically, no particular reason for stimulating saving by higher interest rate. We have here the unique case of "a market for present *versus* future purchasing power, unaffected by any other influence except the desires of individuals about the time-pattern of their consumption" (see Ch. 4-a-4). Theory may be brought into the picture in the following way. If saving and hire-purchase can be regarded as two sides of the same process of redistribution of consumption according to the different time preference schedules of the consumers, then in terms of the pure welfare theory optimum (Pareto-optimum) consumption interest rate will be the one which equalizes saving with consumer credit. By this procedure, the value of the marginal unit of consumption is made equal for savers and spenders (in money terms) and thus, given the institutional framework, the available consumption goods are distributed in an optimal manner. However, practical considerations may lead to different results and, generally, the world of economic policy is usually immensely more complicated than that of matching the time preferences of savers and spenders.[2]

---

[1] In Yugoslavia, where all these conditions obtain more or less, the gross (i.e., without deducting consumers credits) increase in personal savings represented in 1955 about 1% of gross non-private investment. See *Statistical Yearbook of the FPR of Yugoslavia*, Beograd, 1957.

[2] The following may serve as an illustration. In Yugoslavia, the consumption rate of interest is 5—6% and the welfare optimum is apparently never struck because consumer credits are constantly much higher than personal saving which would indicate the redistribution of consumption in favour of the more easy-going one. At the end of 1955, personal saving (saving deposits in banks; data on hoarding are not available) amounted to 14 milliard dinars (insurance institutions collected about 3 milliard dinars in addition), while consumer credits amounted to 28 milliard dinars or twice as much. The reason for the relatively low interest rate for consumer credits is to be found in the deliberate policy aimed at inducing the consumer to buy durable consumer goods like wireless sets, bicycles, household appliances, etc. Because of the low standard of living, large masses of consumers were not buying these products and were not getting used to them. With the gradual increase of the standard of living consumers increased their expenditures but continued to buy the products they knew and which were obtainable in divisible quantities (food, textile, alcoholic drink, tobacco). At the same time, the newly created industry — aimed partly at raising the cultural level of the population (wireless sets) — required an expanding market in order to be able to reduce costs of production.

In the welfare context one phenomenon deserves to be mentioned separately. One may assume that with the degree of inflation, *ceteris paribus*, *nominal* consumption rates of interest will change. But, as empirical evidence suggests, *real* interest rates are likely to change as well. Do these changes express changes in time preferences? Economists answer with *no*, and invent the phrase "money illusion" as an explanation. Unfortunately this does not help us to settle the question of the most beneficial redistribution of consumption; to make corrections for "money illusion" would be as arbitrary as to consider it irrelevant from the welfare point of view. Once again, we reach the conclusion that "preferences of individuals" are practically never actual preferences of individuals but that they always depend on the economic system as a whole. It is, therefore, in the nature of things that mere interest rate cannot redistribute purchasing power optimally. Stabilized economy with constant prices appears to be an essential precondition for such a redistribution which, as a first approximation, may be based on the equilibrium consumption rate of interest.

4. Concluding the discussion on the theory of the interest rate in planned economy, it remains to sum up briefly our findings. Three different rates of interest may be distinguished conceptually and numerically. The first two govern the organization of production, the third one is a device for redistributing consumption. Investment determination rate of interest reflects the aggregate marginal productivity of social capital. It assumes zero value when the economy is pushed on to the path of maximum growth. The allocation rate of interest ensures most productive application of new capital. It is always positive because the

---

The solution of the problem was self-evident. Some economists also argued that in Yugoslav circumstances, an *increase* in consumer credits will help to *suppress* inflationary tendencies. Note also that the amount of consumer credit depends not only on the rate of interest, but also on the comprehensiveness of the list of articles for which the credit is available and on other conditions of credit.

There are some further complications. The gap between personal saving and consumer credits was actually smaller because the population held also 3½ mrd din of government bonds. But this sum cannot be simply added to the savings deposits because the bonds are not negotiable and the population subscribed the loan (it was the time of Cominform blockade) governed by patriotic sentiments and not by savings considerations.

Next, peasant agriculture and private handicraft industry represent remnants of the 'capitalist' system and so distort the equilibrium value of the consumption rate of interest (unless it happens to coincide with that of the allocation rate of interest).

Further, in the period 1952—56 the prices of consumer goods and services were rising at an average rate of 6¼% per annum (in 1955 the increase was 13.8%). Consequently the real rate of interest was negative. Does this mean that spendthrifts were living at the expense of virtuous savers? Hardly. Comparing the statistical data for six Yugoslav states, we find that consumer debt per unit of saving is an inverse function of economic development and the standard of living: the higher per capital income the lower proportion of consumer debt to saving (with the notable exception of one State, Macedonia, where people are poor but extraordinarily thrifty). In Slovenia, which is by far the most developed State, saving deposits were 42% *greater* than consumer debt! It follows that, although the negative interest rate and consumer credits, twice larger than saving deposits indicated that the marginal valuations in money terms were not equal, the attacked social welfare, was probably higher than it would have been if they were equal.

The list of complications is, of course, far from being exhausted.

economy is growing. The optimally organized production leads to a maximum possible *output* of consumer goods; to make the best use of the goods produced their time *distribution* to the consumers should be optimal. Wages, i.e., the appropriation of purchasing power, represent the main device of distribution. But for the individual consumer the time pattern of the appropriation of purchasing power does not correspond to the best possible pattern of consumption. Necessary adjustments are achieved through saving and overspending regulated by the consumption rate of interest which may be negative, zero or positive. Each one of the three interest rates is a device for achieving a local optimum. Together, they make up a mechanism for achieving an optimum optimorum.

Appendix

CAPITAL SATURATION IN A STATIONARY ECONOMY

1. A stationary economy may be conveniently defined as an economy in which tastes, labour, natural resources and the state of knowledge are given and constant, while capital represents the only variable factor of production. Thus the problem of capital saturation represents a special case of the law of variable proportions or, as it is usually called, the law of diminishing returns.[1]

The law of diminishing returns states that, in absence of innovations, the application of successive units of any variable factor to another fixed factor will eventually yield diminishing returns. The phrase "eventually diminishing" is used to indicate the possibility of yielding increasing returns before a certain critical point. As A. Lerner observes, the law is not an empirical generalization but a logical derivation and follows from the necessity that every co-operating employed factor have a positive marginal product (41, 155). If the application of factor A increases product more than the application of factors A and B together (A shows increasing returns, while the constant proportion of A and B leads to constant returns), then B has negative marginal product. If B is indivisible, only the increase in the scale of production may eliminate its negative returns. If it is divisible, its excessive part will be discarded at once. In both cases B must be considered as finite, which means that after the scale of production has been sufficiently increased, the negative returns of B will disappear. At this point all factors of production begin to yield positive marginal products and so the law of diminishing returns becomes operative.

2. This knowledge is not sufficient for the solution of our problem. Taking the shape of the production function, as point of departure, some economists argued that even with the law of diminishing returns operative (which is taken more or less for granted), the growth of output

---

[1] For the discussion of various aspects of this law see J. M. Cassels (46), D. Schwartzman (47), and Chamberlin-McLeod-Hahn "divisibility" controversy (48, 169—212; *Quarterly Journal of Economics*, 1949, 128—43).

may be infinite and the capital saturation point non-existent.[1] This is obvious. One can draw innumerable production functions — take only the family of logarithmetic curves — which satisfy the requirement of the diminishing marginal productivity of capital and yet have no maximum. Thus, the issue appears to be one about the facts of technology.

However, the authors of these curves fail to enquire into their economic meaning. The necessary (though not sufficient) condition for the existence of these perverse production functions is that their third derivatives are positive, in other words, that the *returns of capital diminish at a diminishing rate*. Is this retardation of diminishing returns — or, more precisely, such a degree of retardation as to eliminate the possibility of a maximum — economically feasible? The question may be answered in several ways, but the following answer seems to be the most general and straightforward.

Throughout the analysis I shall be assuming that the law of diminishing returns is operative and this is the *only* a priori assumption to be made. As to production functions, three analytically useful types may be envisaged. If the returns diminish by constant or increasing amounts (third derivatives zero or negative), production functions evidently have maxima and at these points our economy becomes stationary. This case is simple and uninteresting because it provides an obvious answer. We shall, therefore, examine the situation in which the industries operate under the conditions of retardation of diminishing returns and distinguish two further cases which exhaust all possibilities. As no restrictive assumptions are used, the analysis proves perfectly general. After all the industries are classified into three categories, according to the formal properties of their production functions, we shall have to examine the empirical content of the curves obtained. The conclusion follows in the form of a theorem.

3. Consider the case when the industries operate under the conditions of diminishing returns and distinguish two kinds of production functions (P): functions which, at the limit, pass into a straight line with a positive slope, i.e., which end with positive constant returns (α-functions),[2] and all other functions (β-functions).

Next, the law of diminishing returns implies that all additional units of the variable factor, in our case of capital, are in every respect equal. Therefore, depreciation (D) cost — physical replacement of output capacity — will be proportional to the physical capital (K) in existence and as such will be represented by a positively sloped straight line. In the case of "permanent improvements" the depreciation line coincides with the abscissa. Analytically, this represents no difficulty, but empirically it is, of course, an "empty box".

---

[1] F. Knight was one of the first to use a similar argument (31, 224); T. Koopmans used it recently (49, 122—5). Koopmans stated the problem very clearly — which was not the virtue of Knight's thinking — and so I am concerned mainly with his argument.

[2] In Koopmans' example: $P = 0.5\,K + \ln(1+K)$, then marginal productivity is $\dot{P} = 0.5 + \dfrac{1}{1+K}$, which at the limit becomes $\lim_{K \to \infty} \dot{P} = 0.5$, where 0.5 represents the slope of the straight line. P stands for Product and K for Capital.

It follows at once that the point (M) where the slope of a β-function (P) becomes equal to the slope of the corresponding depreciation line (D) represents the point of maximum net output for this particular function taken in isolation. The same applies to those α-functions whose marginal productivity at the limit is less than depreciation per unit of capital. The remainder of α-functions, when considered in isolation, show an infinitely increasing net output. This remainder consists of two

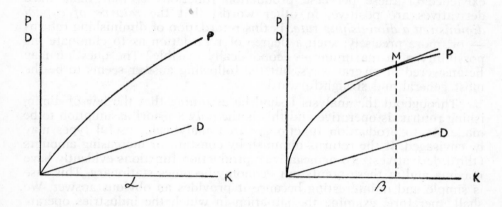

groups of production functions having (αα) both inputs and outputs within the α-sector and (αβ) obtaining inputs from the β-sector. The eventually diminishing net output in the sector β makes for increasing depreciation cost of αβ and thus proves the existence of a maximum point. The diminishing marginal utility of consuming αα-products bends P-curve downwards and so brings a maximum point or ceiling into existence.

4. The last observation needs a short elaboration. Suppose that depreciation costs in the sector αα are zero. Would this mean that equilibrium is reached only when demand is fully saturated and respective goods become free? The answer is no, if labour is also required for production to take place. For, so long as the α-sector needs labour in addition to capital, it is really not independent from the β-sector — where labour must be positively priced — and output will never be expanded so far as to result in free goods. But it is not necessary to assume that the operation of a particular capital good requires labour; it suffices to assume that only the creation of the good itself requires labour. For those people who have to expend their labour on the production of the capital good in question, the sum of services of that capital good — regardless of its eternal duration — has a finite value. After a certain point, this value falls below the opportunity cost of the sacrificed alternative output. At this point, the marginal productivity of capital in this particular line of production, falls to zero.

In order to have equilibrium achieved when the particular services become free, one would have to assume not only the permanency of capital goods and the absence of the current use of labour, but also the absence of any time preference. It suffices to list these assumptions to realize that they do not apply to the world as we know it.

5. If labour is excluded, there is only one more possibility left for ascribing empirical meaning to the sector $\alpha\alpha$: that there are machines which by themselves produce more machines. But such wonderful machines have not yet been invented and it is not likely that they will ever be. Thus the $\alpha\alpha$-sector appears to be devoid of empirical content.

6. Finally, it is possible to envisage a situation where even a β-type production function of the economy has no attainable maximum point. This would happen if the interplay between the falling interest rate and additions to capital were such that it would take infinitely long time to attain the point M. An infinite number of capital additions to attain a finite value of capital means that the additions are infinitely small. As economic systems do not react to infinitesimal changes, this mathematical construction is also devoid of empirical content.

7. The following theorem emerges: *The diminishing marginal productivity of social capital implies the existence of a saturation point where net output is at its maximum and where all goods and services produced are scarce.*

References:

1. D. A. Worcester, "A Reconsideration of Rent Theory", *American Economic Review*, 1946, 258—77.
2. B. Ischboldin, "Zur Grundlegung der modernen Grundrententheorie", *Schmollers Jahrbuch*, 1957, 31—52.
3. L. von Bortkiewicz, "Die Rodbertussche Grundrententheorie und die Marxsche Lehre von der absoluten Grundrente", *Archiv für die Geschichte des Sozialismus und der Arbeiterbewegung*, 1911, 391—434.
4. B. Narain, *Tendencies in Recent Economic Thought*, University of Delhi, 1935.
5. K. Marx, *Capital*, Vol. III, Calcutta, Saraswaty Library, 1946.
6. P. A. Samuelson, *Economics*, London, McGraw-Hill, 1952.
7. J. Mackie, H. Walston, *Land Nationalisation*, London, Fabian Tract 312, 1958.
8. E. H. Chamberlin, *The Theory of Monopolistic Competition*, Cambridge, Harvard University Press, 1946.
9. J. J. Spengler, "Monopolistic Competition and the Use and Price of Urban Land Service", *Journal of Political Economy*, 1946, 385—412.
10. A. Marshall, *Principles of Economics*, London, Macmillan, 1952.
11. G. Cassel, *The Theory of Social Economy*, Vol. I, London, Unwin, 1923.
12. J. A. Schumpeter, *History of Economic Analysis*, New York, Oxford University Press, 1955.
13. R. L. Hall, *The Economic System in a Socialist State*, London, Macmillan, 1937.
14. K. Wicksell, "Cassel's System of Economics", in *Lectures on Political Economy*, London, Routledge, 1946.
15. D. H. Buchanan, "The Historical Approach to Rent and Price Theory", *Economica*, 1929; reprinted in: The American Economic Association (ed.), *Readings in the Theory of Income Distribution*, Philadelphia, Blakiston, 1946. Quotations refer to the book.
16. J. Robinson, *The Economics of Imperfect Competition*, London, Macmillan, 1946.
17. M. D. Brockie, "Rent Concepts and the Theory of Opportunity Cost", *Weltwirtschaftliches Archiv*, Band 72, Heft 2, 1954.
18. K. E. Boulding, *Economic Analysis*, New York, Harper, 1955.
19. L. G. Reynolds, *The Structure of Labour Markets*, New York, Harper, 1951.
20. A. W. Stonier, D. C. Hague, *A Textbook of Economic Theory*, London, Longmans, 1953.
21. E. von Böhm-Bawerk, *The Positive Theory of Capital*, London, Macmillan, 1891.
22. ——————, *Capital and Interest*. London, Macmillan, 1890.

23. ——————, *Recent Literature on Interest*, London, Macmillan, 1903.
24. I. Fisher, *The Theory of Interest*, New York, Macmillan, 1930.
25. J. Robinson, *The Accumulation of Capital*, London, Macmillan, 1956.
26. G. Cassel, *The Nature and Necessity of Interest*, London, Macmillan, 1903.
27. F. A. Hayek, "Utility Analysis and Interest", *Economic Journal*, 1936, 44—60.
28. O. Lange, "The Place of Interest in the Theory of Production", *Review of Economic Studies*, 1935—36, 159—92.
29. F. H. Knight, "Professor Fisher's Interest Theory: A Case in Point", *Journal of Political Economy*, 1931, 176—212.
30. ——————, "The Quantity of Capital and the Rate of Interest", *Ibid.*, 1936, 433—63, 612—42.
31. ——————, "Note on Dr. Lange's Interest Theory", *Review of Economic Studies*, 1936—37, 223—30.
32. O. Lange, "Professor Knight's Note on Interest Theory", *Ibid.*, 231—35.
33. F. H. Knight, "Diminishing Returns from Investment", *Journal of Political Economy*, 1944, 26—47.
34. K. Wicksell, *Lectures on Political Economy*, London, Routledge, 1946.
35. F. A. Lutz, *Zinstheorie*, Zürich, Polygraphischer Verlag, 1956.
36. J. Schumpeter, *Theorie der wirtschaftlichen Entwicklung*, Leipzig, Duncker and Humboldt, 1912.
37. M. Weber, *The Theory of Social and Economic Organization*, London, Hodge, 1947.
38. G. Haberler, "Schumpeter's Theory of Interest", *Review of Economics and Statistics*, 1951, 122—28.
39. R. V. Clemence, F. S. Doody, *The Schumpeterian System*, Cambridge, Mass., Addison-Wesley, 1950.
40. J. A. Schumpeter, *Business Cycles*, New York, McGraw-Hill, 1939.
41. A. P. Lerner, *The Economics of Control*, New York, Macmillan, 1944.
42. B. E. Lippincott (ed.), *On the Economic Theory of Socialism*, Minneapolis, The University of Minnessota Press, 1938.
43. H. D. Dickinson, *Economics of Socialism*, London, Oxford University Press, 1939.
44. G. D. H. Cole, *Socialist Economics*, London, Gollancz, 1950.
45. M. Dobb, "The Question of Economic Law in a Socialist Economy", in *Political Economy and Capitalism*, London, Routledge, 1937.
46. I. M. Cassels, "On the Law of Variable Proportions", *Explorations in Economics*, 1936; reprinted in: The American Economic Association, *Readings in the Theory of Income Distribution*, Philadelphia, Blakiston, 1946.
47. D. Schwartzman, "The Methodology of the Theory of Return to Scale", *Oxford Economic Papers*, 1958, 98—105.
48. E. H. Chamberlin, *Towards a More General Theory of Value*, New York, Oxford University Press, 1957.
49. T. C. Koopmans, *Three Essays on the State of Economic Science*, New York, McGraw-Hill, 1957.

III. THE PRICING OF THE FACTORS OF PRODUCTION
(CONTINUATION)

In Part II we were concerned with the analysis of the non-human factor of production which we found convenient to treat as two separate factors, Monopoly and Capital. Now we proceed to analyze the human factor of production, which we shall also find convenient to dissolve into two separate factors, or, perhaps more correctly, which is a single factor but has two for analytical purposes different aspects, that of Labour and of Entrepreneurship.

The categories of Monopoly and Capital may be attributed a technical sense, which means that they are equally applicable in any exchange economy. But it would be absolutely inadmissible to treat the human factor in the same way because it depends on social relations in production and these relations typically change. If so, which set of social relations should we choose as the basis of our analysis? What are the criteria? How to detect the laws of development? Although my intention is to keep the discussion confined to bare essentials of the theory of planned economy, it proves impossible to avoid the analysis of the social structure of the economic system we are discussing. We thus encounter an undoubtedly formidable problem.

It is clear that only an utmost simplification of the problem of socio-economic development will sufficiently reduce its dimensions to make its meaningful treatment within a chapter feasible. I propose to attempt this in the following way. First, it seems sensible to take an already existing general theory of socio-economic development as a general basis for discussion. In my opinion there can be little doubt that the best *available* theory is still that of K. Marx and F. Engels, known under the name of historical materialism. When we accept the general results of a theory there is no need to go into details while there is a possibility to provide a simple *schematization* which, though dangerous, is useful and helps to preserve the uniform structure of the argument throughout this study. What is left has quite manageable dimensions and consists of points not dealt with by Marx and Engels and of those particularly important from my point of view. Finally, once the relevant system of economic relations is defined, it will become possible to avoid arbitrariness in the analysis of Labour and Entrepreneurship.

73

5. THE OPTIMUM SOCIAL SYSTEM

(a) Schematization of Socio-Economic Development

1. For a long period of time, much longer than that of the written history, human communities could hardly manage to produce enough to survive. In the social relations, then existing, there was no room for "class exploitation"[1].

However, as innovations gradually accumulated, productivity of labour rose. In many communities it became possible to produce regularly more than it was absolutely necessary for survival. Thus, an opportunity arose to live on other people's surplus product. As soon as this economic opportunity became apparent, it was seized by some members of community. And as the other (in- or outside the community) were not willing to part with their surplus product, they were compelled to do so by brute force, they were made *slaves*. Society became a *class* society with the ruling class appropriating the surplus product of the exploited class and using it for its own aims. In this sense, i.e., based on the control of means of living, class exploitation has continued to be exercised in all societies right up to our days and is likely to last for some time to come.

2. A slave is a man owned by another (free) man, owned in the same sense as cows and ploughs. This formal similarity has in those days induced Aristotle to classify slaves — as in our days tempts economists to classify wage-earners — into the same economic category with cows and ploughs, distinguished only as tools which speak as against those which low or are mute. This was a deception of a man who conceived the then existing social relations as only natural and therefore eternal. Ploughs and cows work equally well in all social systems, but human beings do not. For one thing, slaves were very inefficient workers. For another, their reproduction costs were high. On both scores improvements were possible and this is what made *feudalism* a more efficient social system.

The new ruling class had come to realize that in order to extract the surplus labour it was not necessary to resort to slavery. Feudal lords found it quite sufficient to own land, to be able to compel serfs to work for them a certain amount of time. Thus, from the point of view of owners labour force reproduction costs were eliminated because peasant families looked after their own reproduction themselves. The possibility of working for some time on one's own land and of paying the feudal rent not only in terms of labour but also in terms of product and, later, in terms of money, were conducive to the rising productivity of labour.

3. In feudalism the worker was no longer property of the master but was still personally dependent on him, i.e., he was still made to work for him by means of non-economic institutions. The land was not only a means of production, it was also a means of direct political power, because a feudal estate was a sort of a small state headed by a landlord exercising political, military and administrative powers. The serfs were

---

[1] For a different view see Schumpeter, 1, 146.

74

tied to the land and so were not only workers but also subjects of their feudal lords.

The obvious next possibility was to replace personal dependence by market dependence and still to have a smoothly working socio-economic mechanism. After a certain number of violent clashes of antagonistic social forces in various countries, this proved to be possible. Workers, possessing no means of living, have no other choice but to sell their labour force to owners of means of production, i.e., to owners of capital. A new social system, *capitalism*, came into being. At the beginning, the workers had no political rights. Moreover, fines and corporal punishment in the factory, so common in those days, represented a direct continuation of master-serf relations. But after the new system had become more settled, this practice could and had to be discontinued, political rights were granted with no evil effects for the stability of the system. Political and economic power were held firmly by the propertied class, while the free market system provided an efficient barrier for preventing a mass invasion of the higher social strata by the members of the property-less class.

Personal freedom and a *relatively* great social mobility had a tremendous impact on the productivity of labour. Slave and feudal economies, not to speak of primitive society, were almost stationary. Capitalism meant a dramatic change in human history. In the last two centuries, which is about the period of time when the organization of production may be described as capitalist, production of material wealth has expanded more than in all those thousands of years before. Surely, this must have profoundly affected the course of social development.

4. It is hardly necessary to stress that the scheme developed in previous paragraphs is nothing more than a scheme. Its sole purpose was to point at the crucial factor in social development: the relations between men and men in production. Ancient society was characterized by slave labour, feudal society by serfdom, capitalism by wage labour.

Clearly, these relations are not a matter of choice, a matter of ethics or of liking and disliking. There is nothing "natural" in them, for Aristotle thought that slavery was natural, while others think the same for the wage labour. If history teaches us anything, then its lesson says that social relations change, that production expands and that there is a correspondence between these two sets of changes. This correspondence is very complex, but again, if schematized, it may be reduced to the following. The development of productive forces makes a new social system feasible, and once the social change is made, it helps production to expand further. In class societies social changes do not occur by friendly agreement or by means of a rational legislature or anything of the kind, they are outcomes of the strives of antagonistic social classes fighting for their interests. The class whose interests are tied up with the new and superior mode of production emerges victorious and reorganizes the society. In the most developed countries at the end of a social epoch class struggles are likely to result in violent revolutionary overthrows of the old social systems. Once the new social system is more or less established in the most advanced countries, the ruling classes of other countries — unless very much lagging behind the general development

— are likely to submit without civil wars. All this means two things. First, that social development is gradual and that steps cannot be skipped over. Secondly, being tied up with the development of productive forces, the social development — i.e., the succession of social systems — is not reversible.

The process described is not a straight line process. There are temporary setbacks. Prior to the advent of capitalism the world was not a unified whole as it is today and so entire civilizations could have perished without significant consequences for the later development. The scheme is primarily applicable to the European history which has been more or less autonomous and spontaneous and therefore the process could have worked itself out fully. Once capitalism had taken firm roots in Western Europe, it began to spread all over the world by means of trade and conquest. Capitalist institutions were imported into non-European countries whose social systems covered the whole range from primitive society to feudalism and so the most complex social processes were set into being. Perhaps the only universal characteristic of all these processes was that everywhere capitalism was gaining ground against all rival social systems.

But even in Europe slavery, feudalism and capitalism are not three rigid historical systems neatly separated from each other. In each of them the institutions of the other two were known and developed to a certain extent. They are not "pure" systems and they can be classified as separate systems only in terms of predominant institutions. Determinism in development, i.e., in the succession of these systems, only means that, for instance, the uprising of Roman slaves under Spartacus in the first century B. C. and the peasant wars in Europe in the XVth and XVIth centuries could *not* achieve the purpose of their initiators, while the war of the northern states in America for the abolition of slavery in the XIXth century *could not fail* to achieve this goal (ultimately). As concrete events, these are, of course, products of unique historical circumstances and as such unrepeatable. But once irrelevant details are abstracted, a regularity appears and provides a basis for generalizations. It is obvious that any single country may skip stages of development and that this is exactly what many backward countries are doing today. But this fact does not affect the validity of generalizations, for it is only *societies which lag behind* that are able to skip stages of development. Societies in the front line of development cannot accomplish this feat. This observation is intended to serve as a reminding that purely rationalistic blueprints of economic institutions are useless.

Finally, the two-class scheme only focuses attention on the main driving force of social change: the struggle between those who, being the ruling class, are united by their vested interests in the existing social system and wish to preserve it, and those whose prospects are to benefit from the change and who therefore form the opposing social class. But ruling and exploited classes are not necessarily homogeneous, they are not necessarily rigid and between them there are usually a certain number of middle groups which, of course, all must be taken into account in an analysis of a concrete society. The two-class scheme is nothing more than a convenient and very useful *abstraction* of social relations. An attempt to classify neatly all individual members of a given society into two classes would only reveal an extreme naïveté of an overzealous empirical tester. The purpose of the two-class scheme is to provide a simple analytical framework for studying polarization tendencies in the society, with their inevitable result, the fundamental social conflict. By the term *fundamental social conflict* — as distinguished from social conflicts between individuals and groups which are part and parcel of the life in every conceivable human society — I denote the situation where the fundamental principle of social organization involves social conflict between groups which not merely have divergent interests but which are also related to each other as *upper* and *lower* and as *minority* and *majority*. In all class societies it is easy to point at the existence of the fundamental social conflict. And, conversely, whenever we detect the potential existence of the fundamental social conflict,we may confidently expect the development of a class society. We shall shortly have an opportunity to make practical use of the last hypothesis.

(b) State Capitalism

1. Social development did not end with liberal capitalism, but went on. In this context we cannot avoid discussing, if only extremely fragmentary, the problem of the socialist revolution. It is well known that Marx, extrapolating the historical trend, reached the conclusion that socialist revolutions would break up in the most advanced countries. In fact, however, socialist revolutions occurred in relatively backward countries with no particular signs that they will be necessarily repeated — in a violent form — in the most advanced countries. How is one to account for the failure of this prediction which seemed to be so well in accord with the historical experience?

Let us first notice that the failure of the prediction was not at all general. Marx and Engels proved to be right in predicting violent socialist revolutions[1] and they were right in so far as they expected that it would be the most developed capitalist countries where the working class would be able to realize the first items of its socialist program. At the time of *Communist Manifesto* these items were, among others, eight-hour working day, universal suffrage, working class political and trade organizations, free elementary education, social insurance, rising living standard. Today in all advanced capitalist countries these require-

---

[1] In fact, shortly before his death Marx came to expect that it would be exactly Russia to set the example. "Now ... — he and Engels wrote in 1882 — Russia represents the front echelon of the revolutionary movement in Europe" (2, 601). On the other hand Marx was not insisting on violent overthrow of the old social order as *the only* means for achieving socialism. In a speech given in Amsterdam in 1872 he said: "One day workers will take political power in their hands ... But we have never contended that they should achieve this goal everywhere by the same means. We know that institutions, character and traditions of various countries should be taken into account; we do not deny that there are countries like America, England — and if I knew better your institutions, perhaps I would add to them Holland as well — in which the workers may achieve their goals by peaceful means" (95, 154).

ments are more or less satisfied[1], moreover, in a certain number of countries, private ownership of productive means has been partly abolished, through nationalization, certain industries passed into state ownership. But all that was accomplished without a great socialist revolution — though in various countries there has been a certain number of bloody class-clashes of the 1848 type — and this brings me to my second point.

2. The revolution is not a product of development as such but of unbearable social tensions. In the pioneering countries pre-1848 capitalism was frequently generating social tensions in the vicinity of the explosion point. For an illuminating description of the working of a capitalist mechanism in those days one should look up the historical chapters of Marx's *Capital*. However, at that time conditions were still not ripe for the new social system. Later on, socialism became theoretically feasible but social tensions were no more generated to the extent necessary for a violent revolution. Why? I think two crucial, closely related and mutually reinforcing causes may be quoted as an explanation. First, unlike previous economies, the capitalist economy was not stationary; it was expanding relatively quickly providing a possibility for *both* the toiling classes to improve their lot and the owning class to accumulate wealth. Second, the free market proved to be a very successful organizational principle; as it worked impersonally, apparently no one could be blamed for the existing miseries. For both reasons the ruling class found it possible to give political rights to the toiling class without endangering its own position. This meant further easing of social tensions. Gradually, the working class succeeded in organizing itself into trade unions and political parties and the stronger the labour movement became the lesser was the gulf between the owning and the working class. For good or bad, the well organized labour movement saved advanced capitalist countries from socialist revolutions.

3. The situation was different in the backward countries. Here primitive accumulation of capital with the accompanying social conflicts coincided with the relatively high standard of living in the advanced countries, and with the socialist ideologies professed by strong labour movements in those countries. As the Russian 1905 year showed, there

---

[1] E. F. M. Durbin made the following instructive comparison: "One hundred and one years ago — in 1841 — Britain stood at the beginning of the 'hungry forties'. Let us suppose that the representative member of the toiling and starving industrial proletariat had been told, 'In three generations your great-grandchildren will work for eight hours a day (instead of twelve) for an average real wage of three pounds a week (instead of twenty-five shillings); there will be universal adult suffrage (instead of a tiny electorate composed entirely of the rich), and universal and free elementary education (in place of your illiteracy); most of the unemployed will be supported by a state insurance and assistance scheme (instead of being humiliated, as you are, by the Poor Law); there will be regular provision for the sick and the aged (instead of the private charity and starvation from which you suffer); the sons of poor men will go to Oxford and Cambridge at the expense of the state, and working men will enter the House of Commons in large numbers and occupy the highest offices in the state; the recognition of Trade Unions will be the rule, and not the exception; and most members of your class will possess little property'. What would the poor man of 1841 have had to say to all that? He would, I suggest, have laughed bitterly. The prospect would have seemed preposterous to him — unrealisable in its optimism, a foolish dream" (3, 25).

was enough reasons for a revolution. And once the great revolution had begun, it was only too natural that it would not stop short of attempting to accomplish the most radical program which the epoch had produced, that of socialism. For, revolutions are 'locomotives of the history'. They break the ties of tradition, remove the obstacles of vested interests and clear the ground for a free movement towards the limits provided only by the existing revolutionary ideology which reflects material and cultural conditions of the epoch, not just of the country carrying out the revolution. Though, the later implementations of the revolutionary ideology are modified to a great extent by historical peculiarities of the country concerned, the essential fact stands out clearly as demonstrated by the two most momentous national revolutions: in the XVIIIth century the French revolution removed feudal relations and so paved the way toward greater efficiency of the capitalist organization; in the XXth century the Russian revolution removed the next obstacle, private ownership, and improved the efficiency of economic machine even further. Having proved successful, the Russian revolution was likely to be followed by a host of socialist revolutions in other backward countries. Marx expected that capitalist development would lead to the polarization of wealth *within* the most advanced countries and that this will multiply class contradictions to the point of revolution. That, indeed, happened in the earlier stages of capitalist development, but the quick expansion of productive forces helped to check the polarization process before it had gone too far. And so in its later stages capitalist development led instead to a polarization of wealth on an *international scale* by which the class conflict in the backward capitalist countries was magnified and eventually resulted in socialist revolutions.

4. Next we have to investigate further possible changes in production relations. We saw that these relations — abstracting primitive society — passed through three stages: that of complete personal dependence of the worker on the master; that of partial dependence; and that of the complete personal independence of the worker who was working for the master compelled only by the impersonal force of the market. We were able to attribute the increasing economic efficiency to successive stages.

The whole process represents in fact a successive liberalization of the individual from social ties, an equalization of men, a mastering of social relations in a manner similar to that by which nature and its forces were being mastered. If this generalization is meaningful, the next stage may consist in an elimination of all particular private owners of productive means, who, in their role of production organizers, will be substituted by a single owner, the state, which will lead to an equalization of individuals in their relations to the state. This expropriation of private capitalists by the state was what socialist revolution was expected to accomplish. Economic advantages of state capitalism[1] as

---

[1] By "state capitalism" I mean state ownership and direct control and management of all means of production or, at least, of their dominant part. That is an analytical term and as such devoid of ethical — good or bad, right or wrong — and political — democratic or undemocratic — connotations. The same state of affairs others will denote as "state socialism" or as "socialism". For political purposes the difference between "state capitalism" and "socialism" is, of course, great.

compared with private capitalism, are tremendous. Organizing production according to a rational plan the state is able to speed up economic growth two or three *times* (cf. Ch. 10).

The characteristic feature of capitalism is — to use a Hegelian term inherited by Marx — the alienation of human labour. In order to live the proletarian is obliged to sell his inner being, his labour power, and he has no control over the product of his work. The observation implies two things: the worker is primarily an appendage to the machine, he is used to fructify capital; and second, the fate of the final product is governed by blind forces of the market. In state capitalism self-alienation reaches the ultimate possible limits, because the entire society gets proletarianized. But total alienation at the same time provides the means for its own total destruction. For, if not an individual member, the society as a whole is able to control the product of its work through the state. And this is the point which attracts the main attention of socialists. State control is justified not for its own sake but because it is thought to be the only alternative to the chaos of the private capitalist production. However, if it can be shown that a planned economy can dispense with the state control, it will become apparent that state capitalism is only a transitional stage in the development towards another and more efficient social system, that of socialism. Control of production without the state intermediary means control by direct producers, which in turn means that the equality of proletarians is transformed into the equality of masters. The process of human alienation, started in the first class society, comes to an end and in the first *classless* society it is reversed. The work gradually ceases to be

---

Analytically, if the definition is clear, the terms do not matter. "State capitalism/socialism" may be considered as the last stage of capitalist development or as the first stage of socialist development. For reasons which are obvious from the discussion in the text I felt that the first interpretation was more consistent and so scientifically more appropriate. In this I follow the tradition of Yugoslav socialist thinking. Cf. M. Novak saying that the preservation of state ownership "would mean not an abolition of the proletariat but a transformation of all men into proletarians, not the abolition of capital but its universal rule in which it may develop and necessarily develops an exploitation of its own kind" (4, 92). Approaching the problem from another point of view, N. Pašić comes to the conclusion: "Formerly state intervention in the economy was mistakenly identified with socialism. If this criterion were applied to a few recent decades, it would bring into socialist lines all prominent capitalist politicians of the time from Baldwin and Roosevelt to Hitler and de Gaule" (5, 11). A. Dragičević contends that "nationalization of means of production and planned economy are preconditions of socialism, but *only preconditions* and nothing more" (6, 218). Similarly P. Kovač and Đ. Miljević observe that "state ownership and state management by themselves change little or almost not at all the position of the producer in production and his right to participate in the management of the economy... In countries where socialist revolution has been victorious the state, instead of becoming an organ of the working people, may become and becomes an organ of the government and party apparatus, which rules 'on behalf of the working people'" (7, 13). I may add that, in a certain sense, this line of thinking was anticipated already by F. Engels: "The more productive forces it (the state) takes over, the more it becomes the real collective body of all the capitalists, the more citizens it exploits. The workers remain wage-earners, proletarians. The capitalist relationship is not abolished; it is rather pushed to an extreme. But at this extreme it changes into its opposite. State ownership of the productive forces is not the solution of the conflict, but it contains within itself the formal means, the handle to the solution" (8, 313).

"pain", "disutility" and toil and becomes the first need of the man, the assertion of human life. All this, of course, has nothing to do with the *ethical* desirability of such a system. It only indicates a possibility of a superior efficiency of this system. And if one can establish the possibility and economic superiority of a social system, this will mean, in a Marxian framework, to prove its inevitability.

5. Returning to the problem of state capitalism, we have to enquire what are the social forces and processes by which liberal and private capitalism is being transformed into monopolistic and state capitalism. One of them, (an uncomplete) socialist revolution, has already been mentioned. The other, gradual transformation, is by now so well known that a brief review will suffice.

The free play of market forces in competitive capitalism leads to a gradual concentration of production in the hands of smaller and smaller number of firms whose size correspondingly increases. One of the reasons for the greater efficiency of larger firms is purely technological: the increase in output up to a certain point reduces costs of production. The other and by far predominant reason is related to market: a large firm controls a certain portion of market and therefore can undertake planning; a large firm is financially strong which in a market economy means that it commands credit; hence it can exert pressure on weaker partners and in general it can manipulate the terms of buying and selling in its own favour; it is able to survive in recurrent slumps when smaller firms perish. Thus competitive capitalism has been constantly generating tendencies towards monopolization.

Faced with the economic power of employers, workers began to organize themselves into trade unions. In order to be effective, trade unions had to become large organizations and they grew until they reached the absolute limit of a national wide association. At that stage monopoly labour is facing monopoly capital[1].

A similar process took place in politics. In order to have stable government, the number of political parties is being reduced until the whole political life is dominated by two major parties[2]. There is, further, a strong tendency of these two parties to link themselves with the other two monopoly groups and to represent their interests. Thus we are likely to get a "conservative party" favouring interests of private capital and a "labour party" supported by trade unions.

Four giants dominate the social scene in monopoly capitalism: organized capital, organized labour, and two political parties. In so far

---

[1] The two monopolization trends are not necessarily antagonistic to each other. As R. H. S. Crossman, a British socialist, puts it: "... it must be noted that, in modern large-scale industry, there are certain common interests uniting organized management and organized labour. For instance, it is obviously convenient for both sides that power should be concentrated in fewer and fewer hands" (9, 10).

[2] "Two great monolithic structures face each other — describes Robert McKenzie the British scene, adding characteristically — and conduct furious arguments about comparatively minor issues that separate them" (10, 586). It is not difficult to agree with Crossman that in his *British Political Parties* McKenzie "has shown conclusively that the two great parties have developed in accordance with the law of increasing oligarchy which operates in industry, in the trade unions and in Fleet Street" (9, 21).

as political parties clearly identify themselves with two antagonistic social interests, the oligopoly of four reduces to duopoly. The Marxian vision of the two-class structure of society materialized — although with some important modifications due to the bureaucratization process — in the concrete social organization of a modern advanced capitalist country. Capital and labour fight for supremacy. The immediate outcome of this fight is not necessarily known. An extraordinary event, say a serious slump, may suddenly increase the possibility of the abolition of private ownership or, at any rate, disturb seriously the old balance of power in favour of labour. In this case capitalists may resort to fascism, as they did between the two wars. On the other hand, the ruling class may stubbornly refuse to settle political issues by political means, say by banning socialist parties. In this case the working class may resort to a violent socialist revolution. Finally, various countries will be able to preserve the precarious equilibrium between two antagonistic social forces travelling slowly along the road of gradual nationalization of one form or another — first, perhaps, nationalizing "unprofitable industries in need of complete reconstruction", then "industries vitally important for the nation", next "unorganized industries in need of co-ordination", and then again "monopolized industries in which private monopoly cannot be tolerated", and so forth until the last possible candidate for socialization is taken up — and of increasing state control. Widely spread absentee ownership in the modern capitalist economies makes the process relatively painless. Every new "labour" government will have to make another step in the direction of extending public ownership and so private capitalism will be gradually replaced by state capitalism.

6. Here we reach the point where we may resume the main line of argument. The problem of the system of production relations corresponding to a planned economy has been set into its perspective. State capitalism is such a possible system; it is so not only as a logical possibility but also as an empirical reality. But this knowledge is not sufficient for the solution of our problem. We must ask the question: Is state capitalism an *optimum* system under the given conditions? "In the early days of socialist thought — the British socialist W. A. Lewis writes — it was almost an axiom that once property passed from private hands to public ownership all the major social problems were automatically solved; it would be put to purposes conforming more to the public interest, income would be more equitably distributed, economic power would be democratised, efficiency would increase, and the class struggle between owners and workers would end. This view has not survived the experience" (11, 181). Professor Lewis was referring to British experience, but the conclusion may be easily generalized. The main reason for the inadequate working of state capitalism should be sought, I suggest, in the distinguishing feature of its economic and political organization: the rule of bureaucracy. Thus our next task is to analyze the economic consequences of a bureaucratic organization of the economic process.

(c) Bureaucracy and "Office Fetishism"

Analyzing the working of private capitalism and the ideology it generates, Marx laid great emphasis on what he called "commodity fetishism", i.e., a tendency to see relations between men and men as relations between commodities. A closely corresponding phenomenon in state capitalism may be called "office fetishism". It means hiding actual human relations behind impersonal bureaucratic rules, a mystification of activities of office holders. The judgements of the market are infallible and so are the judgements of an official with respect to his subordinates. The holding of office confers upon the incumbent the quality of being cleverer, more honest, more reliable (politically or otherwise), more intelligent, in short: *superior*, to all individuals placed lower in the office hierarchy. The parallelism goes even further. Both free market and bureaucratic structure have their separate lives which cannot be brought under a conscious control. In the case of free market the contention seems fairly obvious. In the case of bureaucracy it may look somewhat puzzling and therefore requires a more detailed enquiry.

1. Bureaucracy, as a social institution, has three fundamental characteristics:

(1) When administrative tasks are simple and undifferentiated, no specialized apparatus is necessary for their execution. In a small social organization the person in authority is able to control social activities — economic, political and military more or less directly. As the community grows in size, a need will arise for a mediating apparatus between the source of authority and the points of execution of orders. As the needs of the community become more diverse and the social life more complex, the need will arise for increased specialization of the members of the mediating administrative apparatus. Thus quantitative extension and complexity of administrative tasks provide "technological" preconditions for the development of bureaucracy. But this is not the whole story.

(2) Like money, the institution of bureaucracy has been known in all social systems, with the exception of primitive society. However, the institution reached its fully developed form — again like money — only in the capitalist system. The relation between the development of money economy and that of bureaucracy is not only that of parallelism but also a relation of mutual causation. As Max Weber, — who was the first after Marx (94) to study systematically, — pointed out, money is a normal presupposition of bureaucracy, it makes regular pecuniary compensation possible and desirable. In feudalism, the administrators — the feudal lords — were in possession of the means of administration. Similarly the soldiers possessed their own arms. In capitalism, the members of administration and army are separated from the means they manipulate and this appears to be related to the separation of the means of production from direct producers[1]. Money, in the sense of capital

---

[1] If the phrase "other things being equal" is interpreted "in the conditions of antagonistic class interests", the following passage from Max Weber may help to illustrate the point: "The expropriation of workers in general, including clerical personnel and technically trained persons, from possession of the means of production depends on the following principal economic factors: (a) The fact that,

accounting, became an institutional basis for both rationalization and de-personalization of human relations. Bureaucratic structures fitted perfectly into this social framework.

(3) The third characteristic of bureaucracy is that it is a product of a particular type of authority. Following Weber in his classification — but placing his scheme into a different theoretical framework — we can distinguish three fundamental types of authority. *Traditional authority* rests on an established belief in the sanctity of immemorial traditions and the legitimacy of the status of those exercising authority under them (12, 301). Loyalty of subordinate members of community is due to the incumbent of the office and not to the legal order. Hence there is a strong tendency to appropriate the means of administration. Where economic development is slow — as it was before the advent of capitalism — changes in social institutions are very small and the whole of social life, including the institution of authority, is likely to be strongly traditionalized. The existence of traditional authority minimizes the possibility of gradual adaptation to the changing conditions of life and so the existing institutional structure — economic, political, religious — tends to come in conflict with the social needs it is expected to serve and the contradictions between the two tend to accumulate. As there is little possibility for solving these contradictions within the traditional framework, a social explosion usually blows up traditional authority and replaces it, for the time being, by the *charismatic authority* of the leader of the revolutionary movement. Charismatic authority rests on devotion to the specific and exceptional sanctity, heroism or exemplary character of an individual person and of the normative order revealed or ordained by him (12, 301). The essence of a charismatic movement is the emancipation from routine and therefore the corresponding type of authority is bound to last briefly and be transitional in character. Charismatic movements either fail and perish or succeed and through "routinization" of "charisma" build new traditionalized systems. Then the cycle may repeat itself.

With the advent of capitalism the mechanism just described ceases to operate. This not in the sense that traditional and charismatic authorities cannot appear any more, but in the sense that they cease to dominate the social scene. Impersonal market and expropriation of means of production and administration destroy personal loyalties to the incumbents of offices. Quick economic development requires flexible adaptations of the social framework which, implying changes,

other things being equal, it is generally possible to achieve a higher level of technical efficiency if the management has extensive control over the selection and the modes of use of workers, as compared with the situation created by the appropriation of jobs or the existence of rights to participate in management. These latter conditions produce technically, as well as economically, irrational obstacles to efficiency...; (b) in a market economy a management which is not hampered by any established rights of the workers, and which enjoys unrestricted control over the goods and equipment which underlie its borrowings, is in a superior credit position... ; (c) from a historical point of view, the expropriation of labour has developed since the 16th century in an economy characterized by a progressive development of the market system, both extensively and intensively, by the sheer technical superiority oriented to the particular market situations, and by the structure of power relationships in the society" (12, 227).

exclude traditionalized solutions, and continuing to occur in a quick succession, make charismatic solutions unlikely. A new type of authority develops, the type which Weber calls *rational legal authority*. Legal authority rests on a belief in the "legality" of the patterns of normative rules and the right of those elevated to authority under such rules to issue commands (12, 300). The rules are universalistic and cover all possible cases of conduct within the jurisdiction of those in authority and define the limits of that jurisdiction. Obedience is owed to the legally established impersonal order, which thus becomes the fundamental source of authority. The authority — T. Parsons comments on Weber (12, 51) — extends to individuals only in so far as they occupy a specifically legitimized status under the rules, an *office*, and their powers are limited to a "sphere of competence" as defined in order. Outside this sphere they are private individuals with no more authority than any one else. Thus a possibility arises for a new and more subtle "office fetishism" to be added to the traditional "commodity fetishism"; one aspect of exploitation relations hidden behind the market to be supplemented or replaced by the other hidden behind the office. The individuals with, as it were, split personality — masters in the office and clients at home, owning nothing and deciding on everything, public servants by title and public masters by position — are *bureaucrats*. The administrative staff, whose constituent members they are, takes a form of a *bureaucratic structure*.

2. Weber distinguished seven fundamental categories of rational legal authority. These categories are nothing but technical or formal characteristics of a bureaucratic structure. They are as follows: a continuous organization of official functions bound by rules; a specified sphere of competence; the organization of offices follows the principle of hierarchy, i.e., each lower office is under the control and supervision of a higher one; rules regulating the conduct of an office may be technical rules or norms; the administrative staff is separated from ownership of means of administration; the incumbent does not appropriate his official position; administrative acts, decisions and rules are recorded in writing (12, 303-4).

These technical features of bureaucracy make it an extremely efficient tool for handling mass administration. Administrative functions can be specialized according to purely objective considerations, and then discharged by functionaries who have adequate specialized training. Business is discharged objectively, according to calculable rules and without regard for persons. From the point of view of those who hold the supreme authority the bureaucratic machine works with unrivaled precision, stability and reliability. The stringency of discipline makes possible a high degree of calculability of results. Finally, the scope of operations of the bureaucratic type of administrative organization appears practically unlimited, and this organization is formally capable of application to all kinds of administrative tasks (12, 309). All this leads Weber to conclude: "Experience tends universally to show that the purely bureaucratic type of administrative organization ... is, from a purely technical point of view, capable of attaining the highest degree of efficiency and is in this sense formally the most rational known means of carrying out imperative control over human beings" (12, 309).

But there is a snag in this ideal-type analysis of a social institution. Bureaucracy is perfectly suited for an imperative — i.e., coercive — control but it does not make sure that the interests of the controller and the controlled are identical. Moreover, there is a strong tendency for these interests to be polarized. A typical bureaucratic structure looks like a pyramid with a tiny top and a large base; with a flow of communications in only one direction, from the top downward; with imperative character of these communications; with two loose ends: the top, where hierarchical relations disappear in the sense that there are no more superiors, and the bottom, where they disappear in the opposite sense, namely that there are no more inferiors; and with no direct communication between the top and the bottom of the social pyramid. "Purely bureaucratic type of administrative organization" begins to assume an ominous outlook of a system full of potential social conflicts. Clearly, Weber's ideal-type analysis appears to be dangerously simplified and misleading. If we are to evaluate the efficiency of the system when developed to ultimate consequences, we must take into account the human relations that the system is likely to generate. In addition, we must consider the disfunctional effects of the system which are determined by its technical characteristics.

3. We have seen how strong the integration forces are in a modern economy of mass production. In discharging administrative functions, the nation-wide bureaucracy behaves in a manner which is not irregular. In fact regularities are marked and we may classify them under three main headings.

(1) Ideally, the bureaucratic apparatus is expected to carry out the commands of the authorities without questioning their validity. This makes for the calculability of results, which is one of the essential preconditions for the superior efficiency of a bureaucratic organization. In practice, however, bureaucracy does not operate in a social vacuum. The calculability of behaviour in a bureaucratic organization rests on the premise that official policy will be faithfully carried out by subordinates. But why should it? True, there is stringency of discipline backed by threat of punishment. But this safeguard is operative only when individual members of the apparatus are involved. It breaks down when the interests of bureaucracy as a social group or even if only interests of the higher strata of hierarchy come in conflict with the policy to be executed. Various consequences follow.

The administrative staff is an apparatus of political rule or of economic management. In either case, if reliability and calculability are to be achieved, the interests of bureaucracy and ruling class must coincide. It is, therefore, natural that in a class society the upper strata of the bureaucratic hierarchy will consist of members of the ruling class or of those aspiring to enter its ranks[1]. Hence we reach the

---

[1] Cf. the illuminating empirical studies by T. B. Bottomore (13), on French higher civil service, and of R. K. Kelsal (14), on its British counterpart. Before the last war the French higher civil service was "A virtual monopoly of the Parisian *grande bourgeoisie*". After the war, in the period 1945—1951, 65 per cent of successful candidates at the admittance examinations came from families in the first two occupational grades (employers and independent professional men; higher civil servants, managers and technicians), which comprise only 9 per cent of the adult

conclusion that a bureaucratic organization, in order to be workable in a class society, must be a class oriented organization. This at once destroys the foundations of rational legality on which Weber built his thesis of the maximum formal efficiency of the bureaucratic organization. Being class oriented, bureaucracy generates social conflict and thus prevents the achievement of maximum efficiency.

Empirical illustrations for the foregoing conclusion can be found without difficulty. The recent history of the most important and most developed capitalist countries furnishes them readily. In Weimar Germany, to quote J. D. Kingsley, "an attempt was made to impose parliamentary control upon a Civil Service but partially committed to the ends the Republic sought to pursue; and the attempt failed disastrously. In France, too, reactionary officials successfully sabotaged the efforts of the Blum Government in finance and foreign affairs; and the Roosevelt Administration was forced to assemble almost a whole new set of officials to carry out the New Deal reforms. No comparable situation has arisen recently in England; but that is clearly because the bureaucracy in its upper ranges has been representative of the ruling class as a whole and because its aspirations have been those to which successive governments were committed" (16, 219). The last statement needs slight correction. British bureaucracy has also had an opportunity to show its class bias; one of them was during the general strike in 1926,[1] another during the second labour government (1929—1931).[2]

It becomes clear that bureaucracy hinders social progress by its very nature. This fact is extremely relevant in the case of socialist revolution. The conclusion reached by Marx that socialist revolution, in order to be successful, must crash and replace the old state apparatus, proves to be confirmed by historical events.[3] There is, however, a practical question: replaced by what? Suppose that the ruling classes are dispossessed and bureaucratic hierarchy is filled up with persons

male population (13, 149). In Britain people born in propertied and professional classes (i.e., families of landed gentry and other persons not gainfully occupied, large and small employers, high and intermediate civil servants, managers, professional persons) held in 1950 71.9 per cent (79.9 per cent in 1939 and 86.0 per cent in 1929) of the highest posts in civil service, while the same occupations comprised only 18.1 per cent of adult male population in the same year (14, 157).

American civil servants are more "middle-class" by social origin, but in one significant respect American bureaucratic elite resembles the other two: in the exclusion of people of working class origin. Workers constitute more than one half of the American society, but produce only 10 per cent of its highest administrators. Cf. Bendix, 15, 29.

[1] Cf. Gerth and Mills: "The general strike of 1926 showed that British bureaucrats will stand socially and politically with the ruling class" (17, 175).

[2] S. M. Lipset quotes George Lansbury, a member of that government and subsequently leader of the Labour Party, saying: "All through the life of the late Government, Treasury officials obstructed and hindered the Ministers in their work. No one can deny this" (18, 259).

[3] S. M. Lipset remarks: "Since the days of Karl Marx, some socialists have maintained that a successful socialist state must destroy the old state apparatus and errect a new administrative organization. In recent times persons who have served in, or studied, socialist governments have suggested that one crucial reason for their failure to proceed more vigorously toward the attainment of their goals have been the 'bureaucratic conservatism' of old civil servants" (18, 258).

entirely unrelated with and even hostile to the old ruling classes. Is the new "classless" bureaucracy likely to behave differently from the old one? Before we attempt to answer this question we must consider two technical features of the bureaucratic action.

(2) In order to ensure precision, impersonality and calculability bureaucracy in action must be governed by rules which are, ideally, supposed to cover all possible cases. In practice, of course, no bureaucratic brain can anticipate and fix, by rules, the infinite diversity of life. Hence there is an inherent contradiction in the system: a completely bureaucratized organization would require that the number of rules is almost as great as the number of concrete decisions; as this is impossible, the number of rules is much smaller and so an important element of imprecision and impredictability creeps into the organization. To cope with this defect those in authority tend to multiply rules whose sheer number and increasing inconsistency with each other have a strong negative effect on those who have to observe these rules and drives them to inactivity. If the number of rules is reduced, the situation is not better. Apart from the increased possibility of evasion, the typical functionary now feels less secure and hence consults the higher-ups more frequently. The behavioural effect of this contradiction is reflected in the tendency to avoid responsibility; by definition, bureaucracy is a-responsible, behaviourally it is non-responsible and irresponsible. The hierarchy of statuses amplifies this effect and adds a new one: not only responsibility, but also work is tended to be avoided; the former is passed upward, the latter downward. A considerable amount of intellectual and emotional energy is wasted in the process.

Nor is this all. The fundamental principle of hierarchy is conformity to rules and authority of the superior. Functionaries are trained to conform, for this makes the bureaucratic organization work. Conformity is clearly a means for the end the organization sets out to achieve. But, for the members of the hierarchy conformity is an essential precondition for their own existence. The result is displacement of goals by means, a typical bureaucrat endeavour to satisfy rules and superiors[1] and not to assist clients. The process is effectively summed up by R. K. Marton: "(1) An effective bureaucracy demands reliability of response and strict devotion to regulations. (2) Such devotion to the rules leads to their transformation into absolutes; they are no longer conceived as relative to a given set of purposes. (3) This interferes with ready adaptation under special conditions not clearly envisaged by those who drew up the general rules. (4) Thus, the very elements which conduce toward efficiency in general produce inefficiency in specific instances" (20, 366).

The disfunctional effects of a bureaucratic organization are magnified as the organization increases in size. In nation-wide bureaucracies

---

[1] Studying the behaviour of a section of American military bureaucracy as participant-observer, A. K. Davis remarks: "Bureaucratic personnel suffer from chronic status-anxiety. Everyone focuses his attention on his superior, whose slightest display of pleasure or displeasure is magnified and distorted downward. The mildest criticism from a superior is often viewed by the recipient as a crushing attack" (19, 389). The same, of course, happens in all other bureaucratic organizations — though it is, perhaps, slightly less pronounced — as every one would know from personal experience.

the process comes to a logical end: the apparatus designed to facilitate control becomes uncontrollable itself. Technically it is simply a consequence of what E. Jaques calls "a paradox of executive work": ". . . the higher the executive, the greater the number of people dependent upon him, but the greater also is his dependence: for the carrying out of his wishes is in the hands of an increasing number of people" (21, 277). Even if at the top of the bureaucratic structure stands a Platonian Philosopher, he will be able to realize his projects only within the limits of the performance possibilities of the apparatus at his disposal. For reasons enumerated the apparatus will tend to handle the tasks inappropriately and thus force the Philosopher to take decisions which may look phantastic to outsiders. But there is no necessity for a national bureaucracy to have a Philosopher as a leader. Perhaps it is more realistic to expect that normally the leader will have much more modest intellectual and organizational capacities. In this case, the main task of the leader may reduce to a permanent struggle for preservation of his own position in the hierarchy — in which case the last trace of conscious control fades away. The probability that this will happen increases when we take into account the next group of disfunctional factors.

(3) The process of administration is not timeless and independent from the size of organization in this respect also. In a large bureaucratic organization, with many intermediary links, there will be a considerable lag between the moment of time when the command is issued at the top and the moment of time when the command is carried out by functionaries at the other end. This lag is doubled when the other-end-officials initiate the process by first transmitting information upwards and then awaiting instructions on how to act. It is trebled or quadrupled if, for some reason or other, information is not properly understood at either end after the first transmission. Often, however, communications will travel the same distance a number of times because at every link in the chain bureaucrats, taking care of their own safety, will endeavour to clear up all controversial points. On their long journeys, informations and instructions get distorted for psychological reasons, in the most ideal case, and for all sorts of other reasons we have examined in (1) and (2). While informations and instructions are travelling up and down, circumstances change and the solution applied may prove grossly inadequate. Both cases reflect another inherent contradiction of a bureaucratic organization, namely that of centralization and decentralization. If the aim is maximum efficiency, decentralized bureaucratic organization is logical and psychological impossibility; logical — because it destroys co-ordination, psychological — because it is impossible to train a man to conform and to assume initiative at the same time. The "balance" is, then, normally struck in favour of centralization. Centralized organization produces the results like those described by M. Chardon in France or those described by the author in Yugoslavia.

All branches of the public service, says Chardon, are organized and staffed so as "to produce words, papers, inaction. No technical consideration directs their efforts; instead, there is an intricate network of routine mechanisms; constant dissipation of forces; chains of costly links on which business stagnates as successive verifications pile up;

men consider, then reconsider; men verify, then re-verify and counter-verify; the least discrepancy gives rise to doubt, to supplementary inquiries, to commentaries, to pointless arid discussions" (quoted from 22, 408). There is a concrete illustration of ultimate effects: "To build a new bridge in place of one palpably unsafe, twenty distinct administrative steps were necessary, with the result that it took fifteen to eighteen months to initiate the construction" (22, 408). In Yugoslavia — during the so-called "administrative period" of 1946—1951 — there was no delay in the *beginning* stage of "building a new bridge" but it reappeared with equal consequences in its *finishing* stage. At any given time a number of half-finished projects were waiting to be completed. Paper-work ind re-verification, with the resulting further multiplication in paper-work, were, of course, common. The conditions in the oil industry, examined by the author, may be taken as characteristic: "Even with their own management and accounting, enterprises were not independent. The Directorate (Federal Government organ) was interfering with all, even with the most trifling businesses and problems of the enterprises, from the calorific value of food in refectories to annual production plans. Frequent changes, complete dependence, wrong economic directives resulting from ... the ignorance of problems of individual enterprises or from the mere *Gleichschaltung* — have transformed enterprises into unmotivated and initiativeless actors of an economic policy conducted by passing them by ... The unfulfilment of plans could always be explained by innumerable 'objective' difficulties ... the number of employed personnel was rapidly increasing without corresponding economic effect, and in the General Directorate 360 (about 20 under the present arrangement) employees were receiving about 170 reports and were sending out circulars in the same proportion ..." (23, Ch. 44-c-2-3). The reports accumulated into volumes of many hundreds of pages in which all the details of a damaged oil-pump could be traced but from which it was absolutely impossible to evaluate the economic situation of the industry. Plans were changed several times a year and in an extreme case an oil refinery got the last version of its annual production plan in the middle of December of the current year.[1]

The French example is typical for the working of governmental bureaucracy in its traditional field. The Yugoslav example is typical for relatively modern cases of entire economies being run administratively. Similar examples may be multiplied at will and, among other things, they also indicate that, as a rule, the more backward the country, the less efficiently bureaucracy works.

4. Bureaucratic organizations may be, and normally are, intruded by elements alien to them. This may and does mitigate the evils of

---

[1] For the British war-time experience in administrative planning, in many respects similar to the Yugoslav experience, see the illuminating book of Professor E. Devons (24). Cf. also W. Eucken for the German experience (25). The most interesting would be the experience of Soviet planning because it has existed for a time long enough to eliminate some, or many, of the defects apparent in the first few years of Yugoslav planning. But I know for no good critical account of the Soviet experience by Soviet authors which I could quote. Scattered evidence suggests that the picture is essentially the same.

bureaucratic administration to a considerable extent. Possible modifications are innumerable and are not our concern here. We are primarily interested in discovering inherent tendencies of the bureaucratic form of organization and for this purpose the "pure" type is best suited. Suppose, therefore, that the social life of a country is organized and controlled by a huge bureaucratic apparatus. What sort of social relations are likely to develop? We need only derive consequences from the foregoing analysis.

The fundamental principle of bureaucratic organization is obedience. The behavioural consequence is obsequiousness towards (i.e. receiving orders from) superiors compensated by arrogance towards (i.e. giving orders to) inferiors. This behaviour is markedly changed at the top and the bottom of the bureaucratic pyramid; the top displays or, at any rate is able to display arrogance, the bottom can choose only obedience. Interests are polarized because what represents maximum freedom of choice for the top at the same time represents minimum freedom of choice for the bottom. The closer the organization conforms to its logical ideal, the greater the span between maximum-minimum relations with the resulting maximization of potential social conflict. Hence there is a possibility of appearance of a sharp social differentiation, the fundamental historical differentiation between the ruling and the exploited class.

This potential conflict then materializes in overt the signs of social stratification. In order to have a stable and efficient system, rulers need loyal bureaucracy. This loyalty upwards is bought by economic privileges and reinforced by status differentiation[1]. Thus there will be a wealthy and powerful minority and a poor and powerless majority. The former will have control over means of production, the latter will sell their labour power in order to live. The former will rule, the latter will be

---

[1] Status differentiation is achieved through ranks and uniforms, through exclusive clubs and exclusive holiday resorts and through other similar means of ostentation. In a more subtle way it is reflected in the absence of criticism upwards: a private is not supposed to criticize a colonel, not even outside barracks. There are, of course, a number of other processes conducive to the perpetuation of bureaucratic polatization — family ties, for instance, are bound to play a significant role — but we cannot discuss them here. One, however, is worth mentioning because it represents an inevitable extension of the status differentiation to international relations. It is the development of a strong nationalism with a tendency of domination. By its very nature bureaucracy is "patriotic". As such it spontaneously proceeds to build the myth of national grandeur, because it is germane to its way of thinking to attribute to various nations various degrees of merit, i.e., to carry out a proper status differentiation, reserving, naturally, the *highest*, or *next to the highest*, rank for its own nation — and because this serves two useful purposes: crediting themselves with the actual and hypothetical achievements of the nation or, what comes to the same thing, of the social organization, domestic bureaucracy proves its own indispensability; assuring the rest of population of their belongingness to a superior nation, or of life in a superior system, bureaucracy tries to provide fictitious strata beneath the bottom stratum, i.e., to transform the loose bottom end of the social pyramid into a pseudo-hierarchical stratum similar to all other above it in order to prevent the development of consciousness of antagonistic interests. In this way the operation of the hierarchical principle transgresses national boundaries and brings about bureaucratization in an international scale.

ruled. And that is nothing else but the classical Marxian two-class structure of society.[1]

We may now answer the question posed in paragraph 3-1: *Even if the socialist revolution radically destroys the old state apparatus and in administrative jobs replaces the members of the old ruling class by the members of the hitherto exploited class, the new society will not necessarily be a classless, socialist society. If the fundamental principle of bureaucratic organization — the principle of hierarchy — is left to operate, in the course of time two social classes with conflicting interests will emerge again.* In order that this be prevented, the state, as an institution whose essence is coercion, must — to use the famous phrase of Engels — wither away. For, the emergence of class antagonism and of a ruling class do not depend on the *ownership* of means of production by the *individual members* of that class, but on class *control* of the means of production and in so far as this control enables that class to exert political — by power backed — control as well.[2]

(d) Associationist[3] Socialism

1. Complete state control means "the subordination of every individual's whole life, work, and leisure, to the orders of those in power and

---

[1] The often quoted Lenin's definition of social classes is also perfectly applicable: "Classes are large groups of people which differ from each other by the place they occupy in a historically definite system of social production, by their relation (in most cases fixed and formulated in laws) to the means of production, by their role in the social organization of labour, and, consequently, by the dimensions and method of acquiring the share of social wealth that they obtain. Classes are groups of people one of which may appropriate the labour of another owing to the different places they occupy in the definite system of social economy" (26, 432—3).

[2] Some economists might prefer to use the term *property* or *ownership* for what I call *control over means of production*. Thus, instead of speaking of private and bureaucratic control, one may speak of private and state ownership. I have chosen my phrase because it describes the essential relation simply and straightforwardly and because, being free from juridical connotations, it is not so ambiguous and misleading as the alternative term. Cf. the following dictum of Marx and Engels: "Communism deprives no man of the power to appropriate the products of the society; all that it does is to deprive him of the power to subjugate the labour of others by means of such appropriation" (27, 46). The meaning of the statement depends on whether we lay emphasis on "the power to subjugate the labour of others" or on "appropriation". Now, if put in this form, everybody acquainted with Marxism will recognize that the emphasis is on the former. But it has often been convenient to transfer it to the latter and in this case surprisingly few people have been able to realize that the conclusion "the power to subjugate the labour of others, vanishes when private property is abolished", is a *non sequitur*. It is here worth drawing the attention to the penetrating Marxian analysis of the essential features of bureaucracy in his *Towards a Critique of the Hegelian Philosophy of Law*. Marx says explicitly: "Bureaucracy owns the essence of the state, the spiritual essence of the society: that is its *private property* (italics Marx's; 94, 272).

[3] Strictly speaking, the attribute "associationist" is unnecessary. I use it only for didactic reasons, because it provides a direct and unambiguous description of the respective social system. "Socialism", like all terms in extensive use, has come to mean such a variety of things — von Mises's usage in the quotation above being an instructive example — that it grossly lacks precision necessary for a scientific term.

office[1]. It is the reduction of man to a cog in an all-embracing machine of compulsion and coercion. It forces the individual to renounce any activity of which the government does not approve. It tolerates no expression of dissent. It is the transformation of society into a strictly disciplined labour-army — as the advocates of socialism say — or into a penitentiary — as its opponents say" (29, 25). If "state capitalism" is substituted for "socialism", the picture that von Mises draws in the passage just quoted is not unlike that emerging from the analysis of pure bureaucratic system in the preceding section. Where von Mises and other economists of the liberal school err is, of course, in the attempts to show that state capitalism should or could be replaced by liberal capitalism. It suffices to compare the capitalist countries of 1848 with the "welfare states" of our days to see at once that the idea is not very commendable. But this is not a correct way of looking at the problem. The essential point is that social institutions change together with the development of productive forces and that, therefore, nineteenth century institutions cannot be applied to a twentieth century economy. State capitalism has proved to be markedly more efficient than the system it has replaced, and this means that the contradictions it generates will have to be solved in a new way.

I must repeat again that the ill effects of state capitalism can be mitigated in various ways and that, therefore, there is no *necessity* that the picture painted by von Mises come true. But there is a *possibility*. And I should only add that this possibility increases — as the historical experience of our century tends to suggest — with the degree of backwardness of the society concerned. The need for the economic development is most strongly felt in the most undeveloped countries where the economy is nearly stationary and the tradition often closer to feudalism than to capitalism. The first element will indicate the need that meagre resources be pooled together, available qualified personnel be put under a single command and the state made responsible organizer of the economic process. The idea that in our century the state plays, or should play, a decisive role in transforming stationary economies into growing economies, seems to command a uniquely large acceptance. But the realization of this idea means creating a powerful bureaucracy. The

---

[1] In fact this happens already in private capitalism as an inevitable result of capitalist development. Compare the following data on the distribution of occupied population in England and Wales before the advent of capitalism and at the end of its *laissez-faire* phase of development (28, 215):

	Late XVIIth c.	1921
Employers	14	4
Employees	34	90
Independents	52	6

It appears that "life, work and leisure" of 90 per cent of the population in the system so dear to von Mises are subordinated "to the orders of those in power and office". — The figures in the two columns are not strictly comparable. The first column is an estimate based on the well known Gregory King's figures and so of doubtful accuracy. But this does not affect the general picture. England of 1700's can be easily substituted by, e.g., Yugoslavia or Russia of the 1920's, and then the proportion of independents (peasants and artisans) rises to about four fifths of the occupied population.

second element indicates that underdeveloped countries had no opportunity to pass through the rationalization and impersonalization process of the capitalist market — which creates the tradition necessary to make bureaucracy work properly[1] — but that there will be a strong tendency to transfer feudal status-consciousness to bureaucratic hierarchies and similarly a tendency to preserve the tradition of a unified political-economic power free from control from below. And that means a strong class polarization. Development requires state intervention and state intervention has a potentially harmful effect — this is just an additional "vicious circle" with which an underdeveloped economy has to cope. The price for "skipping" a stage of development is the involvement in greater risk.

There are a number of policies which in concrete situations may deal with the risks involved in bureaucratization. They are not our concern here. What we must do consists not merely in a modification of the old system but in an outline of a new system which is most likely to replace the old one. The new system must satisfy the criteria of being both possible and more efficient. The essential characteristics of the new system follow directly from the preceding discussion and can be reduced to a single one: the negation of the class polarization principle. The new society, if it is to be more efficient, must be a classless society. It is easy to see that there are two aspects of the problem; one economic and one political. Take the first — first.

2. Von Mises rightly draws attention to one important difference between public administration and economic management (29, 58—62). In public administration there is no market price for achievements. Economic calculus cannot be applied for assessing the success or failure of a bureau. The efficiency of a police department or of a tax-collecting office cannot be established in the same way as the efficiency of a factory. Therefore the activities of the bureaux must be guided by rules and regulations and by the directives of the superiors. The more impersonalized the system manages to become, the closer will it approximate Weberian rational-legal authority.

Compared with public administration, economic management has a great advantage in possessing a fairly objective — within the confines of inescapable market imperfections — yardstick for success and failure in the surplus of return over cost. This makes it possible to avoid bureaucratization even of the very large organizations. As net revenue "can be assertained by accounting not only for the whole business concern but also for any of its parts, it is feasible to decentralize management and accountability without jeopardizing the unity of operations and the attainment of their goal. Responsibility can be divided. There is no need to limit discretion of subordinates by any rules or regulations other than that underlying all business activities, namely, to render their

---

[1] "The tradition and concept of a merit non-patronage civil service was related in many countries to the needs of the dominant business groups, who demanded cheap and efficient service from the state. J. Donald Kingsley has shown how in England the policy of a merit civil service grew with the increase in political power of the business class. The business groups desired an efficient state that would facilitate and protect the development of commerce" (18, 257—8).

operations profitable" (29, 58). This helps to resolve the centralization-decentralization contradiction and to stimulate individual initiative and collective entrepreneurship.

Economic surplus can be used not only as a check of efficiency but also as a direct motivational device. In the conditions of economic welfare that we know, economic motivation is likely to have an extremely strong impact on the performance of individuals and there is no reason for leaving this possibility unexploited.

Profit plus profit appropriation — does this not mean capitalism? Yes, if the institution of capital — in the Marxian sense — is retained as well. But there is no need why it should be. The inner organization of a private (and a state) enterprise represents a bureaucratic pyramid with two loose ends, the unidirectional flow of commands and the workers providing soon a base on which the structure rests. For reasons analyzed earlier the interests of the "base" and the "structure" above it, diverge. To protect their interests workers are compelled to organize themselves into trade unions, i.e., to build new bureaucratic structures in the opposite direction. Thus workers must support two bureaucratic structures which do the job on their behalf. It is a very roundabout method of organizing everyday life. It is easy to see that in so far as the abolition of private ownership removes the source of antagonistic interests, the need for two fighting bureaucracies disappears. Instead, the base can be directly connected with the top through a line of upward flowing specific commands: the Board of Directors is replaced by the Workers' Council. By connecting the two loose ends of a formerly bureaucratic pyramid, the economic organizations are transformed into self-governing associations and Capitalism is superseded by Socialism.

3. It may have been noticed that state capitalism implies, by definition, absence of private ownership and that in spite of this the "loose ends" are left unconnected in the organization of production. This happens because of the internal logic of the bureaucratic organization. "Bureaucratic authority — Max Weber writes — is carried out in its purest form where it is most cleary dominated by the principle of appointment. There is no such thing as a hierarchy of elected officials in the same sense as there is a hierarchical organization of appointed officials. In the first place, election makes it impossible to attain a stringency of discipline even approaching that in the appointed type. For, it is open to a subordinate official to compete for elective honours on the same terms as his superiors, and his prospects are not dependent on the superior's judgement" (12, 307). In other words, the loyalty of the functionaries ceases to be linked upwards and the hierarchical structure tends to disintegrate.

The application of the "principle of appointment" to the very top of a bureaucratic pyramid poses an interesting problem. Three possibilities exist. The pyramid may be truncated, i.e., the organization may be run by a collegiate body which by co-opting new members appoints them to the posts of supreme authority. This collegiate body will normally have one member who acts as a *primus inter pares* and who comes to hold this position by being *elected* by his colleagues (the initiative being taken either by them or by him himself or being prescribed by rules).

The truncated pyramid is a pure technical type of a self-perpetuating bureaucracy. Experience suggests that all bureaucracies tend to develop elements of this type. But there are two further important modifications. In private capitalism, owners of wealth nominate top officials of economic organizations, legally, and to a large extent actually. In state capitalism this function is performed by wielders of political power. So we pass into the sphere of political organization.

Modern political systems, technically denoted as democracies, solve the "top appointment" problem by a fourth method: connecting at regular intervals of a given number of years the two loose ends. This procedure is called *elections* and it produces parties, parliament and government, i. e., the source of supreme authority. There is no doubt that the more efficient this procedure, the greater the chance that the operation of the hierarchical principle will be subjected to some social control. But there is also little doubt that the potential efficiency of the procedure is severely limited. To be effective, the government must hold the office for some time, i.e., it must be stable. To be stable, the intervals between the elections must be long enough and the number of parties reduced. The former excludes frequent communications of commands by definition, the latter implies formation of huge party bureaucracies. Already Weber pointed out that bureaucratization of party organization makes the member of parliament "an agent of the leaders of the party organization" (12, 387). The point is enlarged by R.H.S. Crossman, who in a few words generalized modern experience by noting that the responsibility of ministers to the parliament "is rapidly becoming a constitutional fiction" and by proceeding to say: "Along with Ministerial responsibility, the responsibility of the individual Member of Parliament has withered away ... Now the prime responsibility of the Member is no longer to the elector but to the Party. Without accepting the discipline of the Party, he cannot be elected; and if he defies that discipline, he risks political death" (9, 18).

Due to the long distance, the upward line from the base to the top tends to perform more formal than real connection between the two loose ends of the social pyramid. The obvious remedy appears to be in cutting this distance, in forming independent self-connected structures throughout the system, in forming — to use Yugoslav political parlance — self-governing Communes. In more familiar words, the remedy is decentralization of power. There are very few social activities which require rigid central control. Strictly speaking only activities aimed at the protection of interests of the community against the outside world — belong to this category. Foreign policy is one of them, defense is the other. Practically all other executive functions can[1] be left within the

---

[1] This simple truth is almost entirely neglected in the modern politico-economic literature which is so profoundly influenced by the existence — and apparent inevitability — of colossal bureaucratic organizations. Everyone who dares to take it up is likely to be denounced as an anarchist or a phantast. A refreshing exception — and possibly a display of intellectual courage — is provided by W. H. Morris Jones: "It is ... our present thesis that the most powerful contribution to the solution of the problem of bureaucracy lies in a revival of local government through a reconstruction of its functions and a determination of its areas on the basis of the people's ties and loyalties" (30, 26—7).

jurisdiction of the Communes which are elementary units of economic-political associations. It is, however, hardly necessary to point out that the technical solution, decentralization, becomes possible only in certain social conditions, namely in conditions conducive to the destruction of causes which generate fundamental social conflict.

4. A federation of self-governing associations — political, economic, and any other — this was Marx's vision of socialism as inspired by the short history of the Paris Commune of 1871 (31). As the foregoing analysis shows, this is a possible and more efficient alternative to bureaucratic social organization.

It is important to realize that bureaucratization means more than a mere co-ordination and differentiation of administrative functions. Bureaucracy is an instrument of *imperative co-ordination* — to use a Weberian term once more — based on coercion and, when nation-wide, personified in the state. In the conditions of existence of the fundamental social conflict coercion is an essential element of social organization, indispensable if disintegration is to be prevented. The function of coercion is performed by a special apparatus whose loyalties are tied together on the basis of interests divergent from those of the majority against whom coercion is to be applied. The process is, clearly, self-reinforcing. Rationalizing the experience of the Prussian state, Weber — similarly as his countryman Hegel before him — implied that it represented the end of the possible development of social institutions. Once put in this form, the mistake becomes obvious. Not *every* authority needs be based on coercion. T. Parsons pointed out that professional authority — that of a doctor or of a university professor — is not (12, 52). And this provides the clue for the solution.

In governing a Commune as well as in running a factory there are two types of decisions to be made. One of them represents policy decisions, decisions concerned with valuations, i.e., with setting up a hierarchy of social values. The other type represents technical decisions; once the policy (the "end") is decided upon, technical experts set out to implement it in the most efficient way (the "means"). Bureaucratic authority makes — actually, and often also formally — both types of decisions *uno actu*. If, however, the two types of decisions can be separated, then, without any loss in efficiency, the co-ordination of technical performance will be based on professional authority. And elected self-governing bodies will be engaged in finding out the systems of values which conform mostly to the existing valuations of the members of the community. There is no need for coercion in this scheme. For, the alternative to coercion is not anarchy but a system commanding undivided fundamental loyalties. Common agreement on fundamentals makes possible free disagreement on everything else. Men cease to be "representatives" of bureaucratic organizations and instead begin to represent themselves as freely developed personalities. The destruction of concentrations of power enables to create a society "in which the free development of each is the condition for the free development of all" (Marx).

The "withering away of the state" is a slow process which primarily depends on the rate of expansion of material wealth at the disposal of the community. But once it is started, the class polarization process will be stopped and reversed. Class society came into existence as a result of the rising productivity of labour. The same cause will make it perish.

6. PROFIT AND WAGES

(a) Depicting the Historical Trend: The First Three Waves

After the sweeping generalizations in the preceding chapter it would appear necessary to give some consideration to *concrete* historical events. The following excursus into recent social history will take us outside the strictly defined general framework of the present study, but it seems unavoidable if we are to show that the social theory developed has a definite empirical content. In this section we can do no more than register a certain number of historical events. However, even so restricted, the discussion will prove to be sufficient for our purpose.

1. Examined against the frame of reference discussed in Chapter 5, the amorphous historical continuum of the last two centuries begins to assume a definite structure and the regularities of paramount interest for our subject become apparent. We can distinguish four waves of events which are partly successive and partly superimposed on each other. Our story begins with the first wave which produced a group of prophets of a new social order.

The second half of the XVIIIth century witnessed the advent of a new, capitalist, society. The new society generated new class conflict and very soon the exploited class got its first intellectual defenders. Not quite conscious defenders, to be sure, because, as Engels observes, they at first did not claim to emancipate a particular class, but all humanity at once. The most developed countries of that time, Britain and France, supplied the most remarkable among them. For my purpose I choose to mention three of them, the three whom Schumpeter (32) aptly characterizes as Associationist[1] Socialists. They are Robert Owen (1771—1858), a Briton of Welsh origin, and Charles Fourier (1772—1837) and Louis Blanc (1811—1882), two Frenchmen. All three advocated social reconstruction through producers' associations.

Owen, the most famous of the three, thought of future society as a federation of communes governed by producers. To this view he evolved after two decades he had spent as a manager of a big cotton mill in the Scottish village New Lanark, where he improved the houses of his workers, organized education for their children, reduced working hours, and in general, anticipated the treatment that workers were going to receive on a national scale by more than a century. Owen's ideas inspired the co-operative movement. And in the early 'thirties he was the leading figure in the growing trade union movement, which had only emerged from illegality, and which came to stimulate the formation of self-governing workshops. Under Owen's influence the new Builders' Union was

---

[1] The term was already used by F. A. Neff in 1950 (33) and by L. H. Haney in 1911 (34).

turned into a Guild to carry on the building industry, anticipating thus the future schemes of French Syndicalists and British Guild Socialists. However, after the Grand National Consolidated Trade Union was formed (1833—4) employers and Government acted quickly and in a few months Owenite unionism came to an abrupt end.

Fourier designed *phalanstères* in which capitalists, workers and scientists were to live together in a harmonious community based on the work organized so as to correspond to personal likings and to the capacities of individuals. Louis Blanc, the least original but the most realistic of the three, proposed that the state should undertake to establish social workshops *(ateliers sociaux)* which were to be run by workers. When the revolution of 1848 had made him unexpectedly a member of the Provisional Government in Paris, Blanc tried to put into practice something of this program. But, naturally enough, his bourgeois colleagues tricked him out of the government and skilfully sterilized his activities. Blanc's ideal was an equalitarian society with personal interest merged in the common good. This he summed up as *à chacun selon ses besoins, de chacun selon ses facultés,* the idea which later, in Marx's hands, became famous as the formula of communism.

Associationists were utopian socialists: instead of analyzing the actual conditions of development, they were preoccupied with devising ideal plans for social reconstruction. Consequently, when actual realizations were attempted — and a number of Owenite, Fourierist and similar communities were organized — failure was more or less inevitable. But the Associationists' ideas left a lasting effect on the developing culture of the new society.

2. The appearance of the gigantic figure of Marx on the intellectual scene marks the beginning of the second wave in the historical process under consideration. Marxism is primarily a social theory — or ideology — of the already *emancipated* working class. Thus the essential feature of the new wave is that isolated individuals and their followers are replaced by broad movements: developed capitalist production of the second half of the XIXth century generates trade unions and working class political parties. They differ in details but their programs are basically the same; they require elimination of private capitalist control of the production process.

The profound influence of Marxian thought — which, however, was interpreted in various ways — on working class movements, is well known and there is no point in describing it here. But with respect to my main purpose, that of tracing the development of the institution of workers' management, I should like to mention three movements separately, two of which did not profess Marxism. Although having serious shortcomings, propounding sometimes nonsensical ideas and occasionally being adjusted to reality in a quixotic fashion, these movements express well the fundamental strivings of the working class.

By the end of the last century, the French trade union movement, still in its infancy, came to be strongly influenced by the idea of *Revolutionary Syndicalism.* Syndicalists wanted to place the management of industry into the hands of the trade unions. Trade unions were to be federated locally into *bourses du travail* which would establish a monopoly of labour, presently take over ownership of the industries and run them under local self-governing communes. Syndicalists repudiated parliamentary action, relied on "conscious minority" instead on thoroughly organized big unions and hoped to achieve their aim by general strike. These four characteristics of the movement explain at once why syndicalists came to be equally detested by employers as by orthodox trade unionists, why by disorganizing the working class movement their action inflicted damage on it[1], and why they failed to achieve the goal of workers' management. The industrial militancy of the French syndicalist unions reached the peak in 1902—6, later it receded and after the First World War the ideas were basically modified. In this process not an insignificant role was played by the fact that, as a result of wars, unions multiplied their membership and developed into big bureaucratic organizations.

From France, syndicalism spread to the United States where it developed first under the American Socialist Labour Party led by Daniel De Leon and became known as *Industrial Unionism*. The American movement advocated the organization of all workers into one big union with sections for each industry. Industrial unionism thus overcame two basic weaknesses of syndicalism: it made use of political action and of strong union organization. However, it had weaknesses in other respects, it never exerted great influence on American workers and died out after the First World War.

Syndicalism and industrial unionism spread to Australia, Canada, Mexico and some other countries including Britain, where their influence was reflected in the famous manifest of the Welsh miners, *The Miners' Next Step* (1912), which urged the abolition of capitalist ownership in the mining industry and complete control over the industry by the workers. But in Britain of that time an autonomous British movement — *Guild Socialism* — began to develop as well. Guild socialists opposed state management of industry on the ground that it would lead to bureaucracy and that thereby the social position of wage-earners would not be changed. But they realized that the state is a very important institution which might be turned to very good use: the working class should capture the state and use it to take industry under public ownership. After that, Parliament would hand over the task of administration to the national guilds (former trade unions) within the terms of a Parliamentary Charter. Guilds, as well as communes and other political, social, etc., associations were to be organized so as to allow every individual to participate and to have an effective say. All this was in sharp contrast with the current theory of democracy which, says G. D. H. Cole, the leading theoretician of the movement, "assigns to the ordinary citizen little more than a privilege ... of choosing his rulers, and does not call upon him ... himself to rule" (35, 13).

National Guilds League, formed in 1915, exerted great influence on shop stewards' movement and on several unions. During and after the

---

[1] Accordingly, syndicalism, or anarcho-syndicalism, as it is sometimes called, has become a derogatory word in the working-class vocabulary. It is of some interest to note how the opponents of workers' self-government invariably use this term to denote those in favour of it even if the latter have no connection with syndicalism.

war a number of small guilds were created. The most important in this respect was the movement to reorganize the building industry as a national guild in which employers were to become salaried administrators, subject to election by the workers employed. In the ensuing depression of 1922-3 this movement collapsed, and a year later guild socialism as an organized movement was dead.

3. If the first wave brought to existence individual socialist ideologues and isolated groups, and the second wave produced organized movements, the third wave brings first realizations. Broadly speaking the European revolutions of 1848 mark the time when the working class emancipated itself and asserted itself as a separate social class. It might be supposed that in the revolutions which were to follow the working class would attempt to establish industrial self-government. Let us examine this hypothesis in the light of the events which actually took place.

The era of proletarian revolutions began with the Paris Commune in 1871. The Commune passed a decree by which the industry was to be reorganized on co-operative basis and enterprises run by the workers.

The next in time, the Russian revolution of 1905, produced factory councils which attempted management of enterprises. Both, the Paris and the Russian revolutions were crushed and the workers' management did not survive them.

Different was the destiny of the second Russian revolution, the Great October Socialist Revolution of 1917. It was the first successful proletarian revolution. The resurrected workers' councils of 1905 played leading role in anticipating and carrying out the revolution[1]. Already in November 1917 a decree on workers' control was passed by which the factory committees obtained the right of complete control of enterprises. However, the ensuing civil war, with its concomitant shortages and sabotage required a strict centralization and a military organization of the entire social life, including industry. In 1918 the committees were transformed into organs of the trade unions, and in 1920 they lost the right of participation in management. After that the remnants of workers' control were alive for a number of years, first in the practice of appointing a *red director* (a worker) and later in the managing triangle: director — party secretary — secretary of trade union factory branch. In the late 'twenties Stalin removed even these remnants and in a truly Weberian fashion proclaimed that the essential condition for discipline and efficiency was that the director had absolute and complete control over the enterprise and that he was subject only to the orders from above. *Edinonačalie* (one-man-management) was adopted as basic principle of social organization. Significantly enough, after a short while the gap between workers' wages and managerial salaries was widened several times. Workers' control was eliminated.

The Russian revolution had a strong impact on revolutionary fermentation in other European countries with the result that workers either extorted constitutional and legal reforms or, occasionally, assumed

---

[1] Councils of Workers' Delegates, together with Councils of Soldiers' Delegates, acquired political power and, in fact gave the name to the new *Soviet* state (soviet = council).

(temporary, of course) management of their factories. The most dramatic of all was the Hungarian revolution which gave birth to the Hungarian Soviet Republic in 1918. Here the workers' councils were first created as political organs which later concerned themselves with management in the nationalized undertakings. However, very soon the revolution was crushed and instead of workers' control Hungary got fascist dictatorship.

The same was the destiny of the next revolution, the Spanish civil war, as also was the same attitude towards workers' management. In Catalonia, the enterprises with more than hundred employees (and some other categories of enterprises) were socialized. In 1936, a decree provided for workers' management in these enterprises.

If the revolutions generated by social antagonisms of private capitalism so invariably[1] produced attempts to establish workers' control in the enterprises, one will expect that in the countries in which private ownership has been eliminated social upheavals will generate the same tendency even more clearly. The events in Poland and Hungary in 1956, with the so prominent role that workers' councils played, more than confirm this expectation.

It is frequently said that wherever workers' management has been attempted it has failed. In a sense this is true. But the inference that workers' management should therefore be regarded as an unrealizable utopia — is manifestly false. In no historical period have new social institutions been successfully established at one stroke, without bitter fights against vested interests, and without many failures. What is significant in the events we have reviewed is not the failure to achieve the goal, but their continual recurrence *despite* of all failures.

(b) Depicting the Historical Trend: The Last Wave

1. The three waves described so far could not fail to exert great influence and modify that relatively stable and sanctified pattern of social life which we call *establishment*. Establishment itself began to change and this is the fourth and the surface layer of the historical trend we have set out to investigate.

Various kind of workers' and works councils — the former are composed of workers only and are more usual than the latter which include employers' representatives as well — are as old as the trade union movement. These councils or committees dealt with complaints, welfare work and conditions of employment; they were always advisory, the employer reserving the power of making the final decision. But for a very long time they were only sporadic[2] in occurrence, they did not

---

[1] This absolutely uniform pattern is characteristic for the European revolutions. Asian revolutions proceed in a somewhat different way. This can be explained by the small working class in these countries and by the fact that they have a different cultural tradition.

[2] The oldest works council still in existence in Britain is as far as I know that at Bournville Works of the cocoa and chocolate manufacturing firm Cadbury Brothers Ltd. In this firm works committees were established at the beginning of the century. The aim of the management was defined as *rapprochement* of the employer and worker (36, 2).

represent an institution. Similarly, labour legislation dealing with some forms of workers' participation in the factory organization — almost exclusively confined to welfare matters — can be traced back in several countries (Prussia and Austria, for instance) to the end of the last century[1]. These were also sporadic events and the extent of workers' participation was insignificant. The first landmark in the history of workers' participation in management represent the First World War and the Russian Revolution.

During the war, in order to enhance war production, British and German governments sought co-operation of the unions and — got it. As a result, various forms of management-workers co-operation developed. The events that occurred in both[2] countries are so significant that they warrant a few more words.

2. The three years preceding the outbreak of the war represent one of the most disturbed epochs in British industry, writes J. B. Seymour, the historian of Whitley Councils. At the commencement of the war hundred strikes were in progress (39, 9). It was in this period that syndicalist influence was strongest in Britain and that (in 1912) the miners and the largest of the four railway unions, accepted the demand for complete control over the industry by the workers. It was also this period that the future shop stewards' movement was announced (Glasgow engineers' strike in 1912).

Before the war shop stewards were minor officials appointed by the union from among the men in the workshop; they were to see that their union dues were paid and newcomers organized. They had no power to negotiate grievances neither were they officially recognized by the management (39, 10). Then came the war which, as C. G. Renold tells us on the basis of his first hand experience of an employer, "was regarded by large sections as a capitalists' war and the restrictions, controls and hardships were resented accordingly" (40, 16). It suffices to add that, in 1915, under the Treasury Agreement, after trade union leaders voluntarily pledged themselves not to sanction strikes during the war, the dissent of the rank and file was certain. The big Clyde engineers' strike early in 1915, when the strike committee disregarded superior union officials and won the strike, set the pattern and initiated what became known as shop stewards' movement.[3] The movement brought works committees to a high point of development.

---

[1] For the sake of completeness an interesting early German attempt should be mentioned. The Industrial Commission of the revolutionary National Assembly, which met in Frankfurt in 1848, put forward a resolution asking that Factory Committees, consisting of employers' and workers' representatives, issued works rules subject to the approval of district Factory Councils elected by the Factory Committees in the district. The resolution has never been enacted because the revolution collapsed shortly afterwards (37, 1).

[2] Demand for workers' control in British industry was most acute in the twelve-year period 1910—1922. For a detailed and thorough account of what was happening see B. Pribićević (38). For a standard work on the comparable German movement see C. W. Guillebaud (37).

[3] Characteristic for the mood of workers was the following published statement of Clyde strikers: "We hold the view that the trade union officials are the servants, not the masters, of the rank and file, and that they require some pressure at times to move them in the path the rank and file desire them to tread" (41, 131).

103

Syndicalism, guild socialism, shop stewards' movement, increasing number of working days lost by strikes despite all restrictions — 2 million in 1915, $2^1/_2$ million in 1916, $5^1/_2$ million in 1917 — this alarming situation called for government intervention. In October 1916 a committee (known as the Whitley Committee) was appointed to examine the methods for securing permanent improvement in industrial relations. The following year the Whitley Committee produced its scheme of employers-workers co-operation. For each industry, a National Joint Council and District Councils were to be formed to bring together employers' organizations and unions and in individual establishments Joint Works Committees were to provide a recognized means of consultation between the management and the employees. But, the scheme as a whole, failed to work, except in government departments. "The employers, as a body, have never favoured the scheme... The trade unionists, frightened by the shop stewards' movement, appear to shrink from giving authority to any rank-and-file movement and away from the central organizations" (39, 191). Out of about hundred works committees formed as response to the Whitley Committee recommendations, by 1929 only one half were still alive. After the war, the government rejected the miners' and railwaymen's demand for nationalization and self-government. The first post-war recession, which started in 1921, killed the shop stewards' movement and the guild socialists. The situation was again normalized and the capitalist machine could again work as before. But not quite; the seed had been sown.

3. Unlike Britain, Germany was defeated in the war and the events took the other possible form. The defeat coupled with the tremendous influence of the Russian revolution produced a German revolution (1918). Workers' and Soldiers' Councils sprang all over the country. Frightened to death, employers were ready to go very far only to escape full scale socialism. And so it happened that Germany became the first capitalist country to have a Constitution (July 1919) which among the "fundamental rights" of citizens included the following one: "For the purpose of safeguarding their social and economic interests the wage-earning and salaried employees are entitled to be represented in Workers' Councils for each establishment, as well as in Regional Workers' Councils organized for each industrial area, and in a Federal Workers' Council" (Article 165; 37, 10).

On the basis of the Constitution in 1920 a law was passed making Works Councils (Betriebsräte) compulsory in all establishments with twenty or more employees. The councils were to supervise the working of collective agreements, to enter into agreements on the conditions of work

---

D. Kirkwood, one of the leading members of the Clyde Workers' Committee, told the visiting prime minister Lloyd George at a meeting in December 1915, that they had organized the strike "in defiance of you, in defiance of the Government... and in defiance of the Trade Union officials" (38, 568).

Comparable to the British Shop Stewards' movement was the German Works Councils movement after 1918. And comparable to the statements of Clyde strikers was the following published statement of the striking metal workers in Düsseldorf in 1924: "In a great number of towns, the Trade Unions have adhered to the general strike proclaimed by the Works Councils. Where this has not yet taken place the workers must force them to join the movement. The leaders of the Unions who refuse must be rejected from their offices" (37, 70).

and subjects not regulated by wider agreements, to watch over engagements and dismissals; but also to advise the employer on how to improve efficiency and organization. However, Constitution and laws are dead letters if they are not backed by active social forces. The German working class movement of that time was deeply divided both in its trade union and in its parliamentary section. The majority, who held the power, were undetermined, compromising, hesitating. The state bureaucracy was hostile. This gave the employers breathing space. The results of the revolution were gradually undermined — the slump of 1924 playing not an insignificant part — and then liquidated. The process came to an end in May 1933 when both trade unions and works councils were abolished, which marked the advent of fascism. In our days, unsuccessful or half-successful socialist revolutions — this seems to be the lesson of Hungary, Germany and Spain — end in fascism.

As to the other European countries, it suffices to mention that in the period 1919—1922 for similar reasons similar laws were passed in Austria, Czechoslovakia, Norway and elsewhere. In Yugoslavia, the law on protection of workers (1922) provided for election of workers' commissionars *(radnički povjerenici)* from the shop floor, whose task it was to protect workers' interests and co-operate with the employer. The attitude of employers and trade unions very soon reduced this provision to a mere formality (7, 22). After a period of strikes, a similar solution was reached under the Popular Front government in France in 1936; it meant recognition of workers delegates *(délégués ouvriers)* with the right to meet management every month. In the United States a somewhat different union-management co-operation on production problems began on one of the railways in the 1920's when the union wanted to reduce costs in order to secure work for railway shops. Other firms and unions experimented with similar ideas until the 1929 depression which killed experiments of this kind. A decade later the steelworkers' union developed quite successful co-operation plans in a number of small steel and steel products firms. Steelworkers' scheme survived the last war and continued to be operated in some 50 firms (42, 55).

4. The second landmark in the development of workers' participation in management was provided by the Second World War. Similar to the first war it initiated a cycle, though on a much larger scale. Again governments sought co-operation of workers in order to enhance war production and joint production committees were set up in various countries (Britain, the United States, Canada). Again Britain was victorious and Germany was defeated, and there was a spontaneous development in the former and legislative measures were taken in the latter. Again British miners expected to get self-government; they got joint consultation instead. But there were also several novel features of which the most important is the large-scale nationalization in some countries and full-scale nationalization in a number of others (East European and Far East Asian countries). In all nationalized industries joint consultation between workers and management was introduced as a matter of course.

In Britain two national agreements during the war set the pattern for the establishment of Works Committees: the Committees were to be advisory and were to provide an outlet for the regular exchange of views between employers and employees on welfare and production matters subject to the qualification that terms and conditions of employment were to be dealt by unions on behalf of the workers. In 1947 the National Joint Advisory Council recommended to employers' organizations and unions the setting up of joint consultative machinery where it did not already exist. The recommendation was followed and today there are several hundred Works Committees in existence in Britain.[1]

In Germany the legislature of the Weimar period was not only revived but also pressed a step further: from joint consultation to co-determination (Mitbestimmung). In the two basic industries — coal, and iron and steel — unions achieved parity for workers' representatives in the supervisory board (Aufsichtsrat), a body which appoints the board of management. Moreover, one of the usually three members of the management board, the personnel director (Arbeitsdirector), is nominated by the union (the law of 1951). In other industries workers' representatives are still in the minority, although this minority (one third) may be larger than in the Weimar period. Workers' Councils (Betriebsräte), representing both wage and salary earners, must be elected in all establishments employing not less than five permanent employees (the law of 1952). In order to promote co-operation between Workers' Council and employer, in establishments with more than hundred employees Economic Committee (Wirtschaftsausschuss) must be formed, each side appointing one half of the members.

In France a law passed in 1946 made it compulsory for industrial concerns employing more than fifty workers to establish Works Committee (comité d'entreprise) representing the manual workers and the technical grades. Every act of major management importance must be subject to agreement to the committee. If there is a disagreement the case is to go to arbitration. Similar laws were passed in Belgium in 1948 and in the Netherlands in 1950. In 1946 in Sweden, the unions and employers associations reached an agreement according to which Enterprise Councils were to be set up in firms with 25 or more employees· The task of these councils may be broadly described as joint consultation on all important matters. It is of some interest to record that when in 1923 a Royal Committee proposed to form similar joint production committees both unions and employers opposed the idea and nothing came out of it. After the second war, by 1950, in 2,650 firms, employing 600,000 workers, Enterprise Councils were set up (42, 56—8). Similar joint consultation committees were introduced in Norway (1945) and Denmark (1947) on the basis of unions-employers agreements and in Finland, by a special law (1946).

In a number of other countries the pre-war practice of joint consultation was continued after the war as well or, where it did not exist, it was introduced for the first time. In 1951, the International Labour Office registered more than thirty countries with *permanent* organs of workers' participation in management. The practices vary but have an important

---

[1] Enquiring into the problem of joint consultation in British industry, the National Institute of Industrial Psychology sent questionnaires to 4,719 manufacturing establishments employing over 250 people; returns were received relating to 751 establishments, of which 545 had joint consultation (43, 21).

common feature: apart from a few exceptions they are confined to joint *consultation*.

5. It will be useful to attempt a brief evaluation of joint consultation as it came into being and developed during the last four decades. The following five aspects of the problem seem important.

(1) The *motivation* for the setting up of the joint consultative machinery falls into three distinct categories. The revolutionary pressure from below compels employers and the government of the day to relax the managerial authoritarianism. Being result of a strong clash of interests, the outcome of the fight must be legally sanctioned to remain permanent (although legal sanctions often prove to be a fiction). The German case is typical for this situation.

Next, during the modern totalitarian wars governments are vitally interested in stepping up production and therefore devise and advocate schemes of joint consultation to bridge the gap between employers and workers. This case is typified by British and American practices. With respect to the latter the International Labour Office study says: "The general purpose of the Labour-Management Production Committees was to raise the quantity and quality of output for war production by the joint effort of labour and management in each war plant" (44, 197). The extent to which this purpose was achieved is visible from the following evaluation of the same study: "While there seems to be little doubt that the committees made a substantial contribution to plant output, a number of the committees did not aid to as great an extent as had been expected..." (44, 257). Some 5,000 committees were set up in plants with war contracts. Most of them disappeared with the end of the war.

The third type of motivation is that by individual employers who are not forced *by law* to adopt joint consultation. They adopt it primarily on economic grounds. This point is illuminated by the following statement of C. G. Renold, himself an employer having successful joint consultation in his firm: "In the first place the point should be made that the whole development had its origin in a very practical need — the need felt by the Management for closer contact with its men in the interest of smooth working" (40, 100). This need appears when the concern overgrows one-man management[1]. It becomes urgent in the turbulent conditions of war and industrial unrest. And once the works council is set up it is likely to continue to exist in the ensuing time of military and industrial peace. War has another effect as well: it increases the self-consciousness of the exploited classes and humanizes the members of higher social strata providing thus a psychological bridge between them[2]. Then there is also a small number of employers[3] who are inter-

---

[1] "In many instances the idea took shape in the minds of individual employers or managers faced with rapidly expanding personnel, and was originally intended as no more than a substitute, of sorts, for that direct personal contact which is so easily lost when the pay-roll lengthens and the ratio of skilled and semi-skilled workers increases." This is the testimony of G. S. Walpole, also an employer (45, 39).

[2] The research team of the National Institute of Industrial Psychology records: "A number of the younger executives told us that their favourable attitude to joint consultation had been acquired through experience in the services during the war" (43, 69).

[3] In France they have formed their own organization under the name *Union des Chefs d'Entreprises — Action pour les Structures Humaines* (UCEACT).

ested in joint consultation for its own sake, because they regard it as a humanizing institution. This Owenite type of employers, earlier practically non-existent, is likely to multiply in the degree in which the adverse social pressure — of their equals and of the establishment as a whole — decreases. The example of individual employers, the recurrent interventions of government, the constant improvement of the educational standard of workers, create gradually an atmosphere where joint consultation becomes an indispensable part of the managerial routine. Exactly this seems to be happening in Britain today, as demonstrated by the appearance of yet another type of employers. In the majority of the firms visited by the N.I.I.P. research team "joint consultation seemed to be regarded as an up-to-date technique for improving management-worker relationships" (43, 59). Competition is the essence of capitalism; accordingly, there is nothing to stop a capitalist firm from competing even in improvements of relations with workers. This sounds paradoxical, but such are the conditions of full employment under capitalism. Clearly, if pursued consistently, such a competition must eventually lead to destruction of capitalist relationships, but this will be nothing more than a parallel to the Schumpeterian "creative destruction", the destruction of profits by competition initiated to increase profits.

Nationalized industries and nationalized economies represent a separate case. There joint consultation is an indispensable minimum to make these systems work at all, i.e., to make them socially acceptable. The only development I can visualize is a constant increase of workers' participation in management, either granted by the governing bureaucracy, or fought out by revolutionary means.

(2) What happens to the *discipline* in an organization where executive authority is undermined by everybody's having the right and the opportunity to question the validity of the commands from above by reference to his own set of criteria? This is the very first question our Weberian-minded generation will ask in connection with the practicability of workers' management schemes. For, is it not true that an efficient organization requires obedience, obedience being defined as following "such a course that the content of the command may be taken to have become the basis of action for its own sake" (Weber, 12, 300).

In fact, however, the literature on joint consultation and workers' management[1], including the most detailed field studies, shows no awareness of the "problem of discipline". I can do no better than quote two employers' testimonies: "When I first took the step of introducing joint consultation on a very broad basis into my own works — writes G. S. Walpole — I was told by most of my fellow employers that I was selling the pass to the enemy, and that the first result would be that works discipline would go to the devil. I have found, on the contrary, after two years' experience, that works discipline has improved almost out of recognition, and that every other legitimate interest of ownership has also been catered for in a measure which four years ago I would

---

[1] Cf. W. H. Scott (46; 47), E. Jaques (21), G. S. Walpole (45), C. G. Renold (40), the two I. L. O. studies (44; 48) and N. I. I. P. study (43) for joint consultation, and P. Kovač and Dj. Miljević (7) and the Congress of Workers' Councils of Yugoslavia (49) for workers' management.

108

not have believed possible: production is up, absenteeism is down: wastage is reduced, and valuable time is saved" (45, 166). C. G. Renold explains the mystery of this phenomenon: "The need to base managerial authority on reason rather than on arbitrary power — as is implied in the whole philosophy of joint consultation — has enhanced that authority" (40, 119).

It is hardly necessary to add that the same applies with even greater force to the system based on the philosophy of self-government. For want of quotation — no field study has been made so far — I shall perhaps be excused in backing this contention by my own experience as a member of a workers' council. Self-government substitutes understanding for obedience, agreement for the exercise of arbitrary power. By eliminating capitalist or bureaucratic duality and polarization of interests it reduces tensions and improves co-ordination.

(3) The *success* of joint consultation has been rather limited so far and the reasons for this we shall examine in a moment. The success of German Works Councils of the Weimar period McKitteric and Roberts evaluate by saying that Councils "were useful in protecting the workers' interests, but achieved virtually nothing in the way of genuine participation in management" (50, 9). For the post-war development the same authors state: "Where workers' councils exist the general experience has been that employees take a keen interest in their activities ..." (50, 20). In Britain broad masses of workers are still apathetic, but four fifths of the workers' representatives in councils support the institution and show a keen interest in it (43, 64). It is also significant that the experience in joint consultation has induced chief executives, senior management and workers' representatives to take a more favourable view in 37, 48 and 58 per cent of the cases respectively and a less favourable view in only 9, 5 and 1 per cent of the cases as compared with the view they originally held about joint consultation (43, 65).

(4) Next, there is the problem of the *fundamental relation* between Capital and Labour. This two opposing sides are reflected in the very term *joint* consultation. The initiative on the part of employer to introduce joint consultation in his firm is not infrequently a deliberate attempt to anticipate and check the development of unionism[1]. But even if this is not the aim, joint consultation increases loyalty to the firm, and this loyalty and loyalty to one's class are two different, nay conflicting loyalties[2]. It produces workers' leaders who are not trade union officials and so are outside the grip of the "machinery". Clearly, unions

---

[1] Describing the conditions in the United States I. L. O. study says: "A considerable number of pre-war plans for joint committees in factories had been developed primarily by management in order to interest workers in the successful operation of factories and in many instances had been aimed at undercutting the development of unionism" (44, 185).

[2] The resulting deep psychological conflict of the workers is well analyzed in the already quoted Tavistock Institute study: "... it seemed as though the only time the members of the Council could hold their heads high was if there was a management-worker fight on; if there was no fight they felt guilty, as if they were not doing what was expected of them" (21, 122). "... the desirability of employment with the firm has led workers to look to the management rather than to the trade unions for security of employment, and has aroused in the workers' leaders an acute conflict over loyalties divided between the firm and the trade unions" (21, 179).

will not be enthusiastic about partnership proposals and frequently will be opposed to them.[1] On the other hand, if a union or shop stewards seek to participate in joint committees, employers will fear infringement on their own prerogatives. The hopelessness of the situation lies in the fact that *both* sides are right in their fears. With the employers basically opposed to surrendering their arbitrary power and the unions basically unwilling to assume responsibility for the organization of production — because they gain nothing and lose their independence together with the grip on the membership's loyalties — the *status quo* is likely to be prolonged and potential changes prevented. The logic of the situation is such that unions act in virtual collusion with employers against workers, a collusion which becomes overt in more turbulent times.[2] This sheds new light on the events we have surveyed: formidable social forces have been and will be opposing workers' participation in management.

(5) Trade union paradox represents another illustration of the working of bureaucratic structures. In order to protect themselves in a world of polarized interests, the world whose institutions are against them, workers build strong bureaucratic organizations: unions and parties. Once these organizations are built they acquire their separate interests different from the interests of those who support the whole structure. There is nothing ethically wrong in it, this does not happen because the leaders are wicked; given the institution, the development observed is inevitable. The way out of the impasse is logically easy. The organization must first be used to eliminate the fundamental cause of polarization of interests — in this case to eliminate private control of production. And then the bureaucratic principle of organization must be replaced by self-government. However, actual unions and socialist parties are not likely to follow this course straight away from their own accord. Having become a part of the establishment with a clearly defined role in it, they are not prone to leave the life of routine and rush

---

[1] The following statistics seems significant. In Britain, the initiative for starting joint consultation in about three quarters of all cases has come from management and in only 4% and 4% from workers and unions respectively (43, 161). The percentages are not capable of a simple and straightforward explanation, but basically, I think, they show that the unions are *not* interested in pressing for workers' participation in management.

[2] The conclusion is generalized, but it is, of course, not difficult to point at the concrete historical situations which reflect this type of process straightforwardly. I choose German Works Councils of the Weimar period to illustrate the point. In this connection C. W. Guillebaud, their historian, has to say the following: "To the German masses ... the workers' councils stood for the democratization of the industrial system and the attainment, in the economic sphere, of the same rights of self-government and self-determination as they thought they had achieved by the Revolution of 1918 in the political sphere ... But when it came to the practical working out of the basic and, to the individual workers, the most important part of the structure — the Works Councils, they found that the bulk of the political leaders of labour were in league with the employers to prevent any too wide extension of powers to these Councils" (37, 212—3). The unions were apprehensive of losing leadership (p. 41), and hence were anxious to ensure that the Works Councils do not become really effective; they and their political allies, Majority Socialists, "were backed up to the utmost by the employers, who were at least as much concerned to fetter the Works Councils and to confine them within the organization of the Unions. Of the latter the employers were not afraid ..." (p. 11).

110

into uncertainties of a full scale socialization. Self-government, on the other hand, is an idea so alien to the spirit of bureaucracy that it is clear that it will encounter vigorous resistance.[1]

The situation, however, cannot remain completely unchanged. There is no reason to believe that business cycles have died out. But there is some reason to believe that governments of industrial countries in the second half of our century cannot afford to tolerate heavy unemployment without risking major social upheavals. By curing the slump the first decisive element of change is introduced into the process: the increasing degree of social control. The welfare state is its symbol. However, uninterrupted full employment had a thoroughly anti-capitalist effect: it generates competition in the improvement of management-workers relations. For, the employers are vitally interested in avoiding labour turnover, in escaping strikes and in overcoming the resistance toward the introduction of new processes, while workers feel secure and for this reason are actively conscious of their rights and possibilities.[2] By raising the status of the workers, employers gradually sur-

---

[1] As an empirical illustration I choose two authoritative pronouncements of Unions and Party views in Britain, but equivalent examples could be found without great difficulties in any other country. The following statement of Mr. Gunter in the parliamentary debate on joint consultation in 1950 is by the National Institute of Industrial Psychology evaluated as a "very well expressed trade union view": "There has been an amazing revival of the old syndicalist idea of direct workers' control in certain sections of labour. In my opinion it is impossible to envisage any great development in the sphere of joint consultation if we imagine that this old, wooly idea of workers' control can operate. In the last resort management must be allowed to manage and to make decisions, and must accept the responsibility. What we seek is that their decisions and policy shall be translated to the workers so that they may understand their objectives, and thereby help to ensure that co-operation which can result in much better and higher production. I cannot leave the trade union side without expressing my belief that the majority of trade unionists do not desire to see the establishment of workers' control, as it is sometimes called" (43, 82). The Labour Party 1957 policy document on nationalized industries in the chapter on workers' participation asks the question: Direct Representation? and answers it negatively: "The syndicalist view of industry run by workers, either through their trade unions or through ellected boards, was rejected by the Labour Movement many years ago" (51, 39). Note the reference to "syndicalism" in both instances.

[2] Cf. H. A. Clegg: "To-day industrial discipline is a different matter in all industries from the pre-war period of heavy unemployment. This is often said to be one of the greatest difficulties of British industry to-day. At the same time, full employment has done more to make industry more democratic and to raise the status of the worker than any legislation or any machinery for joint consultation could do" (52, 78). Note however that the concluding antithesis of Clegg is spurious, the causation is different from the one implied. The democratization of the industrial organization produced joint consultation, not the other way round. If so, another straightforward conclusion follows. Once generally applied, joint consultation becomes a social institution and cannot be abolished without social upheavals. But neither can it be petrified in its present form by which the attention of workers is channelized towards welfare matters, while management reserves the right to make the crucial managerial decisions. Very soon workers will begin to insist that this "toilet democracy" be replaced by "proper democracy". C. A. Myers unintentionally describes something of the sort happening in Sweden when he says: "But unless the committees begin to tackle real problems ... the 'stagnation' may turn into disgust and revulsion. 'Toilet democracy', as one person described the current concern for better washrooms, lighting, etc., may suffice for a time, but it is hardly the 'industrial democracy' that labour movement said it was seeking" (42, 71).

render their autocratic power by which their social function loses its content. In this way the second element — the increasing degree of workers' management — is introduced into the process. It is not likely that the process will always develop smoothly. However, in case of revolution, the trend is even clearer.

In the hundred and fifty years that have passed since the first Owenite experiment in New Lanark the relations between employers and workers have been constantly changing. These relations are reflected in the character of meetings between employers and employees which, as British National Institute of Industrial Psychology describes it aptly, "over the last 150 years shows a historical development from deputation and negotiation to consultation" (43, 29), and, we may add, to direct management in the end. This last phase of development supersedes the two-sides character of the meetings and unifies interests of all concerned in the institution of self-government. The last four decades have already produced the first attempts to go beyond mere consultation. German co-determination is the case in point. And the first individual firms have already begun to move even further towards the state of genuine workers' self-government[1].

6. We see that by the time the Second World War was finished the idea of workers' self-government was already in the air; it was not grasped as something distinctively new, it was not yet systematized and not introduced into the university curricula,[2] but it was nevertheless firmly established, like all those great ideas which mark the epoch and whose significance comes to be appreciated only afterwards. In the light of what we have learned from the history of this idea we may be induced to envisage the following hypothetical situation. Suppose a social revolution occurs somewhere sweeping away all the traditional barriers and — like all preceding revolutions — raising the demand for workers' management. Suppose, further, that the respective country is fortunate enough to have workers' management developed before the bureaucratization process, resulting from the socialization of the economy,

---

[1] Duisburger Kupferhütte, where the chairman of the Workers' Council is a member of the Managing Board — is a German example. Olivetti organization is an interesting Italian example. Glacier Metal Company is an outstanding British example. Glacier Works Council constitution says: "The Functions of the Council shall be ... to carry the responsibility of deciding the principles and policies which shall govern the Management of the Factory in the light of opinions of producers and managers, in the light of the interest of consumers, shareholders and the nation at large, and in the light of total Company Policy" (21, 153). In seeking to achieve this aim — the management to surrender the arbitrary executive power and the workers to develop responsible and effective collective decision making instead — both management and workers had to overcome enormous difficulties resulting from their own learned attitudes and from the totally uncongenial institutional set-up in which they were to act. These difficulties are indicative of the profound changes in social relations which are brought about by self-government. The process which took place in Glacier Company is admirably described in the Tavistock Institute study which bears the telling title: *The Changing Culture of a Factory* (21).

[2] In fact, academic economists, both left and right, are still unaware of its impact. Cf. a characteristic footnote-observation of J. A. Schumpeter: "Wild socializations — a term that has acquired official standing — are attempts by workmen of each plant to supersede the management and to take matters into their own hands. These are the nightmare of every responsible socialist" (53, 226).

proceeds so far as to polarize society separating the revolutionary elite from the broad masses. If these circumstances obtain, it is very likely that workers' self-government will become a permanent social institution. Now, the situation described is in fact not so hypothetical. It seems to have materialized in the postwar Yugoslavia.

The decisive period was the first five years after the revolution. A law passed in 1945 provided that workers' commissioners *(radnički povjerenici)*, as legal representatives of the workers, should establish contact with management, government agencies and union branches with the task of protecting the social and economic interests of the workers and helping in advancing the production. The following year the major portion of the economy was nationalized, and nationalization was completed in 1948. In the meantime, workers' commissioners ceased to exist and instead, trade union factory branches got the legal right to put forward proposals to the management. This was a retreat from control to consultation, a dangerous step backwards so much reminiscent of the Soviet development in the period 1917—1920. However, already in 1949 there was a new change: in a number of factories consultation between the management — mostly people who took an active part in the revolution themselves — and workers came to be spontaneously introduced. Parallelly, the fierce attack of the Cominform, launched in the middle of 1948 and continued over a period of several years, acted as a force helping to check the polarization process. In December 1949 the Government and the Trade Unions jointly issued an instruction on the formation of the workers' councils as advisory bodies. Councils were elected in 215 larger enterprises, but soon, other enterprises requested to enjoy the same privilege and by the middle of 1950 there were already 520 councils in existence. In June 1950 the National Assembly passed the law by which the *councils were transformed from advisory into managing bodies*. The working *kolektiv* of every enterprise elects the Workers' Council *(radnički savjet)*, which, as long as it enjoys the confidence of the electors, is a supreme policy-making body in the enterprise. The Council elects its executive committee, the Managing Board *(upravni odbor)*, which is concerned with the day-to-day implementation of the Council's policy; the actual execution of the directives, as well as the job of routine co-ordination of the activities of the enterprise, is left to be performed by the general manager and the expert technical and administrative staff. By this piece of legislation the perennial management-worker antithesis did not cease to exist at once, but conditions were created for it to be resolved. By 1950 it had already become abundantly clear that, in general, bureaucratic organization results in inefficiency and undesirable social relations and thus the introduction of workers' management cleared the ground for a series of institutional changes which were to follow[1]. The subsequent development in other spheres of social life strengthened in turn the new organization of industry. Self-government of producers was extended beyond the immediate working place, all representative organs, from local

---

[1] For industrial self-government see Kovač and Miljević (7). For a general discussion of the institution of self-government and a description of self-government schemes in the rest of the system see L. Geršković (54).

councils up to the Federal Assembly got a second chamber, *Councils of Producers*. In 1953 a change in the Constitution took account of the new social institutions. *Workers' management has become a part of the establishment*.

And this is the point we had to reach before proceeding to tackle the problem of Labour and Entrepreneurship and to discuss the corresponding price categories of Wages and Profit.

(c) Kolektiv-Entrepreneur and Profit

1. It is safe to say that entrepreneurship, and the corresponding category of profit, represent the weakest link in formal economic theory. Classical economists knew only three productive agents, of which one, Labour, was basic. Neoclassical economists formalized the analysis and introduced Entrepreneurship (or Enterprise, or Management) as a fourth agent. But this innovation has always remained controversial[1]. The controversy has centered around the notion of entrepreneurship as a factor of production analogous to land or labour, i.e., as something marketable in physical units which could be used for building up a clearly defined production function. As the concept of the factor of production as used in the present study is not based on the notion of tangible resources, that part of the problem disappears and we pass on to discussing some theories of the entrepreneurial function in the production process.

2. Of all the theories of entrepreneurship put forward only two — those of F. Knight (57) and J. Schumpeter (58) — gained wide acceptance. Knight, continuing a century old line of thinking initiated by Say, maintained that the entrepreneur's contribution to the process of production consisted in bearing non-insurable risks or uncertainties· The entrepreneur is the only agent whose duty is to combine and organize other agents; he takes risks in making price-output decisions and the reward for this activity is profit. This theory has been criticized on two scores. First, even if owner, the general manager as a rule uses other people's capital too and they bear risk as well. And secondly, the theory is not applicable to modern capitalism where the managing director is frequently just an employee of the firm and as such obliged to keep his family budget strictly separated from the profit account of the firm. Of the more recent attempts to repair the theory that of J. H. Stauss may be mentioned. Stauss replaces the individual functionary by the

---

[1] Cf. E. Fels and R. Richter for a recent attempt to show on logical grounds the analytical uselessness of the "factor" entrepreneurship: "We conclude that entrepreneurship, unless nothing but specialized *labour* is meant, cannot meaningfully occupy an argument place in production functions ... Entrepreneurship, the residual, non-routinizable, non-delegable, somewhat amateurish activity cannot be established as a productive factor on a par with labour, land and capital" (55, 221). It appears that "the usual interpretation of entrepreneurship ... by its very nature is *extraneous* to the larger part of economic analysis in much the same way marksmanship is extraneous to ballistics" (55, 203). Schumpeter would have agreed with this, for he thought it was inadmissible to "speak of 'supply of business ability'" and "to draw supply curves for entrepreneurial services even if we believe in supply curves for any other kind of work" (32, 897). For an older criticism see L. M. Fraser (56, 317—29).

firm as an entrepreneur pointing out that the central relationships of entrepreneurship are those of decision-making by the firm (59, 117). However, the source of profit, as positive entrepreneurial gain, still remains to be explained.

To provide an answer to this question was the task which Schumpeter set before himself. While Knight stresses the speculative and, in a certain sense, the passive role of entrepreneur, Schumpeter emphasizes his active and creative role. Enterprise, he says, means carrying out new combinations of productive factors and the individuals whose function is to do this are entrepreneurs. Risk falls on the owner of capital and therefore risk-taking is in no case an element of the entrepreneurial function. The entrepreneur sets up new production function initiating a new cycle of development; he is essentially an innovation and as such creates profits. Among the various possible criticisms of Schumpeter's theory, one is important for our present purpose. It consists in the observation, already anticipated by Marx[1], that real (i.e. non-tautological) innovators and those who reap the profit are frequently, or perhaps usually, different people. The latter, enjoying the power derived from peculiar institutions of the capitalist order, simply appropriate the ingenuity of the former. However, if Schumpeter's innovating entrepreneur who creates profit is a somewhat artificial construct in a capitalist society, why should we not make better use of this undoubtedly appealing concept in the theory of a socialist economy? In other words, we may attempt to make use of the following scheme: capital is socially owned and thus accessible to every entrepreneur after paying the price for its use (interest); entrepreneurs innovate and thus create profits; if the results of innovation are applicable elsewhere, they will be made accessible to other entrepreneurs and after a while profits will be absorbed by consumers and so disappear; this continual "creative destruction" fosters economic development (though it does not exhaust it as

---

[1] The difference in the cost of the first building of a new machine and that of its reproduction, of operating an establishment based on a new invention and of later establishments, is so great "that the first leaders in a new enterprise are generally bankrupted" and only those who later buy them out at bargain prices reap profits. "It is, therefore, generally the most worthless and miserable sort of money-capitalists who draw the greatest benefits out of the universal labour of the human mind and its co-operative application in society" (60, 78). There is another, closely related, criticism. Schumpeter's entrepreneurs-innovators are by implication most successful businessmen. But business leaders are typically recruited from a particular social class. At the time when Schumpeter conceived his theory — the first decade of this century — in the U.S.A., e.g., out of 190 most prominent business leaders studied by W. Miller, 50% came from families described as "upper class", and 45% were sons of businessmen and professionals (61, 206). As Schumpeter would not claim that innovating ability is hereditary, his concept of capitalist entrepreneur amounts to little more than an observation that in private capitalism business is conducted privately. Cf. also the findings of R. Bendix: American business leaders born after 1860 in one third of the cases studied simply inherited business and in the additional 29 to 48 per cent were hired managers (62, 229). The usual criticism of the theory is that individuals who start new businesses, are successful in them and own no capital — which are the three characteristics of Schumpeterian entrepreneur — are so rare in real life that their existence cannot be used for a generalization of capitalist development. For an interesting criticism of a different type see P. Sweezy (63).

in the Schumpeterian scheme). But before we pass to consider this scheme, let us examine more closely the anatomy of the entrepreneurial function. We note in passing, quite in the Schumpeterian tradition, the difference between the entrepreneurial and managerial role: the latter is the routine aspect of the former.

3. N. Kaldor (64, 67), J. H. Stauss (59, 115) and others distinguish three entrepreneurial activities: supervision, co-ordination and decision-making in view of uncertainty. Being interested in the competitive long run equilibrium of the firm, Kaldor seeks for a factor which would be in fixed supply and so cause diminishing returns. He finds this factor in co-ordination because, he thinks, while the other two factors can be increased, co-ordinating ability for the individual firm is given by the brain capacity of its entrepreneur and as such is fixed (64, 69). Thus co-ordination appears to be that function which characterizes entrepreneurship as a factor of production and for this reason should be considered as *the* entrepreneurial function.

Kaldor's treatment of co-ordinating ability as scarce factor responsible for equilibrium has been widely accepted. But this, I guess, happened for *psycho*logical and not for *logical* reasons. For, on closer inspection we quickly find that the choice is arbitrary[1]. The key co-ordinating decisions are made in the same way in a grocer's shop, in the Standard Oil Company and in the Chinese economy at the top of respective executive hierarchies, and the size of the organization makes no difference in the nature of the activity. Hence, if we may agree that supervision, co-ordination and uncertainty-bearing are three elements of the entrepreneurial activity, there is no reason for any one of them to be singled out as more fundamental than others. Incidentally, Kaldor's problem largely disappears in an economy where self-government is the institutional pattern: apart from a few exceptions, the firm is there limited to only one location which makes for an inevitable upward turn of long run cost curves and thus for a determined equilibrium even under conditions of otherwise perfect competition. The three elements enumerated do not seem to exhaust the entrepreneurial activity. It would seem necessary to modify the triadic concept of the entrepreneurial function by adding a fourth element, valuations, which corresponds to what for instance Rama Sastri calls harmonizing diverse interests (66, 4) and which reflects the fact that management involves human relations as well.

In the economy consisting of self-governing entities, managerial functions are not exercised by the particular class of individuals but by the collectivity of the members of the economic organizations, whom we shall call *working kolektivs*.[2] Social valuations and risk-bearing (also an aspect of valuation) are manifest functions of the kolektiv. Supervision is a two-way process in which every member of the kolektiv takes part. The remaining function, co-ordination, is purely technical and as such performed by technical experts, themselves members of

---

[1] For a different criticism see Chamberlin, 65, 187—91.

[2] *Kólektiv* (first syllable stressed) is a Yugoslav term for which there is no adequate English translation and which, therefore, I propose to use as a *terminus technicus*. The nearest English concepts are *team, collective, community of workers*.

the kolektiv. We thus reach the first important conclusion: *The kolektiv qualifies for the exercise of the entrepreneurial function.*[1]

4. Co-ordinating activity is not a purely technical activity *by itself,* in other words, it is not independent from social relations. If supervision is one-way process, i.e., if it is bureaucratic supervision, efficiency of co-ordination diminishes. And changes in efficiency are clearly of paramount importance for economic theory. We may therefore pause to examine the problem a little more closely.

Efficiency of co-ordination boils down to the problem of centralization *versus* decentralization. Bureaucratic authority requires very strict centralization. And this means — as von Hayek, arguing his case for the use of market mechanism, was quick to point out — that the existing and potential resources are wasted due to sheer technical necessity to condense knowledge of facts. For, there is a kind of knowledge "which by its nature cannot enter into statistics and therefore cannot be conveyed to any central authority in statistical form. The statistics which such a central authority would have to use would have to be arrived at precisely by abstracting from minor differences between things, by lumping together, as resources of one kind, items which differ as regards location, quality and other particulars, in a way which may be very significant for the specific decision" (68, 524). Von Hayek suggests that in order to secure the best use of resources known to any of the members of society, the price mechanism must be allowed to operate. Undoubtedly the market provides a much more efficient communication mechanism than an administrative hierarchy. But this is only one aspect of the problem; the other two are: co-ordination of market choices — for they are made in space and time — and communication below the level of the firm. And in order to be solved efficiently the co-ordination problem must be solved in its totality.

In so far as other things are kept equal, independence in decision-making increases efficiency. Then it does not mean splitting and breaking up an organization with the resulting uneconomic and anarchic bits-and-piecesness. It means, on the contrary, maximum economy, because direct initiative and direct responsibility are transferred to direct performers of tasks, workers and junior executives on the level of the firm, kolektivs on the level of the national economy. Administrative control and management cannot successfully react to changes and problems emerging in immediate work; slow as well as inadequate and global reacting causes great economic losses. Inside the firm hierarchical relations exert a depressing effect on individual performers, stifle initiative, undermine the will to work, cause resistance, in short, lower labour

---

[1] It will be useful to illustrate this conclusion by a statistical snapshot of the kolektiv-entrepreneur in action in the particular Yugoslav circumstances of 1956. The agenda of the meetings of Workers' Councils in this year comprised characteristic items in the following proportions: production and investment plan, costs of production and sales, reports of the Managing Board, the use of free funds — 40%; labour relations, discipline, economic criminal — 19%; wage-rates, norms and labour productivity, distribution of profits — 17%; welfare and training — 13%; miscellaneous items — 11% (67, 11). In 1956, the average net profit realized and appropriated by the kolektivs amounted to about 10% of the standard wage bill (computed from the data of *Statistički Godišnjak FNRJ 1958*, pp. 105 and 106).

efficiency[1]. For these reasons initiative and responsibility must be transferred to those in immediate contact with the tasks to be performed. Various social systems have satisfied this requirement in various degrees. And the system of workers' self-government is in this respect surely superior to any other existing alternative. Compared with private capitalism state-capitalist organization proved to be significantly more efficient, as measured by the rate of growth of production, because it could make use of planning on the national scale. Compared with state-capitalism socialist organization will be more efficient because by removing class antagonism it is able to make better use of the existing knowledge, as well as of the intellectual and emotional energy of the members of the community[2].

---

[1] In this field empirical research has only begun. The studies made so far indicate that labour productivity is probably significantly lower in the usual conditions of an autocratic business leadership as compared with the potential conditions in which workers are given an opportunity to participate in the decisions concerning their work. N.I.I.P. reports an American experiment in a textile company where differential productivity in this respect was 54—61 against 76—86 units (43, 217). In another American experiment in a sewing plant Coch and French established respective productivities as about 50 against about 70 units while "the rates of turnover and aggression (were) inversely proportional to the amount of participation" (69, 524). K. Lewin and associates worked out pioneering studies of more general significance, on the differences between "autocratic", "democratic" and "laissez-faire" leadership (70; summarized and including later research in (71) and on the effects of group decision (72). The famous Hawthorne experiments may also be mentioned. The general moral of these experiments is well summarized by R. Bendix: "Controlled observation of small work-groups over a number of years indicated that increased production on the whole seemed more closely related to the morale of the group than to any of the variables (such as differently spaced rest pauses, mid-morning meals, higher pay, variations in illumination, temperature, and so on) which were tested. Morale was related, on the other hand, to the improved supervision, the prestige position of each member of the testgroup and the increased attention which individual problems, opinions, and suggestions received" (15, 78).

[2] The above paragraph is largely reproduced from a study accompanying a model organizational chart which the author prepared in 1952 for a large Yugoslav oil enterprise and which contained detailed comparisons with the corresponding American and Soviet charts (73, 22). Later I examined the same ideas against the shortcomings of centralization in Yugoslav economy. Two distinct periods of development of the post-war economic organization in Yugoslavia — the first, "administrative", period is characterized by strict centralization and ends in 1951; in the second period, which lasts ever since, "free market" and workers' management were developed — provide almost laboratory conditions for testing the conclusions reached above. Unfortunately, no detailed study for the economy as a whole has been made so far. For one significant detail see Ch. 9-b. See also a short study of R. Bićanić (74). I undertook to examine one industry (oil industry). Some of the findings have already been quoted in Ch. 5-c-3-3. Here I add data on the labour productivity.

The centralization of management was largely initiated in 1947, reached its peak in 1950 and, in connection with the taking over by workers' councils, was substantially relaxed from 1952 onwards. The changes of the productivity of labour in the oil industry (production and drilling) against this background are as follows: 1941 — 100, 1946 — 74, 1947 — 96, 1948 — 63, 1949 — 70, 1950 — 59, 1951 — 78, 1952 — 111, 1953 — 163 (23, Pregled 9). Though these figures cannot be taken as representative for the economy as a whole — for a number of reasons oil industry was more sensitive than other industries and the formula I had devised for measuring labour productivity could not eliminate the influence of natural conditions — they nevertheless depict an impressive trend.

5. Though autonomous to a great extent, kolektiv, clearly cannot be *completely* autonomous. In matters of valuations which affect significantly the interests of some other kolektivs there must be a superior representative body to make decisions. This is a very serious and little explored problem, but we cannot discuss it here. In matters with which we are primarily concerned the upwards dependence of kolektivs will be largerly technical in nature. It would be ideal to separate "regulative" functions from "operative" functions and leave the former to the representative organs while the latter should be displayed by the working kolektivs and their associations (7, 60). In this way supreme co-ordination, including the Social Plan together with the financial instruments necessary to ensure its execution, would be vested in Parliament.[1] It should be stressed, however, that a certain amount of co-ordination will have to be done by the specialized state apparatus on the spot in which case regulative functions shade into operative ones. This interference of the state apparatus may be very pronounced in the early days of the new system. But as the process of normalization and institutionalization develops it can be gradually relaxed and reduced to routine activities. Banks play a special role in the overall co-ordination in that they combine customary business criteria with the intentions of the Social Plan. Finally, the Planning Authority supplies enterprises with relevant data which provide elements for their economic policies. The enterprises report their own important decisions which enables the Planning Authority to prepare a new set of data for the use of all concerned. The Social Plan, the banks and the availability of information represent an efficient co-ordinating mechanism which enables smooth functioning of the economy without centralized management. The upshot of all this is that risks and uncertainties are minimized and the entrepreneurial function presents itself in a completely new light.

In the realization of economic plans the main task of the Planning Authority is to preserve normal market conditions. In so far as price fluctuations can be avoided, windfall gains and undeserved losses will be avoided as well (in this, of course, foreign trade poses a thorny problem). And in so far as stability is achieved, *profits and losses of enterprises will depend on productive contributions of kolektivs.*

The next question relates to income distribution. There is no necessity for total amount of gross profit achieved by a particular kolektiv to be appropriated by them as well. The share of profit to be distributed among the members of the kolektiv is function of the incentives it provides. In general we wish to maximize the "supply of enterpreneurship", and we achieve this by institutionalizing a certain scale of distribution which is universally agreed to be "fair". Thus gross profits break in two parts: net profits which as a reward to members of the

---

[1] A similar idea was expressed by Clegg and Chester when they discussed the future of British nationalization: "Parliament should decide what functions can be and should be exercised over an area wider than the individual undertaking and place responsibility *for these functions alone* upon regional and national authorities" (75, 209). The authors stress that "...the future of nationalization depends on discovery and using means to make national ownership and national planning compatible with small-scale operation" (75, 211).

kolektiv are used to induce the supply of productive factor "entrepreneurship" and the remainder if any, which by its nature represents rent and as such is taxed away. Speaking of profit as a price for entrepreneurial services we shall therefore imply net profit, or that part of profit which is left to the free disposal of the kolektiv.

Negative profit, or loss, requires similar treatment. Within a certain range it will be regarded as market penalty for failure to supply the average amount of "entrepreneurship". *In this sense* — and regarding absolute loss only as a special case of a perfectly general opportunity loss — *the entrepreneurial function of a kolektiv involves risk-bearing as one of its essential component parts*, which is reminiscent of Knight's case. However, the reduction of wages below a certain level will be considered as socially intolerable. Then the state — or the Commune more properly — will have to intervene and subsidize for super-losses similarly as it taxed away super-profits. It may also happen that a particular venture is not profitable without the kolektiv being subjectiv.ly responsible for the failure and will therefore require either a permanent subsidy or even liquidation. *In this sense, risk is borne by the owner of capital*, i.e., by the community — and as such reflects the Schumpeterian case in which risk bearing is excluded from the entrepreneurial function.

We reach our second and final conclusion. *Kolektiv-entrepreneur is engaged in a continuous process of technological, organizational and commercial improvements*, being thus essentially an innovator. The supply of innovations is geared to material rewards and penalties. Appealing to the material interests of the people, this institution provides a strong motivation — though, of course, this is not the *only* motivation operating in the same direction — for a constant increase in efficiency which results in greater production which, in turn, increases the well-being of the community at large. Analytically it establishes a separate factor of production whose price is profit.

(d) Wages and Optimum Distribution of Income

1. In the economic process, producers appear not only as *kolektivs* but also as *members* of kolektivs, i.e., as individuals. The productive services of individuals are remunerated by Wages. Profit and Wages are two aspects of pricing of productive services of labour. In passing let us note once more an interesting parallelism. It is possible to classify all factors of production into two categories of which the first describes the technical and the second the human side of the economic process. We have found that in the first category Interest is only a special kind of Rent; we now add that, similarly, Profit is a special kind of Wages.

In the restrictive analytical sense wage-rate is the price of labour. As such it may be supposed to vary in accordance with the relations of supply and demand. In this respect, two separate problems stand out clearly. The first one relates to the allocation of available labour. The mobility of labour, being for well known reasons very imperfect, the desired allocation cannot be achieved simply by manipulation of wage-rates. However, in order to simplify the analysis, and also because pecuniary incentives are perhaps still predominant, it may be taken as a first approximation that the proper allocation is effected by wage-rates. Then, if the supply of a certain type of labour is inadequate, the wage-rate will be increased so as to allocate available labour to those industries where it will be socially most productive. If demand is inadequate, the wage-rate will be lowered so as to restrict supply. This is the gist of the traditional wage theory which then may or may not be recast in marginalist terms. But here I must warn the reader that the allocation criterion serves only for determination of *relative* wage-rates and that it tells us nothing about their *absolute* level. Should children's allowances, social insurance contributions, etc., be included in the wages? Or should, perhaps, wages be subsidized? It may be shown that it is *in principle* impossible to answer this question on the basis of traditional marginal productivity considerations. But this fact does not affect our present argument.

The second problem relates to the distribution of income. In this respect we must ask the question whether there is any reason why *gross* wages used to allocate labour should be equal to *net* wages appropriated by workers.

2. The traditional marginal productivity theory answers the question positively. In order to distribute the available labour force among various industries, the wage-rate must be equal to marginal product of labour *and* equal to marginal worker's valuation of alternative employments. If free choice of occupation is accepted, the second condition is automatically fulfilled. The first condition must be satisfied if maximum output is to be produced. As worker's valuations are assumed to depend on net wages, it appears that net and gross wages must be equal, and no place is left for taxation. If a tax is necessary, it must not be levied as a proportional income tax, let alone a progressive tax, but as a lump-sum tax so as not to interfere with marginalist equations[1]. Exceptionally, individuals with special native abilities (artists, for instance) may be taxed in the usual way, because they will not change their "industry" and so the "rent of ability" can be extracted from them (cf. Bergson, 76, 8—25).

Lump-sum taxes were imposed by Turkish Sultans on Christian peasantry when the Turks conquered feudal Balkan states in Mediaeval Ages. Progressive income taxes are used by modern administrators. Should these historical facts lead us to conclude that Istambul Grand Viziers were more efficient economists than the present-day Chancellors of Exchequer? And is socialist society condemned to have an eternally unequal distribution of income lest it be labeled irrational? To ask these questions is to give an answer: marginal productivity theory is a very unsatisfactory theory and if we wish to explain the events of the actual world, we must try to think out something better.

It would seem to be a fair description of reality if we postulate that inducement to work does not depend on *absolute* wage — a Yugoslav

---

[1] The argument has a logical flaw which usually remains unnoticed. Namely, valuation of the marginal unit of income (wage) depends on total income earned. If a poll tax is introduced, total net income will change and so will marginal valuations. Thus the distribution effects of a poll tax are equally "arbitrary" as of any other tax.

worker is paid three times less than a British worker — but on *relative* wage. Relative wages, in turn, depend on social norms. These norms are to a certain extent independent of the distribution of natural abilities, and therefore the marginal product and marginal wage may differ without affecting the rationality of allocation. Also, these norms change in a regular and empirically observable pattern, which we shall attempt to establish. Finally, we shall probably not distort the fact too much if we assume that workers choose industries according to gross wages and, independent of this choice, accept taxes as a social institution, thus being satisfied with net wages. Let us start our enquiry by undertaking the following conceptual experiment.

3. Two individuals, A and B, are engaged in growing and digging potatoes. Let them be similar in every respect except that B has stronger physique and is therefore a more efficient digger. Let, however, the wage of B be equal to that of A and their sum be equal to the total product of work of A and B, consisting of so many hundredweights of potato. Then, in the world with which we are familiar, B is likely to produce more potatoes than A, but not as much as he would produce under a more stimulating incentive scheme. (A may or may not work with full effort; for the sake of simplicity we assume that he does and that he considers every amount of potato equal or greater than the products of his labour as an appropriate wage.) Take also into account that the length of the working day is institutionally given and that we are interested in long-run effects, i.e., in *performance which will be sustained permanently*.

Next, change the incentive scheme by promising to B all the potato resulting from the extra effort put into work. A theoretical difficulty arises if it is assumed that his production function and his "psychological cost" function are monotonous, the first falling the second rising. In this case in order to extract maximum work out of B, successive marginal wages will have to be made equal to successive costs, not to marginal products, until the total additional product is exhausted by total additional wage. In practice, as the empirical studies of wage-incentive schemes seem to suggest, there is a fairly rigid limit of the amount of effort that will be *permanently* expended on production, a limit not affected by marginal variations of wages. Thus we may promise B all the extra potato and be quite sure that B will work with maximum effort. If both A and B work with maximum effort, the *output* of potato will be maximized. But the maximum *consumption* is still to be determined. Assume that B only insists on a certain *difference* in wages, not on the appropriation of total extra output, and is willing to work efficiently when he gets this wage differential. (In fact this is no more an assumption but a description of actual behaviour; witness: progressive taxation.) Then the difference between the output of B and the wage of B can be given to A. On the assumption of the decreasing marginal utility of income the welfare of the community will be increased when the "rent-content" of B's wages is transferred to A. Assume finally, that any further attempt to redistribute income in favour of A would lower the productivity of B so much that nothing would be left for redistribution. The last assumption, though not without foundation (see next footnote), is very restrictive and we shall abandon it later. Here we use it to complete, in a simple way, the set of conditions for a simultaneous maximization of production and consumption. To make the case more general one could introduce the assumption of the backward sloping supply curve of labour, and perhaps some other assumptions. But these complications would make the analysis more involved without contributing anything to the substance of the argument.

The example reflects the case of piece-rate work. But this type of work is relatively unimportant if the society as a whole is taken into consideration. An engineer, a civil servant or a university professor usually do not produce measurable quantities of goods and services and neither do the workers in many trades, or if they do the quantities produced are not determined solely by the amount of personal effort expended. Also, piece-rates are always derived from an existing or assumed structure of time-rates. It is therefore this more fundamental wage structure we have to establish. To do that it is only necessary to assume that our individuals A and B do not measure their personal production and that managers and accountants do this instead. It will become apparent that the demand for B-type of work is greater relative to the demand of A-type and to the supply of B-type. This will tend to increase B-wage-rates. And that, in turn, will create consciousness of greater productivity of B-work and, consequently, of its greater *social* value. In the market economy the productivity and the social esteem of work are correlated but are not identical. And here lies the source of the difference between gross and net wages and the clue for the solution of our problem.

4. Suppose that the Planning Authority is free to choose any wage system it likes and that it decides to design the system of wage differentials so that it will be generally accepted as "fair" and as such will induce people to work with their maximum (long-run) energy. What is fair depends not only on the vague idea of productivity but also on the characteristics of jobs (dirty, strenuous, dangerous, more skilled and more responsible jobs involve generally greater "disutility" and thus call for higher remunerations). Is the fair-wages policy the right policy to be pursued? The answer to this question depends on what we can say about a theoretical difficulty inherent in the procedure. Namely, it may be assumed that after maximum production has been achieved by a proper system of wage-differentials, it will still be possible to redistribute income between, say, B and A, so that a certain amount of income of B is transferred to A while the resulting loss in product, due to "dissatisfaction" of B, is less than the gain in income of A. In other words, total product is less than maximum but total consumption, in utility terms, is greater than before because the loss of B is more than compensated by the gain of A.

The assumption of a possible discrepancy between production and consumption implies a possibility of a conflict of valuations. For, we assume that A and B have agreed on what are "fair" wages and hence the possibility that another distribution of income will increase total welfare means a conflicting valuation. If two conflicting valuations of equal "rank" are considered, logical deductions cannot provide a solution. However, in our case the "agreement" valuation is more general

123

and includes the "distribution" valuation as a special case, because the "agreement" is reached after a consideration of all possible consequences. Hence, the conflicting "distribution" valuation must be ruled out as inconsistent with rational behaviour.

If A and B have *fully* agreed on what is the appropriate distribution of income, then we know that they will work with maximum efficiency and that no discrepancy between best distribution and maximum output can arise. The argument can be reversed and then we get the following useful result. Assuming that it is possible to induce *both* individuals to supply maximum work, we may find the desirable distribution of income even without asking the individuals explicitly. We need only manipulate wage differentials so as to induce each individual to produce maximum output. But our assumptions are still too restrictive; we must consider a community of many individuals and then we need an additional device to make the problem tractable. Passing from the two-person to a multi-person community we shall assume that A and B reflect *public opinion* with regard to the respective classes of labour. The concept of public opinion raises many questions which, however, we need not discuss here. It will suffice to assume that (1) public opinion exists and (2) that in a homogeneous society the existence of public opinion implies that a great majority of people concerned, are prepared to agree on a particular matter. The first assumption is hardly controversial, while the second is based on empirical observations — supplemented by experiments (Sherif, Asch, Crutchfield and others) — that individual valuations are moulded by and tend to conform to collective valuations. Now, if wage differentials satisfy public opinion, individuals will supply maximum work. There will be some exceptions, but just because they are exceptions they can be disregarded. Accepting collective valuations and supplying maximum work does not imply full agreement. Individuals may have their doubts and private reservations, but these are valuations of the "second" rank because they do not affect general agreement on the remuneration of work. If and when they do affect it public opinion changes and a new "agreement" replaces the old one. Maximum output is thus indicative of the fact that community *accepts* the respective income distribution and so we cannot argue that it *ought* to accept a different one. One modification is needed, however. Public opinion is not an automatic result of individual valuations as such but always of the individual valuations as they arise in a definite institutional system. To solve the problem completely we must design an appropriate institutional system as well. In this respect the economists can advise that the system be designed so as to be conducive to maximum economic equality. There are two reasons for recommending this course. First, historically greater equality was conducive to greater economic efficiency (see Ch. 5). And secondly, the empirically observable drive towards equality (see *infra*) indicates that greater equality means an increase in the welfare of the community. Thus most egalitarian distribution of income consistent with maximum output appear to be two conditions for the *optimum distribution* of income[1].

---

[1] In determining practical policy the following considerations may also play an important role. In a regularly growing economy every change is magnified at compound interest. If the rate of growth is 10% per annum and the planning

5. The desirable distribution of income may be approached from two different starting positions, both of which are found in reality. We can start from an over-equalization — normally the result of a social revolution — and then experiment with the wage-differentials until a "fair" structure of wages is struck. To give this case an empirical content and to provide a suitable appelation call it "Yugoslav Case". In Yugoslavia by 1951 it was realized that over-equalization of incomes had affected production adversely and in the following six years Trade Unions and Government were experimenting in widening wage-differentials[1]. — Or, more usually, we can start from a situation of a very unequally distributed income and gradually reduce inequalities until the point is reached where output begins to shrink. This case may be typified as the "British Case", because British economy provides a good empirical illustration for it. Over the last four decades, inequalities in income distribution have been markedly reduced while no adverse effect on output seems apparent[2].

Both Yu-Case and B-Case imply that equal distribution of income is for some reasons "better" than an unequal distribution. It will be

---

horizon of the community 30 years — both parameters are explained in Ch. 10 — the present reduction of output will cause a total loss in output 180 times greater. Thus if we decide to defy public opinion and to apply an equalization policy which would, for instance, reduce all incomes above the average in order to increase all incomes below the average, we may be virtually sure that *both* sections of the community will lose.

[1] If 1938 is taken as the year of comparison, indexes of nominal salaries and wages in 1951 for various categories of employees were as follows: public servants with university education 280, skilled workers 300, public servants with secondary education 360, unskilled workers 685. The difference in wages between skilled and unskilled workers was reduced by 60%. Average salaries of employees were nearly equalized with average wages. As a result, people tended to avoid responsible jobs and it was evident that incentives for improving the skill were lacking. Equalization was too quick generally and also particularly because even *absolute* standard of living of certain categories was reduced. Thus in 1951 the real earnings of a married couple, both working, were (1939 = 100): business employees 55, government employees 60, skilled workers 76, unskilled workers 224. If three children's allowances are included indexes increase to 84, 76, 111 and 339, but even so the first two categories experienced fall in living standard and, also, children's allowances were not incentives for work. Therefore since 1952 there was a deliberate policy to widen earnings differentials parallel with the increase in social product. The great increase in production (22%) and consequently in real earnings (14%) in 1957 helped to bring this process more or less to an end (if my impression of what is happening is correct). The following table summarizes the events:

	1938	1951	1957
Wages of unskilled workers	100	100	100
Wages of skilled workers	330	133	149
Average wages of all workers	100	100	100
Salaries of government employees	166	103	} 135
Salaries of business employees	200	110	

Source of data: *Privreda FNRJ*, Ekonomski Institut FNRJ, 1954, pp. 349—51; *Information Bulletin about Yugoslavia*, No. 18, 1958, p. 6.

[2] A. M. Carter provides the relevant data (77). Inequality is measured by the percentage of income which would have to be transferred from high to low income groups in order to achieve an equal *per capita* distribution; thus 0% expresses an absolute equality and (almost) 100% an absolute inequality. Carter's inequality indexes of distribution of personal income after tax are: 1880 — 41, 1913 — 38, 1928 — 30, 1937 — 23, 1948/49 — 16 (p. 75). If 33 years before the First World War

necessary to examine these reasons in more detail. In doing so we first encounter the fact that the equalization of income is an observable long-run tendency, an empirical phenomenon capable of measurement. There are two aspects of this phenomenon.

(1) The first aspect is purely technical. Economic development ultimately results in improving the standard of living — including the vitally important educational standard — of broad masses of population. This reduces efficiency differences between various strata of the society. To a certain extent this fact can be illustrated by the relation between wages of skilled and unskilled workers. In underdeveloped countries the wages of skilled workers will be about 120 per cent higher than the wages of unskilled workers; in developed countries this difference is only about 20 per cent[1]. Similarly, the differences in income, resulting from supply and demand relations, between industrial workers and peasants, between university graduates and uneducated masses, between public servants and their domestic servants — will be several times greater in countries at the initial stage of capitalist development as compared with mature capitalist countries. The countries only entering upon the road of capitalist development, like the feudal economies in Europe two centuries ago, show the characteristic picture of economic polarization: great majority of population extremely and *equally* poor and a very small minority very rich. Due to economic development this spire-on-the-box structure is gradually transformed into a ball-like structure by a multiplication of intermediary strata — all sorts of skilled and professional jobs — relative to either of the extremes[2]. For all these reasons earned income will be more equally distributed in developed than in undeveloped countries. This, however, tells us nothing about the tendencies in the distribution of *total* income, because earned income represents only one part of total income. The other part of total income consists of unearned, property income, and the distribution of property income is determined by a complex set of factors. If an oversimplification is permitted, one may assume (1) that capitalist development generates a tendency towards capital concentration, (2) but it also generates a strong social opposition to it, primarily expressed in the growing pressure of the organized working class, (3) that in the absence of fascism the resulting distribution of income is not likely to grow more unequal, and the distribution of income after tax is very likely to

are compared with 35 years after it, one is tempted to conclude that two world wars and one severe slump did the job of equalization effectively. The possibility for further equalization of income lies in the elimination of private property. Private wealth is markedly unequally distributed: in 1948/49 1% of adult population owned 46% of all private capital, while the comparable inequality index was as high as 75.4 (p. 102).

[1] The figures represent medians of relative wages of skilled labour in engineering industry as compared with unskilled urban labour in 15 developed and 15 undeveloped countries listed by C. Clark (78, 526—30).

[2] Compare, for instance, the distribution of family incomes in the U.S.A. and India after the last war. The third and the fourth quintiles of population — rating being from poor to rich — receive 38% of total income in the U.S.A. and only 27% in India. The first two quintiles receive more or less the same proportion of income in the two countries, 18% and 17% respectively,and so the difference in the middle strata is matched by an inverse difference in the top quintiles (79, 22).

grow less unequal[1]. This brings us to the second aspect of the income equalization tendency.

(2) The second aspect is social and, for all I know, a much more important one. Various social systems produce economic inequalities — and economic inequalities provide the very foundation of social inequalities — in various degrees. To substantiate this contention one cannot do better but refer to four representative economies and the inequalities existing there· The spread of earnings in business is limited on the one side by the wage-rates of unskilled workers and on the other by the salaries of general managers. Thus the degree of inequality will be well expressed by the ratios of annual salaries of managing directors of large enterprises to annual wages of unskilled workers. If, in order to take into account factor (1), the respective economies are arranged according to the degree of development, manager-worker ratios are as follows: Yugoslavia 7 : 1, which reduces to 4 : 1 when children allowances are included; the Soviet Union 20 : 1; Britain 10 : 1; the United States 20 : 1[2].

---

[1] Cf. S. Kuznets for an attempt of a systematic explanation supported by some statistical evidence (79). Statistical data are still scanty, but those which have been published support the hypothesis that economic development *ultimately* (Kuznets's evidence suggests that in the earlier stages of capitalist development income inequality is widening) leads to a marked equalization of incomes. Carter's series for Britain describes the history of one country. Kuznets adds data for the U.S.A. and Germany which show the same trend. T. Morgan supplies "cross-section" data for three underdeveloped (Ceylon, Puerto Rico, El Salvador) and four developed (Canada, Sweden, the United States, the United Kingdom) countries. In the post-war years, the richest tenth of the population received the following share of total income (before tax): in the undeveloped group 33—44 per cent, in the developed group 28—32 per cent (80, 161). The difference in taxation further increases the difference in income distribution in favour of developed countries. See also an earlier paper by T. Morgan (81) and the criticism of it by H. T. Oshima (82).

[2] Salaries and wages net of taxes and families·with three children are implied. Because of the paucity of data, not to speak of comparable data, these ratios are only very rough approximations and should be interpreted as indicating only the *order* of magnitudes.

The Yugoslav ratio is based on private information for the managerial salaries; the average monthly wage of unskilled workers was 9,090 dinars in 1957 (*Information Bulletin about Yugoslavia*, No. 18, 1958, p. 6). Some comparable data are published for 410,000 persons employed in civil service, judiciary, schools, health and social insurance institutions, cultural and scientific institutions, communal undertakings, banks and offices of business associations. In this sector, the top-bottom ratio is about the same as in the industrial sector; altogether 34 salaries greater than 50,000 dinars (about £ 50) per month were recorded in 1956. (*Statistički Godišnjak FNRJ 1957*, p. 352).

Published data about Soviet wages are so scanty that the ratio quoted does not indicate much more than that Soviet inequality is greater than British and smaller than American. What is particularly difficult to assess is the very large bonus which the Soviet director gets for various aspects of overfulfilment of the plan. In respect to wages one firm point is the statutory minimum monthly wage of 325 rubles in industrial settlements in 1957 (*Soviet Studies*, 1957—58, p. 351). On the basis of scattered evidence I estimated the average monthly wages of unskilled workers to be 400—450 rubles in 1957. See T. B. Bottomore (83, 39—40). For some pre-war relations, see Bergson (76, 228), Bienstock (84, 93—5), Schwartz (85, 165—7). The extreme top-bottom ratios are occasionally quoted to be several times greater than the one in the text.

6. Having established an empirical trend and recalling the fact that every new social revolution produces a new pressure towards greater equalization, we may consider that the decisive argument has been furnished, that equal distribution of income should be regarded as a standard or as a limiting case of an actual movement. But it is, of course, possible to formalize the analysis and in this case Lerner's approach may serve the purpose well. Lerner assumes that (1) consumers enjoy satisfactions from having things. (2) They choose goods which give more satisfaction rather that those which give less. (3) Marginal utility diminishes with the amount of goods consumed, for otherwise only one good would be bought; it folows that marginal utility of money income is diminishing, because if income is increased, new goods which have previously been excluded, will be bought, and this means that they have been considered less satisfactory. (4) Individuals are equally sensitive to increases as to decreases in income which leaves marginal utility of income unchanged. (5) The satisfactions of different people are similar, i.e., it is not meaningless to say that the satisfaction one individual gets is greater or smaller than the satisfaction enjoyed by another individual. This proposition is incapable of proof, but the only alternative is solipsism which is obviously absurd. (6) Each individual's satisfaction is derived only from his own income and not from the income of others. (7) Total income is distributed independent of the capacity of income-receivers to enjoy their incomes. Or, in the formulation of M. Friedman, if individuals are classified according to the capacity to enjoy income, the probability distribution of income would be the same for all such classes. (8) Total amount of income is unrelated to its distribution (89, 11—40).

The British wages for 1956—57 are obtained by applying the Ministry of Labour index to earnings of unskilled workers in 1952—53 (£ 352) as they were established by a national survey undertaken by the Oxford University Institute of Statistics (86, 142). This produced a figure slightly lower than £ 450. The salary of a representative managing director is taken as £ 12,000 (= £ 4,340 net of taxes). Statistics on directorial salaries does not exist, but it is known that the highest salaries go beyond £ 50,000. The chairman of the boards of nationalized industries get £ 10,000 (= £ 4,040 net of taxes). In 1956—57, *Inland Revenue Report* registers 2,524 earned and 6,270 unearned incomes greater than £ 12,000 (of these 605 earned and 1848 unearned incomes higher than £ 20,000).

American average wage of unskilled workers (non-farm labourers) was $ 2,142 in 1951 (87, 105). Applying Bureau of Labour index for average weekly earnings of production workers (1951 = 100, 1956 = 126) I got annual earnings of $ 2,700 for 1956. A. Patton reports on remuneration of chief executives in 582 firms in 1956 classified in 18 industries and three groups according to profit levels ($ 3, 10 and 40 million). The median of the industrial averages in the last two groups is $ 126,000 (88, 126), which gives a salary of $ 55,000 net of taxes. In nearly one half of the firms surveyed the chief executive is paid about $ 100,000 or more, the upper limit being $ 809,000 (*Business Week*, May 25, 1957, p. 116). The extreme net manager-worker ratio of highest paid managers and lowest paid (non-white) labour approaches 100 : 1.

The respective gross ratios are 27 : 1 in Britain and 47 : 1 in America; in Yugoslavia there was no income tax in 1957, while in the U.S.S.R. tax rates were so small as to leave the ratio substantially unaffected. It should be noted that the relative inequality in the U.S.A. is greater than the ratio suggests, because socialized services are there significantly less developed than in the other three countries. Also, actual inequalities in Britain and in the U.S.A. are understated as compared with those in Yugoslavia and the U.S.S.R. because of the existence of large unearned incomes (including capital gains) in the former countries.

128

Under these assumptions, more equal distribution of incomes will tend to increase the total amount of satisfaction. If total satisfaction is to be maximized, income must be distributed in such a fashion that the marginal utilities of the incomes of all individuals are equalized. Lerner points out that it is impossible to achieve this because there is no way of discovering the relevant marginal utilities. The solution he suggests consists in maximizing "the *probable* total satisfaction, making this greater than the *probable* total satisfaction that would result from any other distribution of income. If it is impossible, on any division of income, to discover which of any two individuals has higher marginal utility of income, the probable value of total satisfactions is maximized by dividing income *evenly*" (89, 29). This because any other distribution is equally likely to decrease as to increase satisfaction; but because of the diminishing marginal utility of income, wrong redistributions result in greater losses than are the gains of equally likely right redistributions. Or, in Friedman's interpretation, before the change in present distribution and assuming that (7) each class of consumers possesses equal capacity for enjoyment of income the distribution of income will be the same making average income equal for all classes. In trying to maximize total satisfaction the most we can do is equalize incomes in every particular class and consequently for every individual (90, 308—9). If we try to redistribute income among the equal-enjoyment-capacity classes of individuals, it is equally possible that the income will be shifted in the right direction — to individuals with greater enjoyment capacity — as in the wrong direction — to individuals with smaller enjoyment capacity — since we have no means to identify classes. However, as marginal utility of income diminishes, the losses of wrong reductions of income are greater than equally likely gains of right increases in income. Thus "if it is desired to maximize total satisfaction in a society, the rational procedure is to divide income on an equalitarian basis" (89, 32).

Lerner's conclusion cannot be sustained because the assumption (8) is not valid; total amount of income *is* related to its distribution. But assumption (8) may be substituted (and assumption (6) modified) by our analysis in sections 2—4. In this way we get a formal proof for the proposition that it is desirable to distribute income more equally because this increases the economic welfare of the community.

7. It remains to sum up the results of the analysis. We have found that two different criteria are guiding the formation of wage-rates. The first criterion is based on a "fair" wage structure. The evaluation of fair wage-differentials changes is a result of an interplay of technical and social factors. The former — the scarcity of superior grades of labour due to biological limitations or due to material poverty of the society — render some grades of labour more productive than others. To more productive labour society attaches higher value because in the world with still very low standard of living, material improvements are highly valued. With the increase of general economic welfare productivity differences decrease for technical reasons (universal education, medical attendance available to everybody, proper diet, shelter, etc.) and in so far as they remain social valuations of more productive labour are likely to grow less important because of the "diminishing marginal utility"

of successive improvements in living standard. In a society not socially polarized it is in principle possible to find out what are these social valuations and to express them in an agreement on "fair" wages. Net wage-rates include not only "efficiency" differentials, but also positive differentials for dirty, strenuous, dangerous, more responsible, etc., work and, conversely, negative differentials for agreeable and leisurely work, i.e., they include "cost" differentials as well. From the point of view of income distribution these wage differentials do not represent inequalities because they cancel out with the costs incurred. Wages as just described are "net" wages and, as such, relevant for the problem of income distribution.

The second criterion relates to the formation of "gross" wage-rates. They serve, as all other prices do, for proper allocation of the productive factor labour. Ideally gross wage is equal to marginal product of the respective kind of labour. In practice, however, the possibility of applying marginal product calculus is rather questionable and so even great "distortions" of gross wages are not likely to affect appreciably the desirable allocation of labour.

The difference between gross wages and net wages represents rent which is taxed away by the Planning Authority. One may say that net wage-rates represent the supply price of labour, while gross wage-rates are its demand price.

The wages of individual workers plus the profits of kolektivs determined as total demand and supply prices for labour services ensure that available labour resources be maximally utilized. Thus total output will be maximized. For the same reason the income distribution is universally accepted as "fair" and, because of the social institutions, is the most egalitarian attainable. In this sense it represents the *optimum distribution of income*.

In a general case the optimum distribution is *historically* determined and so always relative; it is conditioned by the mode of production and changes with it. The analysis shows that today both private and state capitalism are inherently incapable of achieving optimum distribution of income, because by changing the institutions it is possible to improve the distribution of income without reducing output. Thus it is *a priori* impossible to solve the problem of optimum distribution by assuming capitalist institutions. The analysis also shows that production too is likely to be more efficient in socialism than in the other two systems. Thus, the socialist mode of production — workers' councils, planning and the rest — has both properties which we have found to be associated with the historical succession of social systems: it produces greater material wealth and greater equality simultaneously. In the last analysis the problem of the optimum distribution of income reduces to the problem of the most efficient economic system. The ultimate cause of this historical identity ought to be sought in the fact that economic efficiency depends on human motivation in production and so production relations which are *socially* most acceptable on a given stage of development of productive forces produce also the most efficient economic machine.

130

Appendix

NOTE ON THE MEANING OF "SOCIALISM" AND "COMMUNISM"

1. It might have been noticed that I ended my analysis of socio-economic development with socialism. This should not be interpreted as an implied belief that with socialism development comes to an end, but it does indicate my conviction that hardly more than a guesswork is possible about future development and that, therefore, "marginal productivity" of speculation in this sphere must be quite close to zero. Nevertheless, a brief excursus cannot be harmful. It will be used to clear up misconceptions about a problem of long standing.

In the critique of the Gotha Program of the German Workers' Party Marx defined socialism as the lower phase and communism as the higher phase of the classless communist society. The former is characterized by the principle of distribution according to work, the latter by distribution according to needs.[1] This distinction has come to be widely accepted by socialist economists, but no attempt has been made to examine it within a consistently developed analytical framework. What has been done consists mainly in reducing Marx's definition to a rather obvious nonsense. For this reason I find it necessary to append the following few paragraphs.

2. What does distribution according to work mean? We have seen that there is no reason why the decision on how much everyone will get should be left to "the ideal pricing based upon the principle of scarcity" as for instance Cassel would suggest (92, 34). Cassel — like so many other bourgeois economists, as Marx would call them — is unaware of the difference between the supply and demand price of labour, of which the former is a purely social phenomenon. On the other hand it would be equally arbitrary to leave the decision on income distribution to state officials. The manager-worker ratio in the Soviet Union (Ch. 6-d-5-2) suggests that state officials are not likely to distribute income optimally.

---

[1] In a socialist society "the right of the producers is *proportional* to the labour they supply; the equality consists in the fact that measurement is made within an *equal standard*, labour.

But one man is superior to another physically or mentally and so supplies more labour in the same time, or can labour for a longer time; so if labour is to serve as a measure, it must be defined by its duration or intensity, otherwise it ceases to be a standard of measurement. This *equal* right is an unequal right for unequal labour. It recognizes no class differences, because everyone is only a worker like everyone else; but it tacitly recognizes unequal individual endowment and therefore productive capacity as natural privileges...

But these defects are inevitable in the first phase of the communist society, as it has just emerged from the capitalist society after prolonged birth pangs. The right can never be higher than the economic structure of the society and its cultural development conditioned thereby.

In a higher phase of a communist society, after the enslaving subordination of the individual to the division of labour, and thereby also the antithesis between mental and physical labour, has vanished; after labour has become not only a means of life but life's prime want; after the productive forces have also increased with the all round development of the individual, and all the springs of co-operative wealth flow more abundantly — only then can the narrow horizon of bourgeois right be crossed in its entirety and the society inscribe on its banners: From each according to his ability, to each according to his needs!" (91, 22—3).

The criterion for distribution according to work is easily furnished by the theory of optimum distribution of income discussed above. The criterion does not lead to a static distribution, but results in a process. The process is a function of economic development which leads to economic equalization. Once every member of the community is well fed and sheltered, enjoys medical attendance and has access to all educational establishments, the variations in efficiency will be greatly reduced (except for a few exceptions on either end of the scale, which, being exceptions, are not significant). At the same time, increasing economic welfare will tend to diminish the social valuations attached to the differences in efficiency. Thus our manager-worker ratio is likely to undergo a series of continual revisions downwards. How far? Here we break our story for a moment in order to examine the second definition of Marx.

3. Distribution according to needs may be interpreted to mean that "in communist society everybody will work according to his abilities and will get consumption goods according to the needs of a culturally developed man", which is the meaning attributed to the principle by the authors of the Soviet text-book on political economy (93, 596). It is, however, not at all clear who is to determine the standard of a "culturally developed man". The text-book gives another hint: immensely increased productivity of labour will create abundancy of consumption goods (p. 598). That leads us to the most frequent interpretation which simply says that abundancy of goods ensures full satisfaction of needs of everybody and thus renders every other principle of distribution superfluous. But the needs or wants of human beings are limitless and so Marx's communism appears to be an obvious impossibility — a conclusion which critics and protagonists (though for different reasons) have favoured alike. Here we may resume our story.

As efficiency differentiation grows less significant, "cost" differentiation is likely to become more significant in determining income distribution. The wages of miners will relatively rise while the wages of government officials will relatively fall. Further, in a community with a very high standard of living the material incentives and rewards are likely to become less and less important. This will change the orientation of social valuations from the effect of a particular kind of work to the work itself. Strenuous, dangerous, and very responsible jobs — in so far as not eliminated by automation — will carry prestige values — like, say, climbing Mount Everest and exploring Antarctic at present — not to speak of social recognition and great personal satisfaction derived from every well done job as such, and people will come to be motivated by these considerations more powerfully than by wage differentials. If, however, wage differentials lose their function of inducing people to work, there is no reason why these differentials should be operated any further. Then they may easily be substituted by an equal distribution of income corrected for the differences in personal needs — something akin to the operation of the present health service or children allowances. We now see that distribution according to the needs does not imply the meaningless idea of full satisfaction of needs.

Socialism, like all other social systems, is not a rigid structure; it is a process. It gradually shades into communism. In the former,

132

material stimuli are needed to induce people to do work efficiently. In the latter this need vanishes. Increasing leisure-time[1] makes work *as such*, i.e., freely chosen work, more attractive. "Diminishing marginal utility" of expanding income diminishes importance of material stimuli until they are superseded by more powerful valuations of a different kind. Thus defining his socialism and communism as he did, Marx said something meaningful.

References:

1. J. Schumpeter, *Imperialism and Social Classes*, Oxford, Blackwell, 1951.
2. K. Marx, F. Engels, "Predislovie k russkomu izdaniju 'Manifesta Komunističeskoj partiji'" (Preface to the Russian Edition of the 'Manifesto of the Communist Party'), *Sočinenija*, Tom XV, Moskva, Partizdat, 1935.
3. E. F. M. Durbin, "The Case for Socialism", in *Problems of Economic Planning*, London, Routledge, 1949.
4. M. Novak, Uvod u političku ekonomiju socijalizma (The Introduction into the Political Economy of Socialism), *Ekonomski pregled*, Zagreb, 1955.
5. N. Pašić, *Javne korporacije u Velikoj Britaniji i drugim zapadnim zemljama* (Public Corporations in Great Britain and Other Western Countries), Beograd, Kultura, 1957.
6. A. Dragičević, *Potrebni rad i višak rada* (Necessary Labour and Surplus Labour), Zagreb, Kultura, 1957.
7. P. Kovač, Dj. Miljević, *Samoupravljanje proizvođača u privredi* (The Self-Government of Producers in the Economy), Beograd, Savremena administracija, 1958.
8. F. Engels, *Herr Eugen Dühring's Revolution in Science*, London, Lawrence, 1935.
9. R. H. S. Crossman, *Socialism and the New Despotism*, Fabian Tract 258, London, 1956.
10. R. McKenzie, *British Political Parties*, London, Heinemann, 1955.
11. W. A. Lewis, "The Administration of Socialist Enterprises", in *Overhead Costs*, London, Allen and Unwin, 1949.
12. M. Weber, *The Theory of Social and Economic Organization*, London, W. Hodge, 1947.
13. T. B. Bottomore, "Higher Civil Servants in France", in *Transactions of the Second World Congress of Sociology*, Vol. II., London, International Sociological Association, 1954.
14. R. K. Kelsall, *Higher Civil Servants in Britain*, London, Routledge and Kegan, 1955.
15. R. Bendix, *Higher Civil Servants in American Society*, Boulder, Colorado, University of Colorado Press, 1949.
16. J. D. Kingsley, *Representative Bureaucracy*, Yellow Springs, Ohio, The Antioch Press, 1944.
17. H. H. Gerth, C. W. Mills, "A Marx for the Managers", reprinted in R. K. Merton and others (ed.), *Reader in Bureaucracy*, Glencoe, Ill., The Free Press, 1952.

---

[1] From 1800 to 1950 the average working week in the U.S.A., Britain, France and Germany was reduced from about 84 hours to about 45 hours (6, 355). Suppose that in the same period one, now socialist country, has increased per capita income ten times and that its economy now expands at a rate of 10% per annum. Then every successive year now *doubles* the 1800-income. This must have a corresponding effect on the further increase in leisure-time. Note also that increased leisure-time makes the participation of ordinary citizens in self-government schemes technically feasible. All in all, Marxian communism does not seem to be so very far ahead.

18. S. M. Lipset, *Agrarian Socialism*, Berkeley and Los Angeles, University of California Press, 1950.
19. A. K. Davis, "Bureaucratic Patterns in the Navy Officer Corps", reprinted in R. K. Merton and others (ed.), *Reader in Bureaucracy*, Glencoe, Ill. The Free Press, 1952.
20. R. K. Merton, "Bureaucratic Structure and Personality", *Ibid.*
21. E. Jaques, *The Changing Culture of a Factory*, New York, Dryden Press, 1952.
22. W. R. Sharp, *The French Civil Service: Bureaucracy in Transition*, New York, Macmillan, 1931.
23. B. Horvat, *Ekonomika naftne privrede Jugoslavije* (Economics of Yugoslav Oil Industry), Doctoral Thesis, University of Zagreb, 1955.
24. E. Devons, *Planning in Practice*, Cambridge, University Press, 1950.
25. W. Eucken, "On the Theory of the Centrally Administered Economy: An Analysis of the German Experiment", *Economica*, 1948, 79—100, 173—93.
26. V. I. Lenin, "A Great Beginning", *Selected Works*, Vol. IX, London, Lawrence and Wishart, 1937.
27. K. Marx, F. Engels, "Manifesto of the Communist Party", *Selected Works*, Vol. I, Moscow, Foreign Languages Publishing House, 1951.
28. W. F. Oakeshott, *Commerce and Society*, Oxford, Clarendon Press, 1936.
29. L. von Mises, *Bureaucracy*, Glasgow, W. Hodge, 1945.
30. W. H. Morris Jones, *Socialism and Bureaucracy*, Fabian Tract 277, London, 1949.
31. K. Marx, "The Civil War in France", *Selected Works*, Vol. I, London, Lawrence and Wishart, 1950.
32. J. A. Schumpeter, *History of Economic Analysis*, New York, Oxford University Press, 1955.
33. F. A. Neff, *Economic Doctrines*, New York, McGraw-Hill, 1950.
34. L. H. Haney, *History of Economic Thought*, New York, Macmillan, 1911.
35. G. D. H. Cole, *Guild Socialism Re-Stated*, London, L. Parsons, 1920.
36. *A Works Council in Being. An Account of the Scheme in Operation at Bournville Works*, Publication Department, Bournville Works, 1921.
37. C. W. Guillebaud, *The Works Council*, Cambridge, University Press, 1928.
38. B. Pribičević, *Demand for Workers' Control in the Railway, Mining and Engineering Industries 1910—1922*, D. Phil. Thesis, Nuffield College, Oxford, 1957.
39. J. B. Seymour, *The Whitley Councils Scheme*, London, P. S. King, 1932.
40. C. G. Renold, *Joint Consultation over Thirty Years*, London, Allen and Unwin, 1950.
41. H. Wolfe, *Labour Supply and Regulation*, Oxford, Clarendon Press, 1923.
42. C. A. Myers, *Industrial Relations in Sweden*, Cambridge, Technology Press, Massachusetts Institute of Technology, 1951.
43. National Institute of Industrial Psychology, *Joint Consultation in British Industry*, London, Staples Press, 1952.
44. International Labour Office, *Labour-Management Co-operation in United States War Production*, Studies and Reports, New Series, No. 6, Montreal, 1948.
45. G. S. Walpole, *Management and Men*, London, Jonathan Cape, 1945.
46. W. H. Scott, *Joint Consultation in a Liverpool Manufacturing Firm*, University Press of Liverpool, 1950.
47. ————, *Industrial Leadership and Joint Consultation*, University Press of Liverpool, 1952.
48. International Labour Office, *British Joint Production Machinery*, Studies and Reports, Series A, No. 43, Montreal, 1944.
49. A. Deleon, Lj. Mijatović (ed.), *Kongres radničkih savjeta Jugoslavije* (The Congress of Workers' Councils of Yugoslavia), Beograd, Rad, 1957.
50. T. E. M. McKitterick, R. D. V. Roberts, *Workers and Management*, Fabian Research Series No. 160, London, 1953.
51. *Public Enterprise. Labour's Review of the Nationalised Industries*, London, 1957.

52. H. A. Clegg, *Industrial Democracy and Nationalization*, Oxford, Blackwell, 1950.
53. J. A. Schumpeter, *Capitalism, Socialism and Democracy*, New York, Harper, 1950.
54. L. Geršković, *Društveno upravljanje u Jugoslaviji* (Social Self-Government in Yugoslavia), Beograd, Savremena administracija, 1957.
55. E. Fels, R. Richter, "Entrepreneurship as a Productive Factor", *Weltwirtschaftliches Archiv*, Band 78, Heft 2, 1957, 203—21.
56. L. M. Fraser, *Economic Thought and Language*, London, Black, 1937.
57. F. H. Knight, *Risk, Uncertainty and Profit*, Boston and New York, Houghton Mifflin, 1921.
58. J. Schumpeter, *Theorie der wirtschaftlichen Entwicklung* (The Theory of Economic Development), Leipzig, Duncker and Humbolt, 1912.
59. J. H. Stauss, "The Entrepreneur: The Firm", *Journal of Political Economy*, 1944, 112—27.
60. K. Marx, *Capital*. Vol. III, Calcutta, Saraswaty Library, 1946.
61. W. Miller, "American Historians and the Business Elite", *Journal of Economic History*, 1949, 184—208.
62. R. Bendix, *Work and Authority in Industry*, New York, J. Wiley, 1956.
63. P. M. Sweezy, "Schumpeter's Theory of Innovation", in *The Present as History*, New York, Monthly Review Press, 1955.
64. N. Kaldor, "The Equilibrium of the Firm", *Economic Journal*, 1934, 60—76.
65. E. H. Chamberlin, *Towards a More General Theory of Value*, New York, Oxford University Press, 1957.
66. J. V. S. Rama Sastri, *Nationalization and the Managerial Role*, Bombay, Popular Book Depot, 1957.
67. Savezni zavod za statistiku, *Radnički savjeti i upravni odbori privrednih preduzeća 1956* (Workers' Councils and Management Boards of Business Enterprises in 1956), Statistički bilten 77, Beograd, 1957.
68. F. Hayek, "The Use of Knowledge in Society", *American Economic Review*, 1945, 519—30.
69. L. Coch, J. R. P. French, "Overcoming Resistance to Change", *Human Relations*, 1948, 512—32.
70. **K. Lewin, R. Lippitt, R. K. White, "Patterns of Aggressive Behaviour in Experimentally Created 'Social Climates'", *Journal of Social Psychology*, 1939, 271—99.**
71. R. Lippitt, R. K. White, "An Experimental Study of Leadership and Group Life", in G. E. Swanson and others (ed.), *Readings in Social Psychology*, New York, H. Holt, 1951.
72. K. Lewin, "Group Decision and Social Change", *Ibid*.
73. B. Horvat, "Organizacija preduzeća za eksploataciju nafte i plina u nekim zemljama i kod nas" (The Organization of Oil and Gas Exploitation Enterprises in this and some other Countries), *Organizacija rada*, Nos. 11 and 12, 1952.
74. R. Bićanić, "Economic Growth under Centralized and Decentralized Planning: Yugoslavia", *Economic Development and Cultural Change*, 1957, 63—74.
75. H. A. Clegg, T. E. Chester, *The Future of Nationalization*, Oxford, Blackwell, 1953.
76. A. Bergson, *The Structure of Soviet Wages*, Cambridge, Mass., Harvard University Press, 1944.
77. A. M. Carter, *The Redistribution of Income in Postwar Britain*, New Haven, Yale University Press, 1955.
78. C. Clark, *The Conditions of Economic Progress*, London, Macmillan, 1957.
79. S. Kuznets, "Economic Growth and Income Inequality", *American Economic Review*, 1955, 1—28.
80. T. Morgan, "Income Distribution in Developed and Underdeveloped Countries", *Economic Journal*, 1956, 160—4.
81. —————, "Distribution of Income in Ceylon, Puerto Rico, the United States and the United Kingdom", *Economic Journal*, 1955, 821—34.
82. H. T. Oshima, "A Note on Income Distribution in Developed and Underdeveloped Countries", *Economic Journal*, 1956, 156—60.

83. T. B. Bottomore, *Classes in Modern Society*, London, Ampersand, 1955.
84. G. Bienstock, S. M. Schwarz, A. Yugov, *Management in Russian Industry and Agriculture*, New York, Oxford University Press, 1944.
85. S. M. Schwarz, *Labour in the Soviet Union*, London, Cresset Press, 1953.
86. H. Lydall, "The Cycle in Income, Saving and Asset Ownership", *Econometrica*, 1955, 131—50.
87. H. Miller, *Income of the American People*, New York, J. Wiley, 1955.
88. A. Patton, "Annual Report on Executive Compensation", *Harvard Business Review*, No. 5, 1957, 125—36.
89. A. P. Lerner, *The Economics of Control*, New York, Macmillan, 1944.
90. M. Friedman, *Essays in Positive Economics*, University of Chicago Press, 1953.
91. K. Marx, "Notes to the Program of the German Workers' Party", *Selected Works*, Vol. II, London, Lawrence and Wishart, 1950.
92. G. Cassel, *The Theory of Social Economy*, Vol. I, London, T. Fisher Unwin, 1923.
93. K. V. Ostrovitjanov and others, *Političeskaja ekonomija* (Political Economy), Moskva, GOSPOLITIZDAT, 1955.
94. K. Marks, "K kritike Gegeljskoj filosofii prava", *Sočinjenija*, izdanije vtoroje, tom 1, Moskva, 1955, 219—368.
95. K. Marks, F. Engeljs, *Sočinjenija*, tom 18, izdanije vtoroje, Moskva, 1961.

Book Two

THE WORKING OF THE ECONOMIC SYSTEM

IV. THE THEORY OF FIXED CAPITAL COSTS

Enquiring into the working of the economic machine, we shall focus our attention on the phenomenon of economic growth. An expanding economy is likely to display different characteristics from a stationary economy and it will be our business to examine the nature of these differences.

When dealing with the problems of economic growth or with practical planning we need a measure of capital growth. We are accustomed to use the concept of "net investment" as such a measure.

Net investment is defined as gross investment net of depreciation ("capital consumption"). The difficulties of measuring depreciation — changes in prices, the estimation of the life period of capital assets, the changes in technology — are well known. But, providing that these difficulties have been overcome, net investment is believed to be a useful analytical concept. In particular, growing, stationary and declining economies may be described respectively by positive, zero and negative net investment.

However, if we are interested in the changes in the productive capacity of an economy, which is what really matters in an analysis of economic growth, net investment may become a dangerously misleading concept, and a more appropriate measure of change in capital stock seems necessary. The productive capacity of an economy, defined as the potential output of goods and services in a specified period of time, may rise, decline or remain the same regardless even of the direction of the changes in net investment[1].

The fact just mentioned is due to shortcomings of depreciation when used as a macroeconomic concept. The annual gross social product of an economy consists of three economically distinct parts: the first part is used for consumption; the second part serves for replacement of the output capacity of the scrapped fixed assets to make good for, what I shall call, the *actual* capital consumption, i.e., it is used for keeping the gross (productive) capital stock of the economy intact; and, if anything is still left over, there is a third part to be used for new investment which increases the output capacity of the economy. Our attention will be centered on the analysis of the second part of the social product which is usually supposed to be identical with depre-

---

[1] For a helpful graphic illustration of this fact see P. Redfern, 1, 145.

ciation. However, depreciation measures imaginary and not actual capital consumption, if the latter is defined as the reduction of the quantity of capital representing the output capacity of fixed assets. Depreciation may be greater or smaller, and is only by chance equal to the actual diminution of capital assets. In a growing economy, depreciation will always be greater than capital consumption providing in this way also a part of the funds for capital accumulation.[1] It is this characteristic of the expanding economy to the analysis of which we now turn.

7. THE DEPRECIATION MULTIPLIER

(a) Concepts and Assumptions

1. Depreciation conceptually means setting aside a part of the proceeds realized by means of a capital asset — this part is corresponding to the process of imaginary depreciation of the asset — in such a way that the costs of the fixed asset are evenly spread over the output it helped to produce and that by the end of the productive life of the asset the amounts set aside are exactly equal to the replacement value of the asset, which now may be scrapped and replaced by an analogous new one. From the point of view of an isolated firm it is neither better nor worse off after this operation has been performed; there has been no net investment. But in an interconnected growing economy, the process of depreciation is immediately followed by the process of accumulation, the depreciation funds are not left lying idle but are being invested. Thus the economy as a whole is in the end better off.

2. As a measure of the change in capital stock I propose to introduce the concept of "new investment" which is defined as the addition to the gross capital stock which, in turn, measures the productive capacity of the economy. Alternatively, new investment may be derived from gross investment by subtracting replacement investment (investment necessary to replace the productive capacity of the fixed assets scrapped).

However, so defined new investment does not precisely measure the increase in the productive capacity of an economy because it takes time before new investment may be used for new production. We have to distinguish between the "quantity of capital in existence" and the productive capacity proper, namely the "quantity of capital in function" (capacity utilization being constant). As national product statistics are usually computed annually and investment maturation period is longer, there will be some lag effects. Still, this does not represent any conceptual difficulty, but is a technical matter. Moreover, this distortion is an inverse function of the rate of growth and for high rates of growth becomes negligible for all practical purposes (see Appendix I-3).

3. To measure the accumulative effect of the invested depreciation quotas in a stationary economy I propose to use a transformation coef-

---

[1] In a declining economy depreciation will be less than the capital consumption, the difference being capital decumulation.

140

ficient which I shall call "depreciation multiplier" because of the multiplying effect of depreciation on capital formation.

The depreciation multiplier is the number by which the original new investment has to be multiplied so as to obtain the final value of the addition to gross capital stock. The initial amount of new investment is at the same time equal to the net investment in the same period, and in a stationary economy it is also equal to the sum of net investments. In a stationary situation, an initial disturbance will cause a converging oscillatory process. After this process comes to an end, the multiplier will assume fixed value:

$$k = \frac{\overset{\infty}{\underset{}{\Sigma}} I}{I_1}, \quad I_1 = N_1 = \overset{\infty}{\underset{1}{\Sigma}} N, \quad r = 0, \tag{1}$$

where I stands for new investment, N for net investment and r for the rate of growth of investment in the period before the initial disturbance.

4. In order to find out the net depreciation effect all price and technological changes are assumed to be absent. In calculating depreciation the straight-line method is used, i.e., capital assets are assumed to depreciate by a constant amount each year. Thus, productive capacity and maintenance costs of fixed assets are assumed to be approximately the same throughout their service life which is perfectly foreseen and fixed. The scrap value of fixed assets is taken to be zero. Productive capacity is fully utilized. The year in annual analysis and investment maturation period in period analysis are assumed to be exact multiples of production periods and fractions are neglected (all this in order to avoid complications in depreciation and profit generation). However, in the course of the discussion all restrictive assumptions will be abandoned.

For the sake of brevity and also because this is the normal case the *growing* economy will be examined. But it is always possible to define a strict parallelism between the growing and the declining economy and one could speak simply of a "changing economy" as opposed to a stationary one. Unlike in the other parts of the present study, we shall have to make use of mathematical argument. But the mathematics to be used is rather elementary and it will help to simplify the analysis to a considerable degree. The list of symbols used is given in Appendix I.

We shall study first the case of a stationary economy where a once-over change has occurred. Next, the growing economy will be considered.

(b) Stationary Economy with a Single Positive Change in Investment

1. Suppose that the depreciation period is $n = 4$ years and a single amount of capital $I_1 = N_1 = 1000$ has been created. Suppose next that in successive periods gross investment equals depreciation, $G = D$, thus rendering net investment $N_t = 0$, $t = 2, 3, \ldots$. The result of these assumptions is shown in the table below.

141

Changes in Gross Capital Stock (n=4)

Year	Gross Investment	Depreciation	Net Investment	Replacement	New Investment		Gross Capital Stock (End of the Year)
1	1000	—	1000	—	+	1000	1000
2	250	250	—	—	+	250	1250
3	312	312	—	—	+	312	1562
4	390	390	—	—	+	390	1952
5	488	488	—	1000	—	512	1440
6	360	360	—	250	+	110	1550
7	388	388	—	312	+	76	1626
8	406	406	—	390	+	16	1642
9	411	411	—	488	—	77	1565
10	391	391	—	360	+	31	1596
11	399	399	—	388	+	11	1607
12	402	402	—	406	—	4	1603
13	401	401	—	411	—	10	1593
14	398	398	—	391	+	7	1600
15	400	400	—	399	+	1	1601
16	400	400	—	402	—	2	1599
17	400	400	—	401	—	1	1598
18	400	400	—	398	+	2	1600
19	400	400	—	400		—	1600
20	400	400	—	400		—	1600

The change in investment has caused an oscillatory converging movement in gross capital stock. The continual reinvestment of depreciation funds has had a multiplying effect on the initial amount of capital invested in fixed assets. In this case, with depreciation period $n = 4$, the multiplier is 1.6. For $n = 7$, $k = 1.75$; for $n = 10$, $k = 1.82$, etc., k increasing as the depreciation period increases.

2. The changes of capital stock in our model may be described by means of a difference equation:

$$K_t = \left(\frac{1}{n} + 1 \right) K_{t-1} - \frac{1}{n} K_{t-n-1} \tag{2}$$

As the equation is of higher order than the second ($n > 1$), there is no possibility of writing down a formal solution from which one could deduce the behaviour of the system. But a little experimentation with figures will show that, at least within the range of meaningful assumptions, the variations in n will produce similar patterns as the one described by the figures of the table.

142

Within certain limits it is also possible to find the value of K_t. In the first n years K is growing exponentially with the rate of growth $r = \frac{1}{n}$. In the year $n + 1$, original capital has to be replaced, therefore

$$K_{n+1} = K_1 \left(1 + \frac{1}{n}\right)^n - K_1 = K_1\left[\left(1 + \frac{1}{n}\right)^n - 1\right] \tag{2.1}$$

For the next n years the following formula applies

$$K_t = \left(1 + \frac{1}{n}\right)^{t-n-2} K_1 \left\{\left(1 + \frac{1}{n}\right)\left[\left(1 + \frac{1}{n}\right)^n - 1\right] - \frac{1}{n}(t-n-1)\right\},$$

$$t = n+2,\ n+3, \dots, 2n+1, \tag{2.2}$$

After the year $2n + 1$ the expression becomes very complicated. But again some experimentation with various feasible depreciation periods shows that the final value of gross capital stock may be approximated by the following formula

$$K_{\text{final}} \doteq K_{n+1} + 0.3\,(K_n - K_{n+1})$$

$$K_{\text{final}} \doteq K_1 \left\{\left[\left(1 + \frac{1}{n}\right)^n - 1\right] + 0.3\left[1 - \frac{1}{n}\left(1 + \frac{1}{n}\right)^{n-1}\right]\right\} \tag{2.3}$$

Applying the definitional formula (1) we get the value of the multiplier

$$k \doteq \left[\left(1 + \frac{1}{n}\right)^n - 1\right] + 0.3\left[1 - \frac{1}{n}\left(1 + \frac{1}{n}\right)^{n-1}\right] \tag{3}$$

As n grows the k series will converge, i.e., for longer depreciation periods the multiplier will be greater but less than proportionally greater. If the approximating expression holds for all values of n greater than 1 — for which an indirect proof will be supplied later, (15.1) and (15.2) — the limiting value of the multiplier will be *exact* to the first decimal,

$$\lim_{n \to \infty} k = 2.0 \tag{3.1}$$

3. The foregoing example was based on the assumption that capital produced this year will come into productive use next year and thus the depreciation process would start next year too. In practice, the average lag will be longer than one year, and the depreciation allowance has meaning only on the basis of "capital in function" and not simply on the basis of the total capital stock in existence. It seems that a fairly close approximation to reality may be obtained in the following way.

Suppose that the investment maturation period lasts m years and that the last portion of investment in the m years brings total invested capital in the current period into productive use at the end of the period. The productive capacity of the economy during this maturation period is determined by the amount of capital at the end of the preceding period, which also determines depreciation. Gross investment in the period will amount to m annual depreciation quotas on the basis of capital in function ($=$ capital in existence) at the end of the preceding period. We thus get the case represented by the table. If the matu-

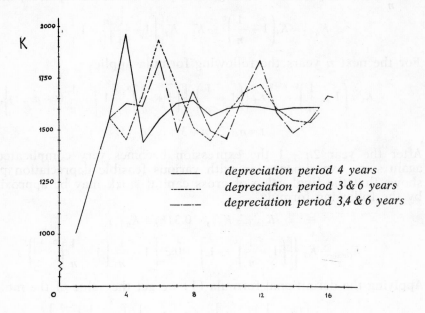

ration period is, say, 4 years, the depreciation period of the model is actually 16 years.

4. The next approximation to reality is to assume that there are two kinds of fixed assets, say equipment and structures, with different depreciation periods. Take, for instance, the depreciation period for equipment $n_e = 3$, and for structures $n_s = 6$ years, which leads to an average depreciation period of $n = 4$ years if we assume that the composition of capital is 1/2 and 1/2 for equipment and structures (see Appendix I-1). The average depreciation period is the same as in Model 1. Thus, by comparison, we shall be able to establish the influence attributable to the additional assumption of various kinds of capital goods.

Model 2 may be described algebraically in the following way

$$K_t = \left(1 + \frac{1}{n}\right) K_{t-1} - \overset{e}{G}_{t-3} - \overset{s}{G}_{t-6} \tag{4}$$

This expression is hopelessly complicated for mathematical treatment. But we can get some idea about the behaviour of such systems by graphical comparison.

An inspection of the graph shows that the introduction of the second kind of capital good has introduced a second peak in the early part of the time path. But the more violent oscillations are a matter of chance because the replacement waves reinforce each other ($n_s = 2n_e$). Therefore, a third model has been introduced for comparison. It is based

144

on the assumption that capital is composed of three kinds of fixed assets in the ratio $1/3:1/3:1/3$ and with respective depreciation periods $n_1 = 3$, $n_2 = 4$, $n_3 = 6$. Thus again there is the same average depreciation period $n = 4$ years.

The graphical comparison suggests the conclusion that, with the introduction of more capital goods with various life periods, the peaks in the initial stages become more numerous and less pronounced, but the oscillations later on are greater. The final value of the capital stock will be about the same[1].

(c) Regularly Growing Economy and the Meaning of the Depreciation Multiplier

1. New investment will not only generate depreciation funds, but will produce profits as well, and the use of these profits to finance successive new investment will help to accelerate the growth of capital.

If into Model 1 we introduce the assumption that there is a fixed rate of profit (in relation to the gross capital stock at the end of the preceding period) and that this profit is used to finance investment, we shall have a continuously growing economy. The steady influx of net investment will tend to smooth out the oscillations. The system will tend to achieve a steady rate of growth and a steady ratio of replacement to depreciation. But instead of a sudden big change we shall assume continuous growth. This is more realistic and also simplifies considerably the mathematics of the argument.

2. Consider an economy with gross investment expanding at a constant rate r. By the time t initial unit investment will increase to

$$G_t = (1+r)^{t-1} \tag{5}$$

Installed fixed assets are scrapped after every n years. Consequently, gross capital stock at time t will be equal to the sum of gross investments accumulated since the time when the assets now scrapped were installed, i.e., since the time $t-n$

$$K_t = \sum_{t-n+1}^{t} G = (1+r)^{t-n} \frac{(1+r)^n - 1}{r} \tag{6}$$

We are next interested in finding out how much of depreciation has been used to finance the process. Bearing in mind that replacement is equal to gross investment made n years earlier

$$R_t = G_{t-n} = (1+r)^{t-1-n} \tag{7}$$

and assuming that depreciation is generated by fixed assets in existence in the previous year

$$D_t = \frac{1}{n} K_{t-1} \tag{8}$$

---

[1] This can be easily proved by treating stationary economy as growing economy with rate of growth $r = 0$ (see *infra*) and by showing that the average n as computed above is equivalent to n in a system with only one kind of assets (see Appendix I-2).

we find that the share of replacement in depreciation is

$$\alpha = \frac{R_t}{D_t} = \frac{nr}{(1+r)^n - 1}, \qquad t = n+1, \; n+2, \ldots, \qquad (9)$$

and consequently the accumulative part of depreciation, i.e., the part which can be used for the expansion of productive capacity, is equal to $1-\alpha$. The formula for α (as well as for other ratios to be derived) applies only after the first replacement, assuming equal life span of all assets, or after the first replacement of the asset with longest life span, in a more general case[1].

3. According to the original assumption gross investment is growing at the fixed rate r. Gross capital stock is growing at the same rate, as seen in the expression (6). Hence, depreciation is increasing at the same rate. Being equal to gross investment n years earlier, replacement is growing at the same rate. Finally, net investment is growing at the same rate because it represents the difference between gross investment and depreciation. In this way, all the ratios between various elements will have definite values.

Some useful ratios worth computing are:
the ratio of gross investment to gross capital stock at the end of the preceding year

$$\beta = \frac{G_t}{K_{t-1}} = \frac{r(1+r)^n}{(1+r)^n - 1}, \qquad (10)$$

the ratio of net investment to gross capital stock at the end of the preceding year

$$\gamma = \frac{N_t}{K_{t-1}} = \beta - \frac{1}{n} = \frac{r(1+r)^n}{(1+r)^n - 1} - \frac{1}{n} \qquad (11)$$

the ratio between depreciation and gross investment

$$\delta = \frac{D_t}{G_t} = \frac{1}{n\beta} = \frac{(1+r)^n - 1}{nr(1+t)^n} \qquad (12)$$

and the ratio between replacement and gross capital stock at the end of the preceding year

$$\frac{1}{v} = \frac{R_t}{K_{t-1}} = \frac{\alpha}{n} = \frac{r}{(1+r)^n - 1} \qquad (13)$$

4. If we had assumed that net investment, and not gross investment, was increasing at a constant rate since the beginning, the same results could hold only as a tendency, only at the limit. In this case the rates of growth of various elements tend to approach the rate of growth of net investment from above in the following order: gross investment, gross capital stock, depreciation.

Being in essence of the same nature as the first assumption, but much more difficult to manipulate mathematically, the assumption of steady growth of net investment will not interest us any more.

---

[1] For the derivation of the average n in an economy with more than one kind of fixed assets see Appendix I-2.

5. The formulae derived above may now be used to elucidate the meaning of the depreciation multiplier. The multiplier measures multiplying effects of an additional investment in a stationary economy. As the gross and net values of initial investment are equal, and all subsequent investments are conceptually made out of depreciation alone — which means that no net investment takes place any more — the multiplier measures the ratio between the gross and net *addition* to capital stock. As initial disturbing investment may conceptually be undertaken at any level of the stationary output, in an equilibrium situation the multiplier must measure the relation between gross and net capital *stock*. Armed with this knowledge we can use our growth equations to derive a precise formula for the computation of the multiplier.

Define k as the ratio between new and net investment both growing at the rate r. Then new investment must be equal to

$$I_t = rK_{t-1} \tag{14}$$

while from (11) we can find net investment to be equal to

$$N_t = \gamma K_{t-1} \tag{11}$$

Consequently

$$k = \frac{I_t}{N_t} = \frac{r}{\gamma} = nr \cdot \frac{(1+r)^n - 1}{(1+r)^n (nr-1) + 1} \tag{15}$$

As the sum of new investment is equal to gross capital stock and the sum of net investment to net capital stock, k also measures the relation between gross and net capital stock. In our stationary model the oscillatory process came to an end when the previous relation between gross and net capital was reached again. With the depreciation period $n = 4$, this relation was 1.6:1.

Now we are equipped to supply the proofs for expressions (3) and (3.1). Suppose that the rate of growth is diminishing towards zero. At the limit, when $r = 0$, a stationary situation will arise and our k will be transformed into the multiplier of Model 1. Therefore the expression

$$\lim_{r \to 0} k = \frac{2n^2}{n+n^2} \tag{15.1}$$

is a simple formula for the multiplier which we can use in place of the earlier clumsy difference equation (2).

If we now ask what is the maximum value of the multiplier, the answer is

$$\lim_{\substack{r \to 0 \\ n \to \infty}} k = 2 \tag{15.2}$$

which is the indirect proof for our coefficient 0.3 in formula (3).

6. We may now sum up our knowledge about the depreciation multiplier. Every single act of investment has multiplying effects so that output capacity is eventually stabilized at a higher level. This is due to the fact that the period of production is shorter than the service

life of fixed assets, which permits output to be used before the need for replacement of the asset arises. As the costs of the asset must be spread evenly over the produce, they will enter into the price as "depreciation". Until the time for replacement comes, "depreciation" can be invested elsewhere generating further depreciation, and so forth. Net value of an asset — or of investment — is defined as gross value net of depreciation. When the total multiplying effect of depreciation is exhausted, gross value (output capacity) cannot be increased any more and a certain balance is established between gross value and net value of capital. This balance depends on the service life of assets, maturation period of investment and the rate of growth, and remains constant so long as the three constituent elements do not change. In a stationary economy the ratio between gross and net value of assets turns out to be the depreciation multiplier itself.

The depreciation multiplier — as the concept is used here — has meaning only in a stationary situation. Technically k may be used to measure the relation between gross and net capital stock in a growing economy, but in this case k loses its explanatory value. To find out the multiplying effect of investment on output we must leave the process to work itself out. This condition is not met in a growing economy, and so we need a different approach. Instead of analyzing the final effect of a *given amount of investment* on the *increase in output*, we shall have to reverse the procedure and analyze *diminishing investment* sustaining a *given output*, i.e., we shall be considering capital costs per unit of output. The method was introduced in the early paragraphs of this section and will be fully developed in the next chapter.

(d) The Conventional Capital Theory

So far we have been discussing the concepts of gross and net capital and investment as they are used in national income accounting. These concepts differ from those used in the conventional capital theory. It seems necessary to indicate the nature of these differences.

1. Capital is defined as the discounted value of expected future returns. The rate of interest is used as the rate of discount. It will be helpful to distinguish two forms of capital. Capital invested in productive assets, which I shall call *equipment*, generates net returns known as profit. Capital in money form, which I shall call *money*, generates interest proper. The productive substance common to both equipment and money I shall call *capital*. Consider first the changes in the value of equipment.

Annual returns from equipment, which, following the tradition, we shall call *quasi rents*, consist of depreciation and profit. The discounted value of all quasi rents represents the value of equipment. Equipment gradually loses its value and the difference between the capital value at the beginning and at the end of an accounting year represents the depreciation of equipment in that year. Depreciation is then equal to the difference between the two respective capitalized streams of quasi rents. The two streams have in common all members but the last, the quasi rent, which would have been realized in the year after the planned expiration of the service life of equipment if there had been no production this year. When discounted for all intervening years, this last quasi rent measures the diminution in the capital value. If interest rate is i, service life of equipment is n and annual quasi rents are equal to 1, the value of equipment at the beginning of subsequent years and the respective depreciation quotas at the end of the same years (implying that quasi rents are realized at the end of the year) are as follows:

Year	Value of Equipment	Annual Depreciation
1	$(1+i)^{-1}+\ldots+(1+i)^{-n}$	$(1+i)^{-n}$
2	$(1+i)^{-1}+\ldots+(1+i)^{-(n-1)}$	$(1+i)^{-(n-1)}$
. . .	. . . .	. . . .
n	$(1+i)^{-1}$	$(1+i)^{-1}$

It is evident that the sum of all depreciation quotas is exactly equal to the original value of equipment which thus can be replaced at the end of the nth year and the process can begin afresh. At this point it will be useful to find out what the rate of profit is. Profit Π is equal to the difference between annual quasi rent and annual depreciation of equipment. Define the rate of profit as the ratio of Π to the capital value of equipment C. Let the age of equipment be j years, so that its unexpired life is $n-j$ years. Then the rate of profit is given by

$$\frac{\Pi}{C} = \frac{1-(1+i)^{-(n-j)}}{\sum_{a=1}^{a=n-j}(1+i)^{-a}} = i, \qquad j=1, 2, \ldots, n-1 \qquad (16)$$

which means that it is constant and equal to the rate of interest.

However, depreciation quotas are not left idle. They earn interest which has to be added to profit and so the rate of profit appears to increase over time. Thus we start with a certain piece of equipment and end with profits, with the replacement fund and with additional interest accrued to this fund. This inconvenient outcome can be escaped if we reinterpret the whole approach. We do not start with equipment but with *capital* in the form of equipment. As the time passes capital gradually flows from equipment into money but total capital sum remains constant, as it is easily seen from the table above. The overall rate of profit also remains constant and is equal to i. This because $\dfrac{\Pi}{C} = i$, and accumulated depreciation quotas earn interest by definition. It follows that our investment in equipment must actually be treated as a money loan. It is either a permanent loan, which means that capital value and interest (profit on equipment plus interest on depreciation fund) to be paid annually remain constant. Or it is the loan which has to be repaid within the period of n years, quasi rents representing annuities.

2. The generalization of capital into a productive substance, not connected with a concrete piece of equipment, may run us into troubles. Consider an economy in which all personal income is consumed and

all profits are invested, and where profits increase at a constant rate. Then capital must increase at the same rate. Consequently, the rate of profit is equal to the rate of growth of capital and is so equal to the national rate of interest. Depreciation is zero because the last quasi rent must be discounted for an infinitely long time. Thus annual quasi rents are equal to profit and increase at the same rate. Now, if quasi rents expand at the same rate at which they are discounted, their sum must be infinite. And an inifinite value of capital is a meaningless result[1].

Attempting another approach, we run into a different kind of difficulties. It is usually assumed that in an atomistic economy the interest rate on the supply side is positively correlated with the amount of saving. On the demand side the interest rate, equal to the marginal productivity of investment, is inverse function of the amount of investment. Thus, assuming perfect foresight, profit will always be greater than interest and so capital will have two values, one lower in the form of money, and one higher in the form of equipment. And two values for the same thing is not a particularly pleasant result. It renders the task of determining fixed capital cost insolvable *in principle*. The sum of all depreciation quotas must exactly cover the original cost of equipment, as, indeed, it does in our table in the preceding paragraph. But if profit is greater than interest and depreciation is equal to the diminution of the capital value, then depreciation is greater than depreciation (= original cost of equipment).[2]

It is, however, not necessary that the rate of profit and the rate of interest are single-valued. In fact, in the real world, we are confronted with a multiplicity of rates, which makes our problem very soon intractable. Perfect foresight, also, is absent in the real world. The consequential fluctuations in expectations and interest rates at once convert our carefully built order of values into a mess in which every

---

[1] It is possible, however, to escape this result if we are prepared to engage in the following mental acrobatic: assume that the rate of interest is given by the rate of growth of capital and *at the same time* assume that growth has been stopped, i.e., that existing *equipment* represents capital we have to measure. As existing equipment has a finite life, the stream of quasi rents will be finite and so will their discounted values. For another possible escape see the footnote to the next paragraph.

[2] Cf. also G. Preinreich (2, pp. 233 ff.). For our purpose Preinreich's argument may be summed up as follows. The rate of interest, the quasi rent of the machine (given the selling price of the product and given operating costs) and its scrap value are known. The time of replacement is unknown. It is determined by the condition that the last quasi rent must be equal to interest on the scrap value. If this condition is fulfilled and the present value of all quasi rents is equal to the cost of the machine, everything is in order. But the market price of the machine is determined by the least efficient pair of all producers and consumers of such machines, and so generally capital value is apt to be greater than cost and profit greater than interest. This fact changes replacement timing (and with it the depreciation calculation) because if the rate of profit is greater than the rate of interest, the machine must be replaced as soon as it ceases to earn the rate of profit on its scrap value. But we do not know what the rate of profit is. The quasi rent profit given depends on depreciation which in turn depends on the rate of interest and the economic life of the machine which in turn depends on the rate of profit. There is no way out of this circle. Consequently, it is in principle impossible to determine depreciation, i.e., the costs of fixed capital. See also F. and V. Lutz (3, Ch. XIX).

150

capital value begins to play to its own tune and in which we are pretty hopelessly lost. In the end, all that is left of the esoteric concept of capital consists in the circular reasoning that the value of capital depends on the rate of interest which is nothing else but the rate of growth of this same capital.

3. Conceptual and empirical difficulties — of which the above are but a few illustrations — inherent in the conventional concept of capital, make capital a notoriously unusable concept in macroeconomic analysis. It appears that national income statisticians have had good reasons not to use this concept[1]. They have been interested — as we are also — in the "physical" characteristics of the economic process. In the last analysis, capital theory not only precludes measurement, but also fails to explain what *is* actually happening; it mystifies rather than explains, for we must always translate the notions of capital into those of the actual production process. In a planned economy, we are interested in the actual output capacity, not in the discounted value; in the rate of growth of actual physical output, not in the market interest rate; in the maximization of consumption, not of capital value. For these reasons, capital theory of planned economy will differ from that describing the working of the (money) capital market[2].

4. Before completing the present chapter it may prove helpful if we consider yet another variant of the capitalization formula, the variant which is frequently recommended — although probably never used[3] — as an appropriate method for calculating depreciation charges (so-called sinking fund method). We postulate that depreciation quotas, accumulated at the ruling rate of interest, be equal to the original cost of equipment (we shall again use the distinction made in paragraph 1

---

[1] Although, some economists are still playing with the idea of evaluating national capital in terms of capital theory. Compare, for instance, the approach of I. Svennilson. The symbols used mean: W = national wealth, P = national product, s = share of saving, i = interest rate. Svennilson starts from the proposition of E. Lindahl

$$W_t \cdot i = P_{t+1}(1-s) + W_{t+1} - W_t$$

which says that the expected national income in the next period is equal to the rate of interest on present national wealth. If national product is growing at the rate r, national wealth will be growing at the same rate. The following formula emerges:

$$W_t = P_{t+1} \frac{1-s}{i-r}$$

In the formula P, s and r are somehow definable and measurable quantities. But what about i? Svennilson — like others — leaves us in the dark about the exact method of calculating the relevant i (4, 323). But even if we got hold of the magic formula, what should we do if — the possibility considered also by Svennilson — it happened to produce i equal or smaller than r?

[2] For an intellectual exercise of how one conceptual scheme can be translated into another see Appendix I-4. There the value of net capital stock (as defined by national income statisticians) in a growing economy is shown to be equal to the value of capital in a stationary economy if the rate of interest in the latter is equal to the rate of growth in the former.

[3] Cf. S. Fabricant reporting that out of 460 large American industrial corporations studied not a single one makes any provision for the interest factor in the time distribution of costs of fixed assets (5, 69).

between equipment and money). Compared with national income accounting method this procedure reduces annual depreciation quotas and increases profits by the same amounts. Depreciation quotas accumulated in the "sinking fund" are exactly equal to the value of equipment to be replaced, but annual depreciation quotas do not correspond to the changes in capital value of equipment and so "depreciation charge" against operating revenue and "the amount written off" of the value of the equipment will differ (cf. 3, 228). To cure this inconvenience we must again reinterpret the original production approach. As usually, all parameters of the system will be assumed to remain constant.

With the productive capacity unimpaired, the amount of profit generated remains constant, because depreciation quotas are also constant. But capital value of equipment declines over time and so the rate of profit increases towards infinity. This rise in profitability is clearly fictitious because it corresponds to no change in economic efficiency. Therefore, we must relate profit to the original or gross value of equipment, because profitability of the first year must remain constant. Now, in the first year, profit is equal to interest because the whole amount of capital is embodied in equipment. Thus the rate of profit is equal to the rate of interest. It follows that capital invested in equipment may be treated as a permanent loan given at an interest rate equal to the rate of profit calculated on the basis of the original or gross value of equipment. Or, conversely, it may be treated as a capital sum to be repaid in n annuities which are equal to annual revenues from equipment (i.e. to quasi rents). In the end we reach exactly the same result as before (paragraph 1).

5. The preceding paragraph has cleared the ground for the last step in the present discussion. We have to establish the relation between the conventional capital theory and the theory of fixed capital costs expounded in this study. It will be convenient to do this by a direct translation of one conceptual scheme into the other[1].

Suppose that we are dealing with the economy as a whole and wish to determine our depreciation quotas so that, if they are accumulated at some specified rate of interest, they provide a fund for replacement and nothing more. Just how is the rate of interest to be determined and how an integrated economy can accumulate depreciation contributions in a sinking fund — is a matter which, we shall pretend, does not bother us. Then we can proceed as follows. Equipment K has to be replaced at the end of the period n; depreciation contributions D's are accumulated at the interest rate i. The sum of depreciation contributions set aside, plus the accrued interest must be equal to the original cost of equipment

$$D(1+i)^{n-1} + D(1+i)^{n-2} + \cdots + D = K$$

$$K = D \frac{(1+i)^n - 1}{i} \tag{17}$$

---

[1] Cf. also E. D. Domar, 6, 166 and 182.

We next find the ratio between annual depreciation contributions and the gross or original value of capital sunk in equipment

$$\frac{D}{K} = \frac{i}{(1+i)^n - 1} \tag{17.1}$$

and then compare the result with (13). The comparison reveals that if the rate of interest is interpreted as rate of growth of gross investment — or, for that matter of gross capital stock — annual depreciation quotas to be accumulated in the sinking fund appear to be replacement expenditures.

8. GENERALIZATION OF THE THEORY

(a) Relativity Properties of Actual (Dynamic) Fixed Capital Costs

1. The key concept in the analysis of economic growth has been that of net investment. Net investment measures the addition to the existing capital with respect to the quantity of capital and its age structure at the same time. The same applies to the net capital stock. A greater quantity of older capital and a smaller quantity of younger capital may be expressed by the same amount of net capital; age is transformed into quantity and vice versa as if they were homogeneous and additive. The consequences are doubly unfortunate: we can neither infer anything directly about the age structure, for its changes are mixed up with quantity changes, nor, for the same reason, do we know anything about the real size of the productive capital. Measuring both at the same time we no longer have the measure for either of them.

It seems, therefore, that the "one dimensional" concept of new investment will do the job more successfully when used in model building or in practical planning. Considering capital as a collection of productive resources, what matters is the change in its quantity. If so, capital consumption is equal to replacement and not to depreciation. Replacement expenditures are the actual capital costs for the community. If then replacement, analogously to depreciation, is measured by its relation to gross capital stock, a series of interesting conclusions follow.

Recalling expression (13) and taking its three limiting values we get

$$\lim_{r \to \infty} \frac{1}{v} = \lim_{r \to \infty} \frac{r}{(1+r)^n - 1} = 0 \tag{13.1}$$

$$\lim_{n \to \infty} \frac{1}{v} = 0 \tag{13.2}$$

$$\lim_{r \to 0} \frac{1}{v} = \frac{1}{n} \tag{13.3}$$

The capital costs of an economy, expressed as a ratio of replacement to existing capital, are falling with a rising rate of growth ($r \to \infty$), and with an increasing length of life of fixed assets ($n \to \infty$), it will also be increas-

153

ing when the rate of growth is slowing down and the life period of fixed assets becoming shorter. This brings a relativity element into the determination of capital cost and with it greater generality.

2. The limit of the last case (13.3) is revealing. When the rate of growth is reduced to zero the economy becomes stationary and in the stationary economy replacement costs are equal to depreciation costs. It follows that *the concept of "depreciation" and the resulting concepts of "net investment" and "net national product" describe in fact a very special case. A generalized theory of growth will build on the concepts of "replacement" and use the resulting concepts of "new investment" and "new national product".*

Our final results may be interpreted also in the following way. If $\dfrac{1}{n}$ measures static and $\dfrac{1}{v}$ measures dynamic fixed capital costs, their mutual relation will be expressed, recalling (13), as $\dfrac{1}{n} : \dfrac{1}{v} = \dfrac{v}{n} = \dfrac{1}{\alpha}$.

In other words, static costs are related to dynamic costs as depreciation to replacement. In the process of growth n "static" depreciation years tend to be lengthened into v "dynamic" years, and the factor of lengthening is $\dfrac{1}{\alpha}$. As α $\left(\alpha = \dfrac{nr}{(1+r)^n - 1}\right)$ varies inversely with the variation of the rate of growth, the time will lengthen or contract depending on whether the change in the speed of the system is positive or negative. When there is no growth, α assumes unitary value, $\alpha = 1$, and the time is contracted to its static limit, $n = v$ (13.3). With the speed of the system tending to increase infinitely, time tends to assume infinite value and, consequently, costs become zero. Finally, unlike in physics, time may be contracted even below its static limit, because, in economics, there is also disinvestment. In this case, dynamic costs will surpass static costs (i.e. replacement needs become greater and greater in relation to existing capital assets) and, at the limit, dynamic costs become equal to the existing capital itself

$$\lim_{r \to -1} \frac{1}{v} = 1 \tag{13.4}$$

It is obvious that from this standpoint the "aging process" has no definite meaning. *Time units, being variable themselves, cannot be used* as units of measurement.

The actual capital costs are thus determined not only by the quantity of originally invested fixed capital but also by its rate of growth and its life span. The third condition may require an explanation, since depreciation costs vary also with the length of the life of the assets. The point is that depreciation variations remain within the field of statics. The difference is clearly visible when (13.3) is compared with (13) and n is allowed to rise; replacement costs tend much quicker towards zero because the expression in the denominator of (13) is exponential and

154

implies multiplication while there is only an adding process in the denominator of depreciation costs (13.3).

3. The generalizing procedure may be completed by letting n be equal to 1. Then replacement cost takes the value

$$\frac{1}{v} = 1, \quad n = 1 \tag{13.5}$$

If the life length of fixed capital is exactly 1, namely if it is equal to the accounting period, then the replacement costs are equal to total capital costs. Now, to achieve final generalization, we have to identify the accounting period with the production period. Fixed capital is thus automatically transformed into circulating capital, into raw material which is fully used in the process of production at once. Raw material costs are a special case of fixed capital costs, a case where the depreciation period is equal to the production period.

(b) Maintenance Cost

1. The theory expounded above is intended to approximate to reality closer than the traditional theory underlying national income accounting. It has been explained so far by means of the simplest possible model which could serve this purpose. Now, assumption may be relaxed and complications may be introduced similarly as, *mutatis mutandis*, in the traditional approach. Thus, for instance, if scrap value of assets is taken into account, or if the sequence of depreciation quotas is represented by a non-linear function, the form of our formulae will change. They will also change if the timing of the replacement has not been foreseen correctly. But all this will not affect the argument. Further, the statistical difficulties in measuring gross investment and replacement or the life span of the assets, are common to both approaches. The discussion of all these and similar problems lies outside the scope of this study. But one of them seems to deserve special attention and hence will be examined briefly before we go further. It is the problem of maintenance costs.

Three different cases may be distinguished: either maintenance costs and output capacity remain unchanged over time; or one of them changes while the other remains constant; or both change. We shall examine these cases in turn. There is actually an additional complication: prime costs may not remain neutral, but may vary with capacity and maintenance costs in any direction. However, we shall neglect this complication for the time being.

2. If maintenance costs are approximately the same throughout the service life of the fixed asset, the capacity of which does not change, they do not represent any difficulty. In this case, maintenance costs may be treated as part of operating costs and the case fits perfectly into the foregoing analysis. Taking into account that our analysis is essentially macroeconomic, such an assumption seems very realistic. The fixed assets of an economy as a whole, of an industry and even of an average firm, are a combination of various kinds of assets installed at various times,

the composite result of which will probably be that maintenance costs will behave in the assumed way. And even if we accept the frequent assumption that the productive capacity of a particular asset tends to decline with the age, we may also assume that the aggregate productivity of the firm tends to increase with age because of the greater experience of workers and management and of many cheap improvements (paid out of maintenance funds) occurring continuously, and tending to preserve the original level of maintenance costs and of output capacity. The usual practice of firms and of national product accounting agencies to compute a straight-line depreciation, are also an indication in the same direction. Thus, until actual measurements are carried out, the safest assumption to be made is the assumption of constant capacity and maintenance costs, which actually amounts to a more general assumption that the absolute net productivity (depreciation net of maintenance, plus profit gross of interest) remains unchanged. (This means that the effects of capacity changes are exactly offset by changes in maintenance costs alone or combined with the changes of other costs if the latter are not assumed to be neutral.) This then may be considered as our introductory assumption.

3. If we assume that the aggregate value of one of our two elements is changing, the complications which arise are more of mathematical than of conceptual nature.

Assume, first, that capacity remains constant while maintenance costs change. The changes in maintenance costs may be accounted for in two ways: either by adjusting aggregate profits or by adjusting depreciation. Both solutions are possible and are found in practice. In the latter case the expected maintenance costs are treated as if they were added to the original value of assets and as if so obtained *total* value was depreciated. The depreciation allowances are equal, but the free part of depreciation (the part available for accumulation) varies with the variations of maintenance costs. In this system maintenance costs are actually conceived as continuation of original investment and are therefore added to the gross national product, while in the first system gross product does not contain maintenance costs but merely reflects changes in maintenance costs.

The second case, with maintenance costs constant while capacity changes, may be reduced to the case above, where replacement changes play the role of maintenance costs changes. This approach may be analytically convenient, because it leads to constant capacity and constant absolute amount of profits and thus leaves us with depreciation as the only variable source of real accumulation. But care must be taken in computing and interpreting replacement costs. Namely, replacement and maintenance costs enter differently into the value structure of the services of fixed assets. Maintenance costs are *added* to pure depreciation to provide the combined funds for the restoration of the original output capacity, while replacement costs are financed out of this fund and as such must be *deducted* from it. Hence it would be a mistake to say that if the decline in capacity happens to be equal to depreciation the difference between depreciation and replacement will disappear. This cannot happen because depreciation must be proportional to output capacity (see Appendix I — 5). It must be emphasized that the effects we are discussing are real effects and so independent from accounting procedures. We may, of course, vary depreciation charges as we like, but we cannot escape the consequence of profit variations automatically compensating every change we care to make.

If we prefer to keep maintenance and replacement costs apart, the appropriate treatment will be to allow the depreciation changes to follow capacity changes, fulfilling in this way the requirement that costs of fixed assets per unit of output should remain constant. But, then, maintenance costs are also costs of fixed assets, and if they have to be spread evenly this will mean that depreciation will have to vary with capacity *and* with maintenance costs; in other words, pure depreciation will have to follow changes in relative productivity of fixed assets.

4. The third possibility is that both, maintenance costs and capacity, change. If they change in the same direction, they may compensate each other's effects or the effect of change of either of them may prevail on balance. If they change in the opposite direction, the effects of the change will reinforce each other. What the final effects on the movement of the system — as compared with our standard model — are likely to be, is quite clear from the discussion in the preceding paragraph.

The assumption of neutrality of prime costs (prime costs per unit of output remaining equal, see paragraph 1) may now also be relaxed. We find that output capacity can be interpreted in two ways: as "physical" output capacity (in terms of gross product) and as "value" output capacity (in terms of suitably defined net product). If prime costs per unit of output remain equal, both concepts coincide and depreciation per unit of time is the same regardless of the basis on which it is calculated. If prime costs per unit of physical output vary with time or with variations in physical output capacity, current gross and net output capacity will differ. In a general case we may take that the costs of fixed asset vary with its value productive capacity. The latter is measured by the value of total product reduced for all non-capital costs, i.e., by quasi rents of the asset. Depreciation per unit of net output remains constant, while per unit of gross output it varies.

(c) Generalization

1. We may now sum up our analysis of the maintenance costs and also relax other restrictive assumptions so as to obtain a perfectly general result.

As indicated in the beginning, the mathematical skeleton of this chapter is based on the assumption of constant output capacity and constant maintenance costs. Common-sense considerations seem to suggest that this is the safest assumption until the empirical measurements of the aggregates involved establish a significant bias in any direction.

If the empirical measurements establish that the aggregate productivity of assets does not remain constant but changes significantly, this will represent no conceptual difficulty, and only the mathematical treatment of the problem will become more complicated. In particular, the establishment of such an empirical fact would in no way affect the fundamental proposition about the relativity nature of fixed capital costs. The time will continue to lengthen or contract and the "same" cost quantity will continue to diminish or increase depending on whether the change in the speed of the system is positive or negative. Only the value of the relativity coefficient α will change. The direction of this change can be established on the basis of very simple considerations.

2. Suppose that the accounting period is equal to the depreciation period of a particular fixed asset, say twelve months. Then the annual depreciation charge and the total cost of the asset become identical and there is no need for a separate depreciation calculation. Suppose, next, that more than one unit of the product will be produced, that prime costs per unit of output remain constant, and that the production period is one month so that the total output of the fixed asset will consist of twelve equal batches of products. If the accounting period is adjusted accordingly, each batch will bear depreciation charge equal to 1/12 of the value of the asset. If depreciation were distributed in any other way, some batches would appear artificially more profitable or less profitable than other. If now we assume a stationary economy, the same conclusion holds *a fortiori*. If depreciation of fixed assets were distributed in time differently from the output of these assets, profits and losses would arise, which is clearly an impossibility in a stationary economy. Thus consistency requires that the cost of the fixed asset be spread evenly over the produce it helped to produce, i.e., that depreciation follow changes in the output capacity (assuming full utilization). Armed with this common-sense conclusion let us now tackle our restrictive assumptions.

3. Take first the assumption of straight-line depreciation which implies that the output capacity of a particular fixed asset is kept constant throughout its service life. Consider the following diagram.

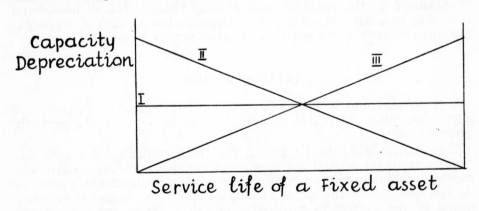

Three possible cases are shown: I output capacity does not change (our model), II output capacity diminishes and III output capacity increases over time. Depreciation, being the cost of the fixed asset, follows its output capacity. Now, because of unidirectional quality of the time flow the first half of the diagram has a greater "weight" than the second. In other words, because of the operation of the depreciation multiplier the amount of fixed investment financed from depreciation funds created in the first half of the life of the fixed asset will have greater total accumulative effect than the same amount in the second half of its life. Thus we reach the conclusion — perhaps surprising at first sight but, nevertheless, perfectly correct — that if in a growing economy the aggregate productivity of assets is declining over time, capital costs per unit of output fall, and vice versa — as compared with the standard case of constant output capacity. Or, expressed in terms of the relativity coefficient α — which, it will be remembered, transforms the capital costs of a stationary economy into capital costs of a growing economy — if in a growing economy the aggregate productivity of assets is declining, α will diminish and the cost quantity will decrease relatively to the standard model; if it is rising, the opposite process will take place; but in either case α will be less than unity and therefore real cost will be lower than in a stationary economy.

For the same reason, the assumption of constant maintenance cost may be abandoned. Maintenance cost, being also the cost of the fixed asset, has simply to be added to depreciation and the respective lines in the diagram have to be adequately redrawn. As we have seen various combinations are possible, but essentially no new problem arises.

Finally, obsolescence, defined as a decline of the output capacity of the fixed asset in value terms, represents no difficulty any more. Once again the lines in the diagram will have to be redrawn. Obsolescence, *ceteris paribus* (i.e. in so far as it is independent of the rate of growth), intensifies the effect of the depreciation multiplier.

4. Our exposition has been based on an analysis of depreciation charges. This approach has been found useful because it provides the necessary link with the traditional national income approach. However, the controversial concept of depreciation is not at all necessary. We need only define capital cost as replacement cost and then try to establish the respective production function. The property of fixed assets to have service life longer than the period of production of a particular commodity they help to create, produces the relativity effect analyzed above, i.e., other things being equal, replacement cost per unit of output diminishes as the rate of expansion of output increases.

With this it might be supposed our task is over. For expository and calculation purposes the stationary and growth models developed in the preceding sections were based on a number of restrictive assumptions. But conceptually they represent a perfectly general case.

(d) Conclusions

1. Our analysis suggests that certain key concepts in macroeconomic analysis need be redefined. Thus the concept of net investment seems to be of comparatively little analytical value (though it may, for instance, be very useful for administrative purposes). The concept is, in fact, misleading, because it does not express what it is supposed to. It is

not consistent with the assumptions of the conventional capital theory — whatever its merits — neither, it does not measure the actual capital input in a changing economy either. It consistently reflects the economic reality only in a very special case of stationary economy. The related concept of net capital stock has similir shortcomings. In so far as net capital stock measures both output capacity and the age of assets at the same time it is often unusable because it tells us nothing about any of these characteristics separately. We therefore need the concept of gross capital stock to measure output capacity and the survey of the age structure of the assets when we are interested in the kind and timing of replacement.

It follows that, for a number of purposes, we need "one-dimensional" concepts of *new investment* and gross capital. New investment is derived from gross investment by subtracting replacement expenditures. New investment measures the addition to the quantity of capital in existence and, with a lag for the maturation period, the addition to the productive capacity of the economy in the respective period. The summation of all new investments gives gross capital stock in existence (including inventories which can be treated in the conventional way).

The concept of new investment is particularly useful in practical planning and in the analysis of economic growth. The output being, *ceteris paribus*, related to the productive capacity of fixed assets — and not to the capital value — such tools of analysis as capital-output coefficients have definite meaning only if computed on the basis of new investment. In a rapidly growing economy, the lag effects, because of the maturation period, are negligible, so that capital coefficient, expressed as the ratio of new investment m years earlier and the increment in output in the current year, approximates to the technological capital coefficient very closely (see Appendix I-3).

For analogous reasons it will be useful to introduce the concept of *new social product*, indicating by it the value of gross social product net of replacement expenditures. New social product represents that part of gross product which can be consumed without affecting the productive capacity of the economy in the period under consideration. In the chapters that follow the term gross social product will be shortened into *social* product, and new social product will be referred to as *social income*.

2. Every single act of investment has a multiplying effect which has been described by the concept of the *depreciation multiplier*. The multiplier turned out to measure the relation between gross and net capital stock. In a stationary economy the multiplier eventually produces a higher level stationary output. In a growing economy the multiplying effect increases with the rate of growth. This is reflected in the fact that depreciation funds surpass replacement expenditures.

As replacement expenditures are made to keep output capacity of the economy unimpaired, i.e., to sustain a certain output, they must be considered as *actual* capital costs of that output. We have found that the dynamic or macroeconomic concept of fixed capital cost implies the relativization of the cost quantity. Capital cost (price and technology changes absent) per unit of output depends not only upon the amount of original capital outlay, but also on the life span of capital assets and on the rate of growth of capital. This theory proved to be more general, comprising the static theory as a special case. Assuming that the service life of assets remains the same, actual (dynamic) costs become identical with depreciation (static) capital costs when the economy ceases to grow and becomes stationary. Compared with the conventional capital theory, the theory developed has the merit of describing economic quantities as they are observed. Consequently, these quantities can be measured, which is of a decisive importance.

3. The greater the speed of economic expansion, the smaller the burden of replacement expenditures. This speed effect might throw some light on the mechanics of industrial revolutions. An industrial revolution is a process of transformation of a stationary economy into a growing economy by means of rapid accumulation of capital. The actual cost of the main scarce factor — capital — per unit of output decreases as the rate of growth of fixed capital increases. The effects are extremely impressive[1]. One could, perhaps, generalize by saying that the real cost of economic development is an inverse function of the speed of development. But this only within certain limits. What are these limits, remains to be explored in the chapters which follow.

Appendices

I. MATHEMATICAL SUPPLEMENT

The meaning of symbols used in the text and in Appendix is as follows:

K = gross stock of capital ($K = \Sigma I$)
G = gross investment
N = net investment ($N = G - D$)
I = new investment ($I = G - R$)
D = depreciation
R = replacement
C = capital value
C = total prime costs
V = present value
Π = profit
a = growth factor ($a = 1 + r$)
c = prime cost per unit of output

d = coefficient of discrepancy ($d = \dfrac{I_{t-m}}{\Delta K_t}$, where ΔK means addition to output capacity)

---

[1] If, for instance, a stationary economy is transformed into a growing economy with the rate of growth of fixed assets of 2% per annum, fixed capital costs per unit of output will on our assumptions decrease by 30%, and they will be reduced to only one half of their stationary level if the rate of growth is 3½% (service life being 35 years and output capacity being constant in both cases).

i = interest rate
k = depreciation multiplier (ratio of gross to net capital stock)
m = investment maturation period
n = depreciation period (life span of capital assets)
p = price
r = rate of growth
t = time

definitional equations: $\alpha = \dfrac{R_t}{D_t}$, $\beta = \dfrac{G_t}{K_{t-1}}$, $\gamma = \dfrac{N_t}{K_{t-1}}$, $\delta = \dfrac{D_t}{G_t}$, $\dfrac{1}{v} = \dfrac{R_t}{K_{t-1}}$.

1. A Stationary Model with Two Kinds of Capital Goods

It is assumed that there are two kinds of fixed assets, equipment and structures, with respective depreciation periods $n_e = 3$ and $n_s = 6$. Capital is composed $1/2$ of equipment and $1/2$ of structures which results in an average depreciation period of $n = 4$. From these assumptions we derive the following table:

Year	Gross Investment		Depreciation	Net Investment	Replacement		New Investment		Gross Capital Stock (End of the Year)		
	Equipment	Structures			Equipment	Structures	Equipment	Structures	Equipment	Structures	Total
1	500	500	—	1000	—	—	+500	+500	500	500	1000
2	125	125	250	—	—	—	+125	+125	625	625	1250
3	156	156	312	—	—	—	+156	+156	781	781	1562
4	390	—	390	—	500	—	—110	—	671	781	1452
5	286	50	336	—	125	—	+161	+ 50	832	831	1663
6	286	130	416	—	156	—	+130	+130	962	961	1923
7	240	241	481	—	390	390	—150	—149	812	812	1624
8	229	177	406	—	286	235	— 57	— 58	755	754	1509
9	253	124	377	—	286	156	— 33	— 32	722	722	1444
10	301	60	361	—	240	—	+ 61	+ 60	783	782	1565
11	285	106	391	—	229	50	+ 56	+ 56	839	838	1677
12	271	148	419	—	253	130	+ 18	+ 18	857	856	1713
13	244	184	428	—	301	241	— 57	— 57	800	799	1599
14	254	146	400	—	285	177	— 31	— 31	769	768	1537
15	265	119	384	—	271	124	— 6	— 5	763	763	1526
16	283	99	382	—	244	60	+ 39	+ 39	802	802	1604
17	275	126	401	—	254	106	+ 21	+ 20	823	822	1645
18	264	147	411	—	265	148	— 1	— 1	822	821	1643
19	255	156	411	—	283	184	— 28	— 28	794	793	1587
20	263	134	397	—	275	146	— 12	— 12	782	781	1563
21	268	123	391	—	264	119	+ 4	+ 4	786	785	1571
22	274	119	393	—	255	99	+ 19	+ 20	805	805	1610
23	270	133	403	—	263	126	+ 7	+ 7	812	812	1624
24	263	143	406	—	268	147	— 5	— 4	807	808	1615

In the first year, 1000 is invested, 500 in equipment and 500 in structures. This composition of capital is assumed to be technologically necessary and is maintained throughout (except for the differences of $+1$ or -1 due to the rounding of the figures). Therefore the average depreciation percentage ($=25\%$) is retained all the time. In the 4th year, the original stock of equipment is replaced and so the first disinvestment takes place in this year. The replacement of the structures in the 7th year causes the second disinvestment and after that the oscillatory movement converges.

One note of explanation should be added. The assumption of the unchanged composition of capital is violated in the 4th year, because in this year disinvestment in equipment is greater than the available amount of combined depreciation, while structures remain unchanged. At the end of the 4th year, the usable output capacity is only $671 + 671 = 1342$ and consequently, depreciation is given by 25 % of this sum. The remainder of output capacity, $1452 - 1342 = 110$, consists of structures, $781 - 671 = 110$, which are left lying idle for one year. For this reason, in the 7th year not all structures installed in the 1st year are replaced but only $500 - 110 = 390$, and the rest of 110 is replaced in the following year together with the structures installed in the 2nd year. After that the process develops smoothly. The discrepancy between existing and used capacity could have been avoided by a more complicated structure of the model.

The model with three kinds of capital goods, depicted by the graph in text (Ch. 7-b-4), has been constructed in an analogous way. In that model, the difficulty described above is practically avoided, because correct, and the obtained proportions of assets almost coincide.

2. Average Depreciation Period in an Economy with more than One Kind of Capital Goods[1]

Suppose that the initial unit investment consists of two kinds of capital goods, G_1 and G_2, and that both of them are expanded at the constant rate r. In what follows subscripts refer to specific investments, G_1 and G_2 are initial quantities, while all other capital letters denote quantities related to the point or period of time discussed. To simplify notation introduce $a = 1 + r$.

By the time t total annual gross investment will increase to

$$G = G_1 a^{t-1} + G_2 a^{t-1} = a^{t-1} \tag{1}$$

Respective depreciation periods are n_1 and n_2. Replacements are equal to gross investments made n_1 and n_2 years earlier respectively and by the time t total annual replacement expenditures will increase to

$$R = a^{t-1} (G_1 a^{-n_1} + G_2 a^{-n_2}) \tag{2}$$

---

[1] In this section I am making use of the proof derived in a similar way by E. D. Domar (6, 182—5).

The ratio of total gross investment to total replacement (= gross investment n years earlier) at the time t must be equal to

$$\frac{G}{R} = a^n \tag{3.1}$$

and it follows from (1) and (2) that this ratio must also be equal to

$$\frac{G}{R} = (G_1 a^{-n_1} + G_2 a^{-n_2})^{-1} \tag{3.2}$$

Gross capital stock at $t-1$ (K, K_1 and K_2 refer to $t-1$) is equal to

$$K = K_1 + K_2 = \frac{a^{t-1}}{r}(1 - G_1 a^{-n_1} - G_2 a^{-n_2}) \tag{4}$$

Depreciation at t is assumed to be the function of capital at $t-1$ and therefore

$$D = \frac{K_1}{n_1} + \frac{K_2}{n_2} = \frac{a^{t-1}}{rn_1 n_2}[G_1 n_2 (1 - a^{-n_1}) + G_2 n_1 (1 - a^{-n_2})] \tag{5}$$

From (2) and (5) derive the ratio between replacement and depreciation

$$\frac{R}{D} = rn_1 n_2 \frac{G_1 a^{-n_1} + G_2 a^{-n_2}}{G_1 n_2 (1 - a^{-n_1}) + G_2 n_1 (1 - a^{-n_2})} \tag{6.1}$$

which must be equal to the ratio expressed by the formula (9) in Chapter 7-c, i.e.

$$\alpha = \frac{R}{D} = \frac{nr}{a^n - 1} \tag{6.2}$$

Taking into account that $D = \frac{K}{n}$, from relation (5) we can derive the average depreciation period for two assets

$$n = \frac{Kn_1 n_2}{K_1 n_2 + K_2 n_1} = n_1 n_2 \frac{1 - (G_1 a^{-n_1} + G_2 a^{-n_2})}{n_2 G_1 (1 - a^{-n_1}) + n_1 G_2 (1 - a^{-n_2})} \tag{7}$$

We must prove that so derived average n can be used for computation of the ratios α, β, γ, δ and v. To do this, we must show that it satisfies the equations (3.1) and (6.2).

Substitute v and z for

$$v = G_1 a^{-n_1} + G_2 a^{-n_2} = a^{-n} \tag{8}$$

$$z = G_1 n_2 (1 - a^{-n}) + G_2 n_1 (1 - a^{-n_2}) \tag{9}$$

It follows from the equality of (6.1) and (6.2) that

$$rn_1 n_2 \frac{v}{z} = \frac{nr}{v^{-1} - 1}$$

$$n = n_1 n_2 \frac{1 - v}{z} \tag{10.1}$$

164

If v and z are substituted in (7), it follows similarly that

$$n = n_1 \, n_2 \frac{1 - v}{z} \qquad (10.2)$$

The value for n is the same in both cases and so the requirements are fulfilled. If α is satisfied, all other ratios must be satisfied as well because they change in fixed proportions. Thus average depreciation period as given by (7) can be used as n in our equations. The conclusion applies also to systems with more than two kinds of fixed assets. It is rather obvious that the formulae are valid only for $t > n$, where n is the longest depreciation period in the system. In other words, the system acquires its simple characteristics with stable relations between various quantities growing at the same rate only after all assets have been replaced for the first time.

3. The Discrepancy between the Addition to "Capital in Existence" now and to "Capital in Function" m Years Later as a Function of the Maturation Period and the Rate of Growth of Capital

Consider a regularly growing economy where technology does not change, productive capacity of once created fixed assets remains approximately constant, assets are scrapped always at the end of the year, the maturation period of every annual portion of investment is m years and its productive life n years. The addition to productive capacity (capital in function) in the year t is given by

$$\Delta K_t = G_{t-m} - R_{t-1}$$

where

$$R_{t-1} = G_{t-n-m-1}$$

and therefore

$$\Delta K_t = G_{t-m} (1 - a^{-1-n}) \qquad (11)$$

Similarly, new investment in the year $t{-}m$ is given by

$$I_{t-m} = G_{t-m} - R_{t-m} = G_{t-m} - G_{t-m-n-m}$$

$$I_{t-m} = G_{t-m} (1 - a^{-m-n}) \qquad (12)$$

Because of the maturation period, there will be a discrepancy between new investment — measuring the addition to capital in existence — and the actual addition to productive capacity (capital in function). The ratio between the increase in capacity in t and new investment made m years earlier may serve as a coefficient of discrepancy

$$d = \frac{I_{t-m}}{\Delta K_t} = \frac{1 - a^{-m-n}}{1 - a^{-1-n}} \qquad (13)$$

It is evident that discrepancy will diminish as the maturation period decreases and the rate of growth increases. If the maturation period is

$m = 4$ and the depreciation period $n = 30$ and if the rates of growth are respectively $r_1 = 1\%$ and $r_2 = 10\%$, the discrepancy coefficient will assume the following values

$$d_1 = 1.081$$
$$d_2 = 1.014$$

In other words, the numerator of the capital coefficient (ratio of investment to increment in output) will be greater by 8.1% and 1.4% respectively if the value of new investment in year t—m is taken as an approximation for the true value of the increment of productive capital (productive capacity) in year t.

In fact, actual discrepancy is smaller because constant technological improvements reduce the influence of past investments which have to be replaced. Thus for high rates of growth capital coefficient computed as a ratio between new investment in t—m and the addition to output in t will approximate technological capital coefficient (defined as the ratio between the gross value of productive assets and the output they produce at normal utilization of capacity) very closely. One should be careful, however, to keep in mind that by this we have not disposed with all other difficulties inherent in the concept of capital coefficient.

4. The Value of Capital in a Stationary Economy With a Positive Rate of Interest (Capital Theory) Equal to Net Stock of Capital (National Income Accounting)

Consider two investment projects. The first consists in buying a brand new asset (K) which has to be replaced every n years (i.e. at intervals n, $2n$, etc.). The second consists in buying assets of balanced age composition and paying out for renewals every year[1]. The present value of capital outlays in the first case is given by

$$V_1 = K[1 + (1+i)^{-n} + (1+i)^{-2n} + \ldots] = \frac{K}{1-(1+i)^{-n}} \tag{14}$$

The present value in the second case is given by

$$V_2 = C + \frac{K}{in} \tag{15}$$

where C is the sum which has to be paid immediately while $\frac{1}{i} \cdot \frac{K}{n}$ is the present value of the infinite stream of annual replacements which in a stationary economy with a balanced age composition of assets are the same every year. If we postulate that both alternatives have equal value, V_1 must be equal to V_2 and therefore

$$\frac{K}{1-(1+i)^{-n}} = C + \frac{K}{in}$$

$$\frac{K}{C} = in \frac{(1+i)^n - 1}{(1+i)^n (ni-1)+1} \tag{16}$$

---

[1] Cf. D. G. Champernowne and R. F. Kahn, 7, 107—8.

166

Substituting r for i we find that the ratio expressed by (16) is equal to k in (15), Chapter 7-c. It follows that the ratio of the value of a set of new fixed assets to the value of the same set of balanced age composition in a stationary economy with a positive rate of interest (capital theory) can be interpreted as the ratio between gross and net capital stock in a growing economy (national income accounting) provided that the interest rate is interpreted as the rate of growth.

5. The Impact of the Changing Output Capacity on Depreciation, Replacement and Profit

Consider the case of a linear decline in output capacity. Let depreciation period be $n = 4$, the price of the product $p = 1$, constant prime costs per unit of output $c = 0.4$ and maintenance costs in the narrow sense (cleaning, oiling, etc.) to be zero. Two different cases can be distinguished: A. either the capacity of the firm (plant) is maintained indefinitely, or B. the capacity is left to decline until after n years wholesale replacement takes place and the changes in the capacity are compensated by replacement investment outside the firm (or in a new plant). Thus A can be conditionally interpreted as the maintenance and B as the replacement case. Within the first case two possibilities arise: capacity may be kept constantly at the same level with no need for wholesale replacements at constant intervals, or such a need may exist in addition to maintaining capacity within intervals.

A. Maintenance:

Year	Capacity	D	R	Cost	Total Cost D+C + (R)	Product	Profit	D—R
1	4 — 3	1	1	1.6	2.6 (3.6)	4	1.4 (0.4)	0 (1)
2	3 — 2	1	1	1.6	2.6 (3.6)	4	1.4 (0.4)	0 (1)
3	2 — 1	1	1	1.6	2.6 (3.6)	4	1.4 (0.4)	0 (1)
4	1 — 0	1	1	1.6	2.6 (3.6)	4	1.4 (0.4)	0 (1)
Sum		4	4		10.4 (14.4)	16	5.6 (1.6)	0 (4—4)

B. Replacement:

Year	Capacity	D	R	Cost	Total Cost	Product	Profit	D—R
1	4 — 3	1.75	1	1.4	3.15	3.5	0.35	0.75
2	3 — 2	1.25	1	1.0	2.25	2.5	0.25	0.25
3	2 — 1	0.75	1	0.6	1.35	1.5	0.15	—0.25
4	1 — 0	0.25	1	0.2	0.45	0.5	0.05	—0.75
Sum		4.00	4		7.20	8.0	0.80	0

The brackets in A refer to the case where the plant has a definite service life at the end of which it must be completely replaced. Then annual "replacement" costs represent maintenance costs incurred to preserve capacity intact until retirement. Total annual costs consist of depreciation, prime cost and "replacement" cost (3.6 altogether) and profit is equal to the difference between product and total costs. Funds must be provided for both depreciation *and* replacement (maintenance), replacement has to be added not subtracted from depreciation. At the time of retirement, the combined depreciation is equal to 8. Half of this sum has already been spent on periodical renewals during the lifetime of the plant by which its capacity was maintained. The other half is available for the complete replacement of the plant, about to be scrapped, by a brand new similar plant.

The case without brackets in A refers to a capacity maintained indefinitely (roads, for instance). Wholesale replacement costs, and with them pure depreciation, disappear. This change is reflected in the profits which are increased by the same amount by which the combined depreciation is reduced. This is one of our limiting cases where n tends to infinity.

The case B explains why replacement, when identified with maintenance, ought to be treated differently from the wholesale replacement (which we usually imply when we speak of replacement). B corresponds to the brackets variety of A with the difference that capacity is not maintained but is left to decline. Observe that the product, D + C, and the profits are exactly twice lower than in A. This is because a linear decline in output capacity renders the average capacity of B twice smaller. The depreciation follows the decline in output capacity which, with the assumed unit prime cost constant, leads to constant profit per unit of output. Total depreciation is equal to total replacement but its distribution in time is different. The last column shows that in the early years, depreciation exceeds replacement. As this surplus can in the meantime be invested elsewhere with multiplying effect, total depreciation in fact exceeds total replacement. Also the depreciation of a declining capacity exceeds in its multiplying effect the depreciation of a plant with constant capacity. For, such an alternative plant would eventually produce the same output of 8 units, but in the early years its output would be relatively smaller and also the funds available for investment (depreciation and profit).

II. A NOTE ON THE HISTORY OF THE PROBLEM

1. Economic theorists encountered the phenomenon of discrepancy between depreciation and replacement in a growing economy a long time ago. One of the first to state the problem clearly was K. Marx. Marx's views may be seen from the following passages:

"A portion of the constant capital which is calculated to be used up each year, and enters as wear and tear into the value of the product, is in fact *not* used up ... Where therefore much constant capital, consequently also much fixed capital, is employed, there exists in that part of the value of the product which provided the depreciation of the fixed capital, an *accumulation fund*, which ... can be used for the provision of new fixed capital ... This accumulation fund is not found at levels of production and in nations where there is no considerable amount of fixed capital. This is an important point. It is a fund for the constant introduction of improvements, extensions, and so forth." (8, 353—5).

Marx's attention is here completely absorbed by the task of laying down the conditions for realization of surplus value. The phenomenon just described is to be used for the same purpose, namely "...if the total capital employed in machine-building industry were large enough to replace the annual wear and tear of machinery, it would produce much more machinery than is required each year... therefore,... even if in this sphere of production the capital invested in it is only reproduced, continuous accumulation in the other spheres of production is necessary" (p. 355). Apart from this application Marx did not elaborate further his observation. Cf. also Marx's letter to Engels and Engels's reply of 24th and 27th August 1867, and *Capital I*, Ch. 13—2.

2. In a planned economy one would expect an extensive use of the concept of new investment, both theoretically and practically, because every well made plan reveals considerable difference between net and new investment[1]. But such an expectation is only partly justified. In Yugoslavia, for instance, the Statistical Office collects and publishes net investment data, and the Planning Bureau makes little use of the data so presented, but corrects them for the amount of the accumulative part of depreciation.

The same dualism in practice, without much theoretical treatment, seems to prevail in the U.S.S.R. too. As an illustration I shall quote A. I. Notkin, the author of a well known book on the theory of reproduc-tion. He deals with the subject in a rather elementary way and says: "... if fixed capital funds are increasing every year, the sum of annual depreciation is always greater than the replacement value of capital physically scrapped... This means that a certain part of social work, expressed in a determinate part of the depreciation fund and which will ultimately be used to replace fixed capital, is, for the time being, the additional source of accumulation and en-larged reproduction parallel with the surplus product produced in the given year... Systematically and quickly increasing the volume of its fixed capital, it (socialist economy) increases systematically and quickly the absolute difference between the size of the deprecia-tion fund and the value of the reproduction of actually scrapped fixed capital. The accumulation of this difference in money form expresses that fact that a certain part of social past and living labour, applied in past years to production of machines, structures and other elements of fixed capital now in function, is temporarily being freed from the process of the simple reproduction and is used for enlarged reproduction of fixed capital..." (10, 104—5).

Notkin clearly insists on the static identity of capital costs, but makes no attempt to explain the resulting "difference in money form". He makes no attempt either to examine the behaviour of this difference under various conditions.

3. Our problem will necessarily be encountered by the estimators of national income and wealth. Thus in his study on the inter-war growth of national wealth of Croatia I. Vinski estimated that new investment[2]

---

[1] I myself encountered the problem for the first time when I tried to solve some problems of enlarged reproduction in a planned economy (9, 28—9).
[2] To Dr. Vinski I owe the term "new investment". By now the term has become firmly rooted in the Yugoslav economic terminology (cf., e.g., F. Vasić, 11).

in the period 1919—1940 was 1.67 times greater than net investment. Commenting on this difference Dr. Vinski says that "... on the whole ... (it) does not represent new value, viz. the increase in social wealth of Croatia, but means simply maintaining the existing value of fixed capital assets in Croatia" (12, 13). What he had in mind seems to be essentially the same as the argument of P. Redfern, whom I shall quote next at some length.

Before embarking on actual measurement, which is the main purpose of his study, Redfern discusses the implications of various theoretical solutions. His final decision is in favour of the traditional solution. Of the alternative solution, with which we are concerned here, he says the following:

"It might ... be assumed that an asset, if properly maintained, retained its full value until it was ultimately scrapped; capital consumption would then be represented simply by the assets going out of use and net investment would represent the difference between new assets installed and existing assets scrapped. This assumption clearly has an element of truth in it ... But the method has major drawbacks. Firstly *net* investment would take no account of the ageing process of an existing asset which was not scrapped. The assumption would thus ignore what has been described as the "two-dimensional" nature of capital: the essence of the productive asset is that it continues to render services over a long period; its value is related not only to the service it renders in a given year, but also to the number of years over which it can be expected to remain productive. The second disadvantage of ignoring the ageing of assets is that it would imply a level of net profit and of national income fluctuating erratically according to the incidence of the scrapping of assets" (1, 142).

Evidently, Redfern, like the other authors quoted, takes for granted that the "ageing process" should be measured simultaneously. But why should it be?

From the point of view of an individual firm, with all the uncertainties about the future, the soundest way of calculating capital costs is on the basis of actual price paid (or which might be paid) for a capital asset spread over the lifetime of the asset. This is the only firm point of calculation. That it is highly appreciated by the firms is clearly shown by the deeply rooted practice of depreciating assets taking into account the original (or replacement) price and the expected lifetime. But why should this individual business accounting practice be obligatory for national product accounting?

It is, first, conceptually unsustainable. A firm may spread the costs of capital outlay over a number of years simply because there are many other firms from which to borrow the initial capital or to which to lend the idle depreciation funds. But a nation must calculate differently. Assuming a closed economy — because of limited international mobility of factors of production national economies are practically closed, and this is perfectly true for the world as a whole — over the long period accumulated, replacement expenditures are not made out of depreciation allowances, neither are new investment outlays met out of accumulated

170

profits or of borrowed capital. Both of them are paid out of *current* national product.

Further, the "two-dimensional nature of capital" is only a great nuisance in an economic analysis of growth. One or two examples might illustrate the point. Take first the problem of age structure.

According to the Yugoslav capital census at the beginning of 1953, gross capital stock was depreciated to about the same extent in building and transport industry, 47.4% and 49.7% respectively. Can we infer anything about the age structure from the comparison of these figures? Clearly not. If we look directly at the age structure of these two industries, we shall find that assets older than 32 years represented 31.7% of all assets in transport and only 4.8% in building industry. Similar figures may be produced for manufacturing and mining as compared with state farms. If we are interested in finding out when and how much of capital assets have to be replaced, net capital stock or aggregate depreciation fund tell us practically nothing. On the other hand, the changes in gross capital stock, although one-dimensional, will give us some practically useful information about the ageing process: if there is negative new investment, no matter what is the value of net investment, this will be a clear indication that the assets are on the whole too old to be compatible with growth. Output will begin to increase only after new investment has become positive. Clearly, this can only be seen retrospectively. If we want to predict, special surveys of the age structure are necessary.

Consequently, net values are of no help in assessing the age of capital assets. They are of no help in assessing the quantity of them either. So, for instance, according to Redfern the net value of the British fleet was in 1953 greater than in 1938, but the gross value was smaller. Because of the war, the losses were not fully compensated, but, on the average, the fleet was "rejuvenated". Again it is hard to see in which sense is this information analytically useful. As the age structure of the fleet is not specified, we can infer nothing about the future changes of its output capacity[1].

The final argument of Redfern (the possibility of the erratic fluctuation of national income) is, I believe, an accidental lapsus in reasoning. Our task is to measure economic phenomena as they are really occurring. If the movement is erratic, why should not this be reflected in statistical series? Now, if one defines national income as that part of national product which may be consumed without diminishing the productive capacity of the economy, i.e., without causing decline in the total output of the relevant period — which, it is true, is usually implied (Cf. 13, 219), but is actually inapplicable to the conventional definition — then national income will statistically be derived from gross product by subtraction of replacement expenditures.

4. Finally, growth economists and model builders will have to deal with our problem too. The pioneering investigation in this field has been

---

[1] The above remarks are not intended as a request that net capital estimates be banned. On the contrary, I think we ought to be grateful to national income statisticians for every information they care to provide. But it is desirable to make it clear what can and what cannot be done with a particular piece of information.

undertaken by E. D. Domar. In his paper on the econometric approach to economic growth Domar introduced his approach by saying:

"In a growing economy ... even with constant prices and correct depreciation charges (computed according to the straight-line method), the latter (depreciation) will considerably exceed replacement expenditures" (14, 33).

In two footnotes, Domar quotes formulae for the ratio between replacement and depreciation and for the ratio between depreciation and gross investment from an earlier (1951) unpublished paper. These two formulae correspond to our α and δ expressed in the continuous form.

A year later (1953), Domar dealt with the same problem in a paper especially dedicated to it (6). The paper represents an admirable discussion of the subject. But Domar failed to realize the general theoretical implications of his new approach. He thought he was describing a particular and not a general case. Thus he writes:

"If the productive capacity of the asset remains more or less intact to the end, our assumption that replacement takes place in one operation is not far from reality. On the other hand, if its productive capacity declines gradually over time, its replacement by other assets (not necessarily within the same firm) is likewise a gradual process, and should the latter happen to move along a straight line, R and D become identical. If its capacity should decline particularly fast in the early years, replacement will exceed depreciation. *Thus the usually assumed identity of R and D, even in a growing economy* (with constant prices), *is not necessarily wrong* ... Within a reasonable range, it should be looked upon as a more or less extreme case, the opposite extreme being our present approach. As usual, the truth lies somewhere between them" (6, 167; italics mine).

However, this time exceptionally, the truth lies in one of the extremes, and the error in reasoning will be obvious from the foregoing analysis, in particular from the discussion in Chapter 8-c and Appendix I-5.

Almost concurrently with Domar, R. Eisner published his first paper on the same subject (1952), and since then a number of other contributions in the field has appeared (15; 16; 17; 18; 11).

References:

1. P. Redfern, "Net Investment in Fixed Assets in the United Kingdom 1938—1953", *Journal of the Royal Statistical Society*, 1955, 141—82.
2. G. A. D. Preinreich, "Annual Survey of Economic Theory: The Theory of Depreciation", *Econometrica*, 1938, 219—41.
3. F. and V. Lutz, *The Theory of Investment of the Firm*, Princeton, Princeton University Press, 1951.
4. I. Svennilson, "Capital Accumulation and National Wealth in an Expanding Economy", in *25 Economic Essays in Honour of Erik Lindahl*, Stockholm, Ekonomisk Tidskrift, 1956.
5. S. Fabricant, *Capital Consumption and Adjustment*, New York, National Bureau of Economic Research, 1938.
6. E. D. Domar, "Depreciation, Replacement and Growth", *Economic Journal*, 1953, 1—32; reprinted in *Essays in the Theory of Economic Growth*, New York, Oxford University Press, 1957. Quotations refer to the book.
7. D. G. Champernowne, R. F. Kahn, "The Value of Invested Capital", *Review of Economic Studies*, 1953—54, 107—11.

8. K. Marx, *Theories of Surplus Value*, London, Lawrence and Wishart, 1951.
9. B. Horvat, *Marksove sheme realizacije i socijalistička proširena reprodukcija* (Marxian Schemata and the Socialist Enlarged Reproduction), Seminar Paper, Economic Faculty, University of Zagreb, January 1950.
10. A. I. Notkin, *Očerki teorii socialističeskogo vosproizvodstva* (Outline of the Theory of Socialist Reproduction), OGIZ-GOSPOLITIZDAT, Moskva, 1948.
11. F. Vasić, "Neto i nove investicije" (Net and New Investment), *Ekonomist*, 1957, 33—54.
12. I. Vinski, *Investicije na području Hrvatske u razdoblju između dva svjetska rata* (Investments in Croatia in the Inter-War Period), Ekonomski institut — Zagreb, 1953 (mimeographed); Ekonomski institut, Beograd, 1955, (with an English summary). Quotations refer to 1955 edition.
13. J. E. Meade, R. Stone, "The Construction of Tables of National Income, Expenditure, Savings and Investment", *Economic Journal*, 1941, 216—33.
14. E. D. Domar, "Economic Growth: An Econometric Approach", *American Economic Review, Papers and Proceedings*, May 1952, 479—95; reprinted in *Essays in the Theory of Economic Growth*, New York, Oxford University Press, 1957. Quotations refer to the book.
15. R. Eisner, "Depreciation Allowances, Replacement Requirements and Growth", *American Economic Review*, 1952, 820—31. The comments by M. Gordon with the rejoinder of Eisner, *Ibid.*, 1953, 609—21.
16. —————, "Accelerated Amortization, Net Profits and Growth", *Quarterly Journal of Economics*, 1952, 533—44.
17. E. Schiff, "A Note on Depreciation, Replacement and Growth", *Review of Economics and Statistics*, 1954, 47—56.
18. H. Neisser, "Depreciation, Replacement and Regular Growth", *Economic Journal*, 1955, 159—61.

V. THE OPTIMUM RATE OF INVESTMENT

In the preceding chapters we established the property of the economic system in motion to generate ever larger output per unit of fixed capital used as the speed of expansion increases. The next natural step is to enquire whether there is any limit for the speeding up of economic expansion. At this stage of our enquiry we may actually expect to establish the existence of two limits: one "physical" and one "valuational". The existence of the physical limit reduces to the problem of the maximum rate of productive investment — the problem which, to my knowledge, has not been tackled so far. The determination of the other limit is identical with what is often called optimum rate of saving. The problem of the optimum rate of saving has received some, if not considerable, attention. Basically, two different approaches have been used.

It has occasionally been suggested that saving decisions have to be made by individual consumers faced with the resulting rate of interest[1]. If we formulate it in this way, it becomes at once clear why the arrangement defeats its own purpose: as J. de V. Graaff puts it, consumers

---

[1] Cf. A. Lerner: "Within the socially determined limits... consumers can be allowed to distribute their consumption through time in the same way as they can distribute it between different consumption goods at the same time. The principle that price should correspond to cost demands that consumers postponing consumption should get interest on their postponement in accordance with the increase (if any) in product that is made possible by the postponement, while consumers who anticipate consumption should suffer a corresponding diminution of consumption or discount. The thriftiness or otherwise of the consumers can then be observed in the degree to which consumption is postponed or anticipated — as shown by the debits and credits of consumers with the state bank — and the authorities could, if they wished, take this index of time preference into account in deciding the rate of accumulation of capital. It might, for instance, be decided to keep the rate of investment at that level which corresponded to a rate of interest at which postponements of consumption, or lendings by consumers, exactly equalled their anticipations or borrowings" (1, 73). These remarks provoked the following reaction by O. Lange: "Mr. Lerner's interesting proposal how the time preference of the consumers could be ascertained in a socialist society and how the rate of capital accumulation could be regulated accordingly deserves full attention" (2, 143). Eleven years later F. J. Atkinson, apparently ignorant of the passages quoted, reproaches Lerner, Lange and other socialist economists for being "arbitrary" and not allowing "that the rate of investment in a socialist state may be decided either by the government or by the voluntary saving habits of the populace" (3, 83).

acting separately are simply not equipped to make rational saving decisions (4, 105). If the amount of saving that one consumer undertakes at a given rate of interest is a function of the goods and services which he expects the savings to be able to purchase in future years, then the consumer is unable to make a consistent decision; because future market conditions depend on savings of other consumers and he has no way of knowing what other consumers intend to do[1]. And this is not only a matter of welfare economics subtleties, but a very real problem. Keynesian economics sheds some light on its economic importance. In the process of organization of social life there are certain decisions whose nature requires that they be made collectively if they are to be consistent, i.e., that they take into account all the consequences they involve. To the list of activities which traditionally involve social action — health protection, school attendance, and the like — we must add the determination of the rate of saving. However, there are still other reasons why it is impossible to achieve a consistent solution of the saving problem on the basis of the individual savers' decisions. The following two properties of the economic machine make for this impossibility. First, the volume of saving is assumed to be determined by the rate of interest. The rate of interest is equal to the marginal net productivity of investment. But because of the diminishing marginal productivity of investment, interest does not exhaust the net benefit of saving (investment). Thus savers get only a part of the new product resulting from investment, which must affect their marginal valuations in making saving decisions. Secondly, even allowing for the deduction of the "investment surplus", savers still do not get the full award for their abstinence from consumption, because as production increases real wages rise as well and a part of the new product is distributed as additional *wages*. It follows that in order to be consistent, saving-investment decisions must be made for the system as a whole; in other words, they must be made collectively.

The second, more frequent, approach is based on various explicit considerations concerning utility maximization. "Present sacrifices" are compared with "future gains". The social welfare function is somehow defined and then the conditions for its maximization are examined[2].

---

[1] Nevertheless, the assumption that private saving decisions somehow represent the proper standard for what the community actually wishes to save — is still deeply ingrained in economic thinking. Compare Professor Lewis saying: "Even a rich country like the U.S.A. was saving in the 1920s only about 10 per cent of its income. In deciding, therefore, that the Russian people should save as much as 25 per cent, the Russian Government was imposing upon them an obligation which only the strongest measures, backed by unassailable state powers, could enforce" (5, 16). In the early thirties saving in the U.S.A. was negative and could, value judgements apart, be taken as an equally valid standard for comparison. And the same applies to all other saving rates up to, say, more than 20 per cent in the post-war Japan. An additional problem arises from the fact that in the U.S.A. virtually all saving is done by the richest ten per cent.

[2] The first to offer a solution on these lines was F. Ramsey in 1928. Ramsey compared potential satisfactions in the state of "Bliss" (the maximum obtainable rate of utility) and the satisfactions of current income (6). The present author feels

The snag in this approach is that utility is immeasurable and therefore welfare functions are empirically unascertainable. Consequently, the determination of the optimum rate of saving becomes inevitably something of an intellectual exercise yielding no criterion for the purpose of practical economic policy. Therefore, in practical work another approach is often used. In planning economic development some constraints are usually postulated, e.g., that consumption must not fall below a certain level, or that heavy industry must be expanded at a certain rate; they are arbitrarily defined and then, considering them as data, the saving decision is reached.

Thus, so far we have been left with a choice between three alternative solutions; the first two—determinate, but either irrational or impossible, the third one—practically possible but theoretically indeterminate. It is the scope of the chapters which follow to examine the possibility of a solution which would be rational, practicable and determinate.

9. THE OPTIMUM RATE OF INVESTMENT

(a) The Concept of the Absorptive Capacity of the Economy

1. In the present chapter we shall be concerned with the establishment and characteristics of the physical limit of productive investment. For a start let us define a few basic concepts which will be used throughout the analysis.

(1) Gross social product and, consequently, the additions to gross social product, will be conceived and computed as net of services not intimately connected with material production (such as public administration, defence expenditures, etc.; transport and trade services are included). This definition of *GSP* is adopted partly with regard to available empirical data and partly because it simplifies analysis. A more adequate concept of social product will be elaborated in Chapter 11.

(2) The phrase "productive investment" will mean investment producing an increment in *GSP* as defined in the preceding paragraph.

(3) In addition to the general distinction between investment and consumption, two further distinctions will be made. Thus, social product will be considered to consist of four different parts. They are:

doubtful whether this method may be mentioned in serious economics. But other economists seem to have less inhibitions on this account. J. E. Meade accepted Ramsey's idea, rechristened "Bliss" into "glut" and reached the following conclusion: "... the condition for the optimum rate of savings is that the present rate of savings should be increased if the present rate of savings ... multiplied by the present marginal utility of income is less than the excess of the rate of total utility ... which will be enjoyed by the community in the state of glut over the rate of total utility which it enjoys in present conditions" (7, 98).

Of the other solutions that of Professor J. Tinbergen should be mentioned. Tinbergen derives his solution from particular assumptions about the shape of utility functions (logarithmic and hyperbolic) and the value of the "psychological discount" (time preference). See also O. Eckstein (9).

(a) Investment in the material factor of growth which causes expansion of productive fixed and circulating assets. This part of *GSP* will be referred to as "investment".

(b) Investment in the human factor of growth (termed *A*-factor) which increases the ability of the society to produce material goods. To distinguish (b) from (a) it may be called "productive expenditures".

(c) and (d) The remainder of social product is divided between personal and communal consumption. As a matter of fact, parts of (c) and (d) are physically identical with (b). The reason for putting certain consumption goods and services into (b) is that their consumption leads to an increase in *GSP*. If these consumption goods and services lose their positive productive effect they will be classified as (c) and (d). The (c) and (d) parts of *GSP* will be referred to as "consumption".

(4) In accordance with our definition of economics in the *Introduction*, it will be assumed, that maximization of consumption, as just defined, is the sole aim of the society's productive efforts. This will imply that if there is a choice between smaller and greater consumption, other things being equal, the society will choose the alternative with greater consumption. If other things are not equal, the society will face a choice — i.e., maximum consumption as against maximum military strength — the consideration of which falls outside this paper and, indeed, outside the scope of economics.[1]

2. I next propose to consider the maximization of production through time. Production is maximized with respect to a specified period, the length of which is determined by some physical properties of the economic process.

Maximization involves not only the allocation of factors of production now, but also the adjustment of their various rates of expansion in the future. The potential effect of the optimum adjustment of the growth rates of factors is defined as the absorptive capacity of the economy. The easiest way to use this concept is to conceive the economy as a giant productive capacity capable of being expanded at a certain *maximum* rate, also at a lower rate, but *not at a higher rate*. Any additional inputs (investment) would not produce additions to but *reductions* of output. Or, applying (with caution) the conventional terminology, marginal productivity of investment will become zero or negative.

Zero marginal productivity of investment does not necessarily mean zero marginal productivity of capital. The latter is a static (in the sense that we may consider only marginal, i.e., infinitesimal changes of capital,

---

[1] Failing to make this distinction in his implicit reasoning and generalizing German experience of the Nazi period, W. Eucken arrives at the conclusion that in a planned ("centrally administered") economy the limits to maximum investment are set by the subsistence levels of the population (10, pp. 176, 177, 181, 190). It is obvious that in a system in which the Government undertakes to make valuations *instead* of the population, bombs and aeroplanes having highest priority in its scale of preference, consumption goods will perform exactly the same function as raw material or as fodder for the cattle. This means that the greater part of the economic problem has been assumed away. But even so Eucken is mistaken. The living standard of the population is lowered towards "Subsistence Minimum" not because investment is increased (assuming marginal productivity of investment positive), but because consumption pattern is changed: cars and eggs consumed by individual consumers are replaced by aeroplanes and bombs consumed by the Government.

or an increment in capital is considered with respect to an infinitely long period) while the former is a dynamic concept. It means even less that the rate of interest is zero. In fact, the belief that the positive rate of interest is an evident proof that the marginal productivity of investment is still positive — seems to have prevented further exploration of the practicability of production maximization. It has been observed that, in normal circumstances, the rate of interest has never vanished; it has existed with investment expenditures however large. It was therefore believed that only an extraordinarily high rate of investment would drive the marginal productivity of investment towards zero[1]. And an extraordinarily high level of investment would imply an extraordinarily low level of consumption. Hence one has to weigh "present sacrifices" with "future gains" and this is the domain of the utility calculus.

However, the actual economic process is somewhat different.

(b) Investment-Production Function

1. Investment is made to increase production. There is therefore some relation between the addition to the output stream and the productive investment which has caused it. There is also a time lag between the cause and the effect known as the maturation period of investment *(m)*. The ratio between additional output[2] in the current year (ΔP_t) and investment[2] made m years earlier (I_{t-m}) we shall term "production coefficient" $(p = \dfrac{\Delta P_t}{I_{t-m}})$. The change of p as a function of investment will be called "investment-production function" *(IP)*. This function may be diagrammatically represented in the following way:

It is fortunate that here we are able to make use of an empirical diagram[3]. The need for representing three variables in a two-

---

[1] Cf. Clemence and Doody saying: "The matter (the limit to the use of capital at a zero interest rate) may appear to be of little practical importance, since everyone agrees that such a limit, if it exists, has never been approximated" (11, 30). Cf. also P. Samuelson: "A zero rate of interest is a little like an 'absolute zero temperature' in physics. We can imagine getting close to it, but we can hardly imagine actually reaching the limiting state of a zero rate of interest. Thus, interest is a basic phenomenon that would not disappear in the most ideal economic world" (12, 673).

[2] Output is defined as gross product and investment as addition to the stock of productive capital, i.e., statistically, as gross investment net of replacement. However, in the following empirical illustrations, gross investment figures will be used because of the lack of reliable data for new investment.

[3] The diagram refers to Yugoslav economy and is taken from an unpublished study of the author prepared for the Federal Planning Bureau. The investment (gross) and production (gross) figures (prices: 1952) are 4-year averages (period 1947—1957); the maturation period is four years. The data refer to industry (manufacturing and mining). The production coefficient for the whole economy increased in the same period from 0.18 to 0.37 (gross investment does not include investment in houses, schools, hospitals and similar non-commercial objects and gross product does not contain the value of services). Industrial rather than whole economy *IP*-function is shown because the period is too short to eliminate the influences of the agricultural weather cycle from the latter.

or an increment in capital is considered with respect to an infinitely long period) while the former is a dynamic concept. It means even less that the rate of interest is zero. In fact, we hold that the positive rate of interest is an evident proof that the introduction productivity of investment still prevails, or seems to have prevailed, but a corporation of capital in normal circumstances. It has been observed that if this exists, I would investigate exceptions being very large. It is satisfactory to observe that rolls to extraordinary profit do survive it would drain the national product in a short... Perhaps this sum of... And I am convinced that high level of investment would imply in other equilibria low level of consumption. Hence one has to switch present sacrifice to wealth accumulated, and thus to also the structure of the ruling concepts.

How can the level of autonomous wealth be suppressed different?

The investment-feed-back function

Investment is made to increase production. There is therefore a relation between the allocation to the output stream and the production increment which it has caused. There is also a time-lag between the enlargement and the increment which will be a period of adjustment θ. The ratio between additional output in the current period (t_P) and investment until some years earlier $(t-4)$ will be

$$ P_t = \frac{\Delta X_t}{I_{t-4}} $$

which we term the relation of increment function for the year t. This empirical method of description faithfully represented in the column we exhibit below that one can tell the operation of an empirical function, when needing measuring three variables in a two-...

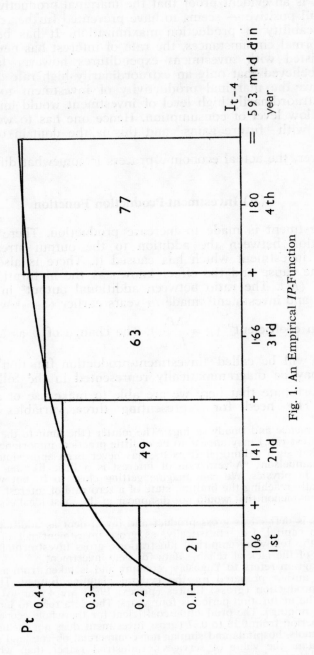

Fig. 1. An Empirical IP-Function

dimensional co-ordinate system has made for a little unusual construction of the diagram; it is, however, perfectly simple once the meaning of it is grasped. The ordinate shows the values of the production coefficient which in four (adjusted) years has risen from 0.2 in the first year to 0.43 in the last. The abscissa shows successive doses of investment expressed in milliards of dinars. The additions to social product are related to investments made four years earlier (maturation period). In each successive year the "dose" of investment has been increased, bringing the total for the whole period equal to 593 milliard dinars. If we multiply the "investment doses", represented by the segments of the abscissa, by the respective production coefficients, we get increments in output which, in the diagram, are represented by the areas of the respective columns. The figures inside the columns indicate the size of these increments. The total increase in output in the period under consideration is equal to the sum of the areas of the four columns, $\Delta P = \sum_{1}^{4} \Delta P_t = 210$ milliard dinars. It is this last figure which will become our main object of analysis as we proceed. Finally, the interpolated curve is intended to approximate to continuous changes in the production coefficient. The area under the curve is, of course, equal to the sum of the increments in output, $\int_{0}^{593} p(I)\ dI = \sum_{1}^{4} \Delta P_t$. The main lesson this diagram teaches us consists in the demonstration of the possibility of great changes of production coefficients. In four years the value of p has increased by more than 100 per cent. This is obviously not due to technological changes only[1]. Thus, we have to investigate the characteristics of our *IP*-function more carefully.

2. The assumption from which we started was that the absorptive capacity of the economy was limited: additional investment beyond certain limits brought about negative increments in output. Thus we

---

[1] In this particular empirical example the spectacular improvement in p may be tentatively explained as follows:

(1) The most important impulse was given by the far-reaching economic reorganization started in 1951—52. The managerial system with the rigid administrative central planning and control (more or less a copy of the Soviet economic organization) has been gradually replaced by a combination of workers' councils management plus global planning through market instruments plus some central decisions concerning major investment projects.

(2) The tempo of investing has been slowed down and the know-how has been gradually improving.

(3) Changes in the structure of investment occurred: after the basic industrialization program was accomplished by the first Five Year Plan (1947—1952) relatively more was invested in extensions and relatively less in new factories. And the capital productivity of extensions was about 50% higher.

As (3) is clearly accidental and (1) has already been analyzed in Chapters 5 and 6, it is (2) which will occupy our attention in the present chapter.

may say that *IP*-function depends on the quantity of investment *(I)*, the absorptive capacity of the economy *(A)* and the speed of their expansion $\left(\dfrac{dI}{dt}, \dfrac{dA}{dt}\right)$, or in symbols

$$p = f\left(I, \frac{dI}{dt}; A, \frac{dA}{dt}\right)$$

Investment has to be absorbed by the economy. How well this will be done depends on the human factor *A*. The complex factor *A* may be made a function of four basic factors (policy variables) and of their changes: of personal consumption, health, knowledge and economic and political organization. In addition, all other relevant characteristics of the economy may be conveniently lumped together as a single exogenous factor E^1. Thus we get:

$$\left(A, \frac{dA}{dt}\right) = g\left(C, \frac{dC}{dt}; H, \frac{dH}{dt}; Kn, \frac{dKn}{dt}; O, \frac{dO}{dt}; E, \frac{dE}{dt}\right)$$

The meaning of *A*-factors may be described very briefly in the following way.

(1) *Personal consumption* has great incentive value in a poor society. It may, therefore, influence productivity appreciably. It may be added that in a growing economy the alternative to be chosen normally lies in the direction of an increase; the possibility of a decrease of consumption cannot normally arise in a rationally constructed scheme of economic development as will be shown presently. (The only two probable exceptions seem to appear in societies with extreme inequality in the distribution of income or in societies where mass enthusiasm has been created; in both cases total consumption may temporarily stagnate or even decline without causing a contraction of *A*.)

(2) That the improvement in the *health* standard leads to an increase in productivity of labour — is notorious. A suitable generalization will be provided by quoting the estimate of J. J. Spengler that the potential productivity of the population of underdeveloped countries would rise 20—30 per cent if the age composition and state of health of their people could be "Westernized"[2].

(3) Factor *knowledge* comprises all degrees of skill, including scientific research. The experience of planning seems to suggest that knowl-

---

[1] The exogenous factor *E* has been inserted to make the algebraic presentation formally correct. As, by definition, *E* is not a policy variable, we shall not be concerned with it and we shall always assume that *E* is somehow given and known. In actual planning, of course, the analysis of *E* is of extreme importance.

[2] Spengler also compares the estimate of D. Ghosh for India, where about 22½% of the national income is spent on maintaining those who die before the age of 15, with that for England, where the corresponding percentage is only 6½% (13, 351).

edge (and certainly not investment resources)[1] is the most important scarce factor in underdeveloped countries with otherwise favourable social climate. Thus growth of "know-how" is likely to pose limits to the general economic development.

(4) The last factor, *termed economic and political organization*, refers to the institutional set-up of the economy. Inadequate economic organization and political discontent and instability are likely to upset the productive effect of all other factors and so minimize the value of A. But factor O may also considerably increase the value of A, which happened, for instance, in India as a result of having achieved independence, or in China after social revolution. Factor O is usually taken as a datum in the economic analysis, and nothing prevents us from following this traditional line here too. Yet, there is also some justification in assuming that in a rationally organized society, the shaping of such an important productive factor will not be left to the haphazard play of blind social forces, but will be undertaken with at least some degree of rationality as is the case with factors C, H and Kn. Planned economy may be assumed to experiment not only with micro but also with macro-organization. And the effects are likely to be very tangible, as our analysis in Part III appears to suggest. In any case O is an important limitational factor.

3. The foregoing considerations show that A is in principle measurable and that in practice its value can be well approximated. The next step in the analysis consists in an examination of the relation between A and I. An image of a vessel (A) into which liquid (I) is poured from outside — springs to mind. In fact, the picture is a little more complicated. The vessel itself produces the liquid, which in turn causes the expansion of the vessel. This feedback operates with diminishing force and the movement comes to an end when the vessel is filled up and additionally generated liquid is uselessly spilt. This is the point of optimum.

In other words, A and I are obviously interrelated. Investment makes possible the expansion of the community's absorptive capacity and A imposes limits to the productive application of I. The absorptive capacity may now be redefined to mean the ability of individuals and of the society as a whole to manipulate the stream of output increments. This ability is limited because there is a given level and a limited speed of potential expansion of the will to work, of the state of health, of the number of skilled workers and scientists and of the institutional

---

[1] This is also visible from the structure of IP-function. Investment is something relative, it is the share of investment in social product which is analytically meaningful. Given enough time, the share of investment may be increased as far as we like (short of 100%). The question is only whether the economy will absorb it. We are accustomed to think of investment as an independent factor of growth. However, in a rationally organized economy it would be more appropriate to treat it as a product of growth. Given A, the economy is able to produce any amount of I which can be productively applied.

readjustments. Being limited, A may be taken as a datum (although a changing one) and I may be defined as its function, $I = f(A)$. So defined investment is the *maximum investment which can be productively applied* in a given economy. Thus the *optimum* path of the investment-production function will be given by

$$P_{opt} = F[I(A)]$$

In this way the optimum rate of investment is determined.

(c) Maximization of Output Increment

1. For the purpose of application it will be necessary to reformulate slightly the last result using the inverse functional relationship of I and A. The problem will now be formulated as follows: try various quantities, collections and sequences of I and for each of them adjust A in the optimum way. Then A becomes a function of I, $A = \varphi(I)$, and various possible *IP*-functions will be expressed by $p = \Phi[A(I)]$. Our task is now to integrate all these functions and to find the maximum integral

$$\text{Max } \Delta P = \text{Max} \int_{0}^{Im} \Phi(I) \, dI$$

The maximum integral represents the maximum possible increase in production in a specified period of the length m. As any other combination of investment would result in a smaller addition to output, this integral provides the formula for the optimum rate of investment.

There is also a third alternative method of finding the optimum rate of investment. Define capital coefficient as $k = \dfrac{1}{p}$. Increment of output in a specified period is derived from

$$I = k \, \Delta P$$

where k is an average capital coefficient computed with respect to the period as a whole. Capital coefficient is functionally related to investment. After a certain point, further increase in investment will increase the value of k. Until the relative increase of k is less than the relative increase of I, the change is worth while, because ΔP will be expanding. The optimization rule follows directly:

$$\eta_{kI} = 1$$

i.e., investment expands until the elasticity of capital coefficient with respect to investment becomes equal to one.

2. The choice we shall have to make may be clarified by recalling our *IP*-diagram.

184

Again, as in Fig. 1, the areas under the curves represent total additions to social product in a period of so many years. All alternatives are considered with respect to the same period of time. In this period various amounts of total investment may be undertaken and, given the total amount, various combinations of successive yearly investment doses are possible. In fact, the number of conceivable variations in both

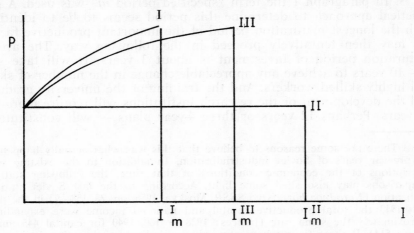

Fig. 2. The Choice of an Optimum *IP*-Function

categories is unlimited. We shall not bother about the second category of variations, and from the first we choose three representative cases. But before we proceed let us make it clear that we are not analyzing the curves themselves but the areas under the curves. In drawing the curves it is only necessary to observe the following rule: given the length m of the period under consideration and given the total amounts of alternative investments in this period, I_m^I, I_m^{II} and I_m^{III} distribute investment over time in such a way that the total potential output increment is maximized in every case. In other words, to be comparable with each other, the curves should be optimum curves with respect to the chosen total amounts of investment. Now, suppose that our curves satisfy this condition. Then their shapes become irrelevant, and in searching for an optimum optimorum the relative areas have to be compared. The three representative areas in the diagram are chosen so as to represent the following relation between respective additions to social product: $\Delta P^I < \Delta P^{II} < \Delta P^{III}$.

The first of the three *IP*-curves may be conveniently termed the "underplanned solution" (historically the capitalist case); the second one the "overplanned solution" (historically, perhaps, the Soviet case); the third one represents optimum. The first solution shows the lowest rate of growth. Capital productivity (p) is higher than in either of the remaining two solutions, but the total increment of output is lowest due to underinvestment. The second solution achieves much higher rates of growth than the first one but, because of investment, negative

185

outputs have been produced[1]. This becomes clear when alternative II is compared with alternative III where smaller total amount of investment creates larger addition to social product. The area under curve III is the largest and therefore this alternative should be chosen in formulating investment decision (granting that the sole aim of economic planning is production maximization).

3. In paragraph 1 the term "specified period m" was used. A good practical approach to determine this period seems to be to identify it with the longest maturation period of the important productive factors. We may then tentatively proceed in the following way. The average maturation period of investment is about 3 years. It will take some 4 — 10 years to achieve any appreciable change in the number of skilled and highly skilled workers. And the training of the university graduates and the development of the research institutions will require more than 10 years. Perhaps 12 years or three 4-year plans — will constitute the

---

[1] There are some reasons to believe that this was what actually happened in the pre-war years of Soviet industrialization. In addition to the existing verbal descriptions of the economic conditions of that time, the following statistical comparisons may also shed some light. According to the last Soviet statistical publication (*Narodnoe hozjajstvo SSSR*, Moskva, 1956, pp. 28, 158—9) in the period 1928—1940 the total productive capital and national income were expanding at approximately the same rate (indices: 1928 = 100, 1940 for capital 445 and for income 514). If these figures have any value as indicators, then they indicate that in the whole period of twelve years the production coefficient remained substantially unchanged (as it is assumed in the diagram above, curve II). It would seem plausible to assume that at the beginning of planning in the U.S.S.R. the production coefficient and the share of investment were not substantially higher than those at the beginning of planning in Yugoslavia. Further, according to the same source, the cumulative annual rate of expansion of total (?) investment (*kapitaljnye vloženija*) in the period 1929—1940 (no figures for 1928) was 17%. The rate of growth of gross investment (housing, etc., excluded) in Yugoslavia in our four adjusted years was 10% and the production coefficient in the next 4-year period increased from 0.2 to 0.4 (it will be recalled that p computed on the basis of new investment would be more correct). If on the basis of these data Soviet and Yugoslav IP-curves are constructed, their shapes turn out to be very similar to those of curve II and curve III in the diagram. The whole comparison is obviously very hypothetical. But it seems to suggest a possibility of an overinvestment practice in the U.S.S.R. in the first phase of industrialization.

It may also be noted that only in a situation of overinvestment, when the increments of output become negative, the popular belief that high level of investment is incompatible with high level of consumption — is a correct description of facts. Overinvestment cuts consumption at both ends: the total product is smaller than it otherwise would be, and in this smaller product the share of investment is greater than necessary. This might help to explain another feature of the Soviet economic development, namely the relatively slow expansion of personal consumption, which hasty critics of the system identified with *every* planning for rapid growth. The explanation becomes particularly plausible when we recall that the already diminished total volume of consumption was further diminished by relatively heavy defence expenditures and large communal consumption in general, so that not much was left for personal consumption. Consider the Yugoslav example again. Instead of doubling production coefficient it could (hypothetically) have been kept constant and the amount of investment could have been doubled (increasing its share to more than 40% of *GSP*). In this hypothetical case, all additional investment would have meant equal loss of consumption without any gain in the higher rate of growth.

planners' horizon[1]. Then within this period the expansion of A and I will have to be adjusted in an optimum way.

The maximization over the whole period may mean that there will be no maximum at any of the three sub-periods. The productive factors are always flexible to a certain degree. The students may be sent to factories instead of to the universities and the output of the current year will be increased. Or we may plan the development of an industry with short maturation period but with bad production coefficient; the output in the sub-period will again be increased. Therefore, optimum and maximum in the sub-periods have to be carefully distinguished.

4. This also calls for a careful handling of the concept of marginal productivity of investment *(mpi)*. To achieve maximum output *mpi* has to be made zero. But in any sub-period and for any *individual* business *mpi* may be greater than zero. That explains the secret of the positive rate of interest in a situation of a zero or negative *mpi*. We may here resume the argument of Chapter 4-c.

The allocation interest rate is the price for the scarce factor of production called capital, when capital is being distributed among alternative uses. But this interest rate has nothing to do with the marginal productivity of the *social* capital (entire capital treated as a whole). If investment is pushed beyond the frontier of A, the additional factory, being a modern one, may very well earn substantial profit. But at the same time the process described by the curve II in Fig. 2 will take place: external diseconomies *with respect to the economy as a whole* will outweigh the positive contribution of the *additional factory*. Additional investment simply reduces the general efficiency of the economy and, for that matter, of the capital employed. This is a reduction in total, and not only in marginal product; of the absolute amount, and not only of the last unit of investment as compared to the last but one. The distinction is similar — but not more than similar — to that between marginal product and marginal revenue in the theory of the firm: marginal value product may be greater than marginal cost, and still the firm will experience a decrease in profits because marginal revenue is less than marginal cost. Long before an additional factory is earning zero returns additional investment will cease to be productive. Thus one may conceivably speak of two *mpi* (determining two interest rates): one with respect to the last unit only, and another with respect to the economy as a whole. The latter determines the optimum rate of investment. In this respect the empirical *p*-curves should also be handled with caution. Reconsider our diagram.

---

[1] In fact, planners' horizon can be determined quite exactly (theoretically). The principle is essentially the same as in engineering design. The economic mechanism is not an absolutely precise machine; on the contrary, the adjustment tolerance of its cogs is quite considerable. On the other hand, additional gains in the precision of planning are rapidly decreasing with the extension of the horizon. The point where these "precision gains" become equal to the existing "tolerance margins" of the economy, represents the limit of the desirable length of the planning period. It should be borne in mind that a long-period plan is not at all absolutely binding. Every year, the horizon is extended for another year and the plan will be adjusted to new circumstances.

187

5. In every successive investment period the amount invested may increase, increasing at the same time the value of p (see Fig. 1). As p is rising throughout the period, one is tempted to say that marginal productivity of investment is rising. But taking the period as a whole, the optimum IP-curve may lie below or above the actual curve (see Fig. 2). If the actual curve lies above the optimum curve (curve I) marginal p is positive, and all potentialities of the system have not been exhausted. If it lies below (curve II) then, although marginal $p = 0$, the true value of mpi is negative; overinvestment has occurred. An analytically meaningful definition of mpi will then read as follows: the marginal productivity of investment represents the (positive or negative) change of (actual or potential) total increment of output caused by an additional unit of investment anywhere in the maximization period. In other words, mpi has meaning only with respect to the whole maximization period.

It should also be noted that the concept of mpi is used here in its gross formulation; rewards for no factors have been deducted. Thus $mpi = \dfrac{dAP}{dI}$; it is a change of physical output per unit of additional investment. This is the consequence of our basic assumption that the absorptive capacity of an economy is measurable by the volume of the total increment of physical output which the economy is capable of achieving in a specified period. In this framework there is no practical need for a net concept, as the following considerations will show.

Assume that relevant functions change monotonously. Assume also that we have to choose between two programs, one of which yields greater total output while the other produces greater absolute amount of consumption goods (investment is assumed to be always most efficiently adapted to the purpose at hand). At first sight the second program is preferable. But in fact the second program is not likely to be possible in the world as we know it. The absorptive capacity of the economy being a function of total product, the difference between A_1 and A_2 — as corresponding to the first and the second program — will increase exponentially and it seems always possible to point to a moment of time when A_1-program will produce both greater total output and more consumption goods. This would be impossible only if all extra-output of A_1-program were absorbed by extra investment (i.e., $P_1 - P_2 = I_1 - I_2$) leaving nothing for extra consumption. But in this case, with the passage of time, the share of investment in output could be increased to any percentage short of 100%. That would involve either an extraordinary increase in capital coefficient or a spectacular increase in the rate of growth, neither of which seems likely. We may conclude by saying that as long as capital coefficient, compatible with productive investment, and the attainable rate of growth remain within relatively close limits, the choice of maximizing production involves the maximum rate of growth of consumption as well.

188

(d) The Nature of Period Maximization

1. There is a difficulty, already touched upon, in the procedure of period maximization. Because of the interdependence of the factors and the time lags the maximization has to be carried out with respect to infinity. There is logically no possibility of confining it to a single period. We may, for instance, plan the output of university graduates today for the beginning of the twelfth year. But what about all the intervening years? If, say, in the eleventh year we again reduce the expenditures on the university training (and send students to factories)[1], the output of the first twelve years may be overmaximized, but it will certainly not be maximized in the course of the next twelve-year period and in the course of the two periods combined.

It must be possible to design a rule which will prevent overmaximization of the kind just described. One can proceed in the following way. First, construct *IP*-curve on the strict maximization principle. Estimate the difference of the potential future productivity of factors when expanded further as compared with the state in the first *IP*-curve. If the resulting loss of output in the current maximization period is less than the next period's increment due to present readjustment, the change is worth making. Now, it is obvious that the productivity in the next period cannot be estimated with precision. To achieve a precise estimation one would have to draw the *IP*-curve for the next period as well, and to do this draw one more *IP*-curve for another period ahead, and so forth *ad infinitum*. As we cannot predict infinity, we have apparently encountered an unsurmountable difficulty.

2. Yet, is this difficulty really different from that inherent in any prediction? Can we say we *know* what is going to happen tomorrow, or even next hour? — As soon as we leave the static world, we are in the world of approximations, all differences in precision are only differences in degree. We choose the length of our maximization period not because we pretend to *know* the pertaining *IP*-curve, but because the procedure is operationally simpler and yields better *approximations* than if we deal with a much shorter or with a much longer period. In the same way we do not *know* the *IP*-curve of the next period, but we have some elements to estimate the *approximate* productivity of factors which are of interest for us. The further we go into the future the less certain our approximations are — but also the less relevant for our present position.

The difficulty encountered is, therefore, not peculiar to this particular approach. It is the "aporia" of the real world, and may be escaped only in a static world with no changes. And if we prefer not to follow the recipe of the ancient Eleatic philosophers and eliminate movement as logically wrong — we are left to accept things as they are and to conceive planning as an infinite process of gradual approxi-

---

[1] This, naturally, does not imply regimentation, but refers to those marginal changes which may be achieved by material stimulation or destimulation or, in this case, by changing the standards of admission. Besides, these changes — being marginal — are probably practically not very important, and the whole problem is much more a problem of theoretical principles than of practical application.

mation. The task of the economist is to design methods which will increase the degree of approximation in a dynamic world — not to remove change from it.

10. THE OPTIMUM RATE OF SAVING

(a) The Evaluation of Present Sacrifices

1. So far we have been discussing the maximization of production rather theoretically and without any reference to consumption. But — as it is often said and may well be said once again — it is hardly a practicable proposition to push investment so far as to make $mpi = 0$. This would imply an exceptionally great increase of investment, which then involves considerations of present sacrifices of consumption. If it were for only one or two per cent of social product to be added annually to already existing investment funds, the whole thing might have practical value. Otherwise, who can make consumers agree to refrain from consumption for the sake of future generations?

Here we may pause for a moment. It is exactly those one or two per cent which are needed. To demonstrate this, a simple model will be constructed. The model will be as crude as it is simple, but it will give us an idea of the order of values, and this is all we need.

2. Suppose there is a regularly growing economy with the share of gross investment in social product $s = 15\%$, gross capital coefficient

$$k = \frac{G_t}{\Delta P_{t+1}} = 3 \text{ and, consequently, with the rate of growth } r = 5\% \text{ per}$$

annum. Suppose next that each year one and two per cent respectively are added to investment fund causing the following year an additional increase in output and increasing thus continuously the rate of growth of output; k is supposed to remain unaffected by these changes. On these assumptions output and consumption will be changing in the following way:

Year	Pattern I			Pattern II			Pattern III		
	Output	s in %	Consumption	Output	s in %	Consumption	Output	s in %	Consumption
0	100	15	85	100	15	85	100	15	85
1	105	15	89	105	16	88	105	17	87
2	110	15	94	111	17	92	111	19	90
3	116	15	98	117	18	96	118	21	93
4	122	15	103	124	19	100	126	23	97
5	128	15	108	132	20	105	136	25	102
6	134	15	114	140	21	111	147	27	108
7	141	15	120	150	22	117	161	29	114
8	148	15	126	161	23	124	176	31	121
9	155	15	132	173	24	132	194	33	130
10	162	15	138	187	25	140	216	35	140

Increase in investment has not reduced the *absolute* amount of consumption. But in the first year the change in investment policy *relatively* reduces consumption. Since then the rate of growth of consumption is constantly increasing. It will take 9 and 10 years respectively to surpass the level of consumption of the original pattern of growth. The result is not substantially altered if the share of investment or the capital coefficient are changed (see Appendix).

The figures and the implications of the model call for a brief explanation. No empirical studies from which we could take empirical values for k corresponding to the conditions stated are available. Nevertheless, we know something. We know that Patterns I and II are likely to produce gross capital coefficients lower than 3, in which case the differences between the two patterns are somewhat overestimated in the table. Next, A is not likely to be expanded by exactly one or two per cent every year until suddenly after the tenth year the absolute limit is reached. Instead — assuming that we start with full capacity utilization, which is also not necessarily the case — the successive increases in the share of investment are likely to occur at a diminishing rate. The effect is that the highest annual differences between II and III as compared with I will be reduced. Further, the foregoing analysis has shown that capital coefficient is an increasing function of the rate of investment. But we have no detailed information about the shape of this function. It seems plausible to assume that productivity of new investment is fairly constant for various shares of investment and that it drops sharply in the vicinity of the point of "full capacity" operation, i.e., when the limit of A is reached. In this case the average values of k in various situations will not be very different. However, whether great or small the capital coefficients of Patterns II and III must be higher than that of I. This effect has been taken into account — although I do not know how adequately — by assuming constant *gross* capital coefficient. From the discussion in Part IV it is clear that by speeding up the rate of growth, while *productivity of fixed capital is kept constant*, we must decrease gross capital coefficient. And conversely, keeping gross capital coefficient constant, implies that "technological" capital coefficient (based on new investment, $k = \dfrac{G-R}{\Delta P}$) is declining.

Theoretically it is possible that in a rapidly expanding economy gross capital coefficient is lower than in a slowly growing economy, but I do not know whether this is empirically feasible. Our model implies that by the end of the period the average productivity of investment in Patterns II and III decreases by about 9 and 13 per cent respectively (see Appendix).

After all these influences in one direction or another are considered, the numerical example above appears to be sufficiently realistic — as far as the present state of knowledge allows realistic examples of this kind — to permit some conclusions.

2. The differences in the consumption during the whole period are relatively small; the greatest, in the middle of the period, is of the rank of 6%, which indicates the lag of only one year. The crop fluctuations

in underdeveloped countries, the industrial fluctuations in developed countries, and the unproductive expenditures of government such as defence, not to speak of war expenditures, in both of them, are all in excess — frequently far in excess — of this difference. Bearing this in mind, it is realistic to expect that if a nation is asked to accept a program which envisages that a certain level of consumption will be achieved in the fifth instead in the fourth year, with all the good consequences afterwards — it will wholeheartedly accept this program. By accepting this program we shall push the economy on the path of maximum rate of growth. For, this program implies an annual increase of investment at the rate between 12% (Pattern II) and 18% (Pattern III), and exactly in this range the maximum rate of expansion of A is likely to lie, as demonstrated by the Soviet and Yugoslav economies which, as the empirical evidence appears to suggest, occasionally even overshot the mark of productive investment[1].

The general result of the analysis so far consists, then, in the conclusion that the production maximization is not only a theoretically determined but also a practicable proposition. The final question to be answered is: where maximization of production is likely to lead and what are its theoretical implications?

(b) "Underdeveloped" and "Developed" Economies

1. The maximization discussion has hitherto implied the case of an underdeveloped economy. This assumption has now to be stated explicitly by defining the underdeveloped economy as one where the share of investment is less than optimum and/or the level of A-factors is low (as compared with already achieved standards in other countries). In this sense all existing economies are underdeveloped. And this will not be surprising if one takes into account the transitional state of today's world economy.

As the economy expands, the level of A-factors will rise, and this will change their productive functions. Once poverty economics is left behind, and people are well fed, have reasonable leisure time and enjoy a healthy life, factors C and H lose their place in IP-function. They are no longer productive agents but only ends in themselves.

Further, it seems reasonable to assume that, after a while, every socio-economic system in its development reaches a stage of relative stability and that this applies to the planned economy as well. At this stage economic and political organization will be more or less stabilized,

---

[1] The Soviet case was already discussed in an earlier note. The Yugoslav case refers to the period of the first Five Year Plan when, with the then given state of A factors, as some case studies suggest, an investment program, too large to be productively absorbed, was carried out. Gross investment (housing, etc., excluded) in the period 1947—1952 was expanding at the rate of 15% per annum. The share of gross investment in gross product reached already in 1951—52 the mark of 30%, and since then this share has not been achieved again. The productivity of labour and capital was low, even declining. Since the end of the first F.Y.P. (1952) the tempo of investment has been gradually slowed down, and the rate of growth of output has increased.

all major potential innovations in this sphere exhausted, and the system will perpetuate itself almost automatically. Thus factor O may be dropped out too.

In this way A will be reduced to Kn, which remains the only limitational factor of growth. The "intellectual capacity" of a community will provide unsurpassable limits to the productive application of investment and so to the speed of expansion of its economy.

2. The last statement may cause some difficulties. For, it is obvious that potential knowledge is unlimited and that, therefore, expenditures on research, however large, must be productive. Therefore Kn expenditures would absorb the whole social product, and thus the criterion for the distribution breaks down.

However, this is not so. The ultimate result must not be confused with the speed of change. Skill and knowledge will always be increasing, but the physiological substratum and social habits pose quite definite limits to the *speed* of the change. Besides, the increase in knowledge in which we are interested increases production and the increase in production requires continual readaptation of the whole social structure. This may not be evident in a slowly expanding economy. Yet, suppose that the rate of growth is 10 %. Then in a generation of two 12-year periods output would increase 10 times. Our children would have to manipulate 100 times greater output and our grandchildren, a 1,000 times greater output. An underdeveloped and poor country of today would after only 70 years manipulate an annual social income of some $ 100,000 *per head of population* — do not these figures sound startling? Obviously, there is a physical limit to the rate of expansion to which society is able to adapt itself.

3. The process of development may be advantageously described diagrammatically in the following way:

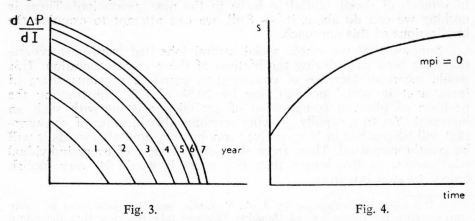

Fig. 3.   Fig. 4.

The Transition from a Low- to a High-Investment Economy

The left-hand diagram indicates the increase of the share of productive investment in every successive year (denoted as years 1 to 7). The continual increase of s pushes *mpi*-curve every year to the right. These impulses tend to decrease. If then all *mpi*=0 points are plotted on an s-time diagram, the resulting curve will increase at a diminishing rate (Fig. 4). The rapidly growing first section of the curve (which may also have an S-shaped beginning) shows the transition from a low-investment and unplanned economy to a high-investment and planned economy. After all economies of adjustment of I and various A-factors are exhausted and Kn is left as the only source of the further expansion of A, the slope of the s-curve will tend to flatten. As s can never reach 100 % the further rise of s-curve can proceed only at a decreasing rate, i.e., the curve will approach assymptotically a fixed limit at infinity. In this second stage, after the new level of a high-investment economy has been reached, the share of investment may for all practical purposes be taken as constant.

Here we reach the point where welfare considerations may be profitably introduced into the discussion.

(c) Production Maximization and the Conventional Welfare Theory

In the preceding sections we were concerned with the factual analysis. To complete our theoretical picture, we have to evaluate the factual results in terms of welfare economics. The obvious question is whether there is any necessity that the optimal rate of saving be equal to the optimum rate of investment? Let us first clear up one elementary misconception about the nature of the economic process.

1. It is frequently argued that the absolute limit to maximization of economic welfare is reached when the whole social capital is used during this generation's lifetime and nothing is left for the next generation· It is said that there exist no economic criterion for judging how much of social capital to leave to the next generation[1]. There is nothing we can do about it. — Still, we can attempt to examine the implications of this approach.

Suppose that the whole social capital inherited from past generations has been used during the lifetime of the present generation. This would mean an increase of consumption equal to previous share of investment in social product, say by 20 % of *GSP* (abstracting the problem of physical composition of capital consistent with such an increase). Yet in a rapidly growing economy this increase of consumption will be reached in four or five years anyway, and afterwards it will be greatly surpassed. Thus, from the point of view of every individual who expects to live longer than five years it would be very foolish indeed to stop investing.

---

[1] The following statement by J. de V. Graaff may be considered as fairly representative for this school of thought: "We can take the view that the group demarcated by the horizon really is (in a very strict sense) the only one in whose welfare we are interested. Then it is reasonable to suppose that terminal capital equipment (equipment left over when the horizon is attained) will be zero. Maximization of the welfare of a group over a given period of time implies, in strictness, utter exhaustion of all physical capital by the end of that period" (4, 97). And also: "If we decide to exhaust physical capital by the turn of the century, the optimum rate of investment over the intervening years may well be zero; if we plan to leave posterity well provided for, it may be very great" (4, 101).

Next, the question of how much capital to leave to the next generation does not arise at all. With every new-born baby the horizon of the "present" generation is shifted forwards and this shifting goes on *ad infinitum*. Clearly, we have to formulate our basic question somewhat more meaningfully.

2. Suppose that we wish to maximize consumption within our lifetime. This is the most general assumption we can make (apart from tautological statements that we choose what we prefer). The lives of all members of a community represent the life of a generation. "Generation" may be defined in several ways. For our purpose it seems most appropriate to define a generation as the community of individuals alive at a certain moment of time and its life span, as a time interval at the end of which at least one half of individuals now alive will still be living. In this way every individual gets "one vote" in making saving decisions. If then, for instance, the life expectancy at birth is 60 years and the population is stationary, the life span of a generation will be 30 years. In developed countries it will be longer because life expectancy is higher and population is generally growing. In the backward countries it may be somewhat shorter, because, although the population is increasing fast the life expectancy is low, frequently below 40 years. Perhaps we may take 30 years as our standard. Next, let us see what are the implications of the maximization of production decision in terms of the conventional welfare theory.

3. It may be argued that the decision to push the economy into the part of maximum growth is a once-for-all decision, and that therefore generalizations about it, in the traditional manner, do not have much sense. Probably nearest to common sense would be to ask the referendum-question as it was formulated in Section a-2. But even such a question is still much too formal to have a real value for the economic theory and policy. This is so because the affirmative answer implies not simply a choice with respect to economic welfare but also a choice with respect to different socio-economic institutions; to achieve maximum growth the economy must be planned. However, once this basic decision has been made and the economy starts moving along the path of maximum growth — and this has been our assumption — formal generalizations about economic choices have sense and shed a new light on the traditional welfare theory.

The choice we face in such an economy is formally the same as before: either to invest more or to invest less as compared with the original investment pattern. The first alternative is dismissed at once because it leads to negative increments in product, with a consequence that everybody loses and nobody gains. The second alternative implies that *IP*-function has been shifted to maximize consumption in a particular sub-period. In this case some individuals would gain at the expense of others and, possibly, at the expense of their own future consumption. In physical terms this gain is always incomparably smaller than the resulting loss, because the gain, being temporary, is finite, and the loss, being permanent and, moreover, expanding, is infinite. The problem is a little more complex in utility terms.

Traditional approach would imply that saving has to be pushed to the point where marginal disutility of saving becomes equal to marginal utility of investment. In an economy on the maximum growth path marginal productivity of investment *(mpi)* is zero. With $mpi = 0$ marginal utility of investment *(mu)* is zero too. If this is so, marginal disutility of saving *(md)* must also be zero at this point. If it were positive, it would be necessary to reduce investment to make $mpi = 0$ and $mu = md$. This conclusion applies to every moment of time. Hence it would never be possible to achieve maximum rate of growth. But this would contradict our starting assumption.

Thus the first choice of maximum growth implies that marginal disutility of saving is zero. If in a growing economy $md = 0$ at one time, it must be zero forever, because increasing consumption implies decreasing marginal disutility of saving and, by definition, *md* cannot diminish below zero (and even if it could, this would not change the final conclusion). Therefore, if maximum growth alternative is chosen once, it will be chosen ever more. Every other policy would be inconsistent.

4. Two further important implications should be noted. First, in a situation of maximum growth, traditional utility considerations become irrelevant. And, second, once the first choice of optimum *IP* is made, traditional utility logic becomes invalid: disutility of saving does not change (continuously) with the welfare of the community and therefore $md = 0$ and cannot decrease with increasing consumption. These results, being a mere logic, are perfectly general. If in some countries — for some *historical* reasons or others — the decisive first choice has not yet been made, this cannot change the *logical* structure of the set of concepts used. It suffices to accept that the initial decisive choice as feasible and all consequences follow at once as generally valid. Contrary to traditional assumptions, marginal disutility of saving is *not always* positive and is *not always* decreasing with increasing consumption. If there is no regularity no *a priori* theory can be built up and all statements become tautologies: the choice has been made because it has been preferred. If there is a regularity, then $md = 0$ is a universal characteristic of utility function, and as such renders utility considerations irrelevant. In fact, what appears to be wrong is not the concept of utility as such but the mode of its marginalist application in the field of macroeconomic investment choices.

5. Now, there is no need to assume production maximization to render traditional welfare considerations irrelevant. It suffices to assume that every individual wishes to maximize consumption within his lifetime which means, given the one-man-one-vote assumption, that the population wishes to maximize consumption within one generation's lifetime. We again encounter the same difficulties. The maximum output of consumer goods within, say, thirty years, is completely determined by the technological features of the respective economies. Thus an independently determined function of the marginal disutility of saving may prove to be inconsistent and is in any case irrelevant.

(d) A Macroeconomic Welfare Theory

1. Judging by the logic of the conventional welfare theory, our goal of maximizing consumption within one's lifetime would appear to be irrational. As there is evidently nothing irrational about the goal as such, we are bound to conclude that the apparently queer results we get are due to an inadequate axiomatic system. If a revision is to be made, at least three possibilities are open to us to show that the choice of maximum consumption (production) will or should — the difference will be made clear in a moment — be made.

We may, first, embark upon a sociological argument. If the analysis in Chapter 5 is correct, only those social systems which achieve relatively high rates of economic expansion are likely to survive. Thus, it is the societies which have maximized the rate of economic expansion that are going to dominate the future world scene.

However, this argument, although logically valid, will not sound convincing for everybody. It requires agreement about the original sociological propositions. And, also, it applies to a very long long-run.

2. The second approach is based on an empirical generalization and the answer it yields is, I think, decisive. We observe the characteristics of the world in which we live and find that the maximum possible rate of growth is achieved when investment expands at an annual rate between 10 and 20 per cent. We next compare the difference it makes when from the traditional pattern of growth — say a constant rate of growth, no matter whether high or low — we pass over to the path of maximum growth. If our numerical example can be taken to indicate the order of magnitudes, the adverse influence on consumption in the early years of transition appears to be relatively small. The total negative difference of Pattern II in the first nine years amounts to 19. This loss has to be weighed against a gain of 2,400 in the following twenty one years, assuming that the average life span of a generation is 30 years, that the rate of gross saving is eventually stabilized at 25 % and gross capital coefficient remains constant. (On similar assumptions, Pattern III yields negative difference of 40 in the first ten years to be set against positive difference of 6,000 in the subsequent 20 years.)[1] Now, there is no logical necessity that 19 of the first nine years be exchanged for 2,400 of the following twenty one years. It may be argued that smaller income in the first period makes 19 in utility terms larger than 2,400 added to higher income in the second period. But in the present world such a value calculus is extremely unlikely, and we may be virtually certain that exchange will take place.

At this point it is possible to give the following formulation to our theoretical hypothesis. The characteristics of the economic process are such that the ceiling of productive investment is reached relatively

---

[1] The same choice may be expressed in yet another way. If non-induced increase in labour efficiency can be taken to be relatively small — witness: pre-capitalist development — the rate of interest which ought to govern the saving decisions of the community as a whole is approximately equal to the inverse value of capital coefficient. In other words, the rate of interest is 30—40—50 per cent (referring to that section of investment curve where capital coefficient remains approximately constant).

quickly. They are also such as to render community's time preference — whatever the reasons for its existence — smaller than necessary to equalize saving with the optimum rate of investment. In other words, the willingness to save is potentially greater than the rate of productive investment. Thus the rate of saving will be governed by the rate of investment which renders the optimum rate of saving identical with the optimum rate of investment. It is not *logically* necessary for this to happen. And it is obvious why. We deal with two separate systems. The *objective* characteristics of the world are such that there is a limit to productive investment. The *subjective* valuations of the community in question may conceivably be such as to set a different limit for saving. If saving limit is lower, there will be a discrepancy between the optimum rate of saving and optimum rate of investment; if it is higher — and this is my thesis — the two must be equal in a rationally organized world. It follows that the postulated identity is more than a welfare economics truism; it is a falsifiable, i.e. *theoretical*, proposition about some actual properties of the real world. If by observing the actual planned economies — such as Polish, Yugoslav, Indian and the like — we find that they are invariably, or at least generally, navigated along the maximization path, we may accept the proposition as true. If observations fail to confirm our theoretical result, the theory must be discarded as false and we shall have to think of something better instead.

3. With the knowledge derived from paragraph 2 we may proceed to consider the third, formal, approach with clear conscience. Similarly as in the case of stationary economy (Ch. 4-b-5) an axiomatic system can be postulated from which the maximization of production choice follows as a logical necessity. We must first get rid of pure time preference. This is a relatively easy job because there is a quite general agreement that pure time preference is "irrational". In the words of Professor Meade, "in 1950 Mr. Smith may prefer enjoyment in 1950 to enjoyment in 1951, although Mr. Smith in 1951 is equally certain to prefer enjoyment in 1951 to enjoyment in 1950" (7, 100). Thus pure time preference ends in inconsistency.

We must next come to grips with the "rational" part of the time preference which arises from the fact that in a growing economy community is becoming richer. The reasoning runs as follows: investment means sacrifice a part of present consumption — when income is low — for larger consumption in the future — when income will be higher. As the marginal utility of lower income is higher than the marginal utility of higher income, there is no way of finding out, on *a priori* grounds, whether a particular investment satisfies utility equation or not. The crucial element of the argument is that lower income has higher marginal utility. In this connection we must ask the question: how is the relevant income to be determined? Is it the income we earn the day when we make investment decision, or is it the income of the corresponding month, or year, or perhaps all previous income we have earned in our life? Clearly, any time period we postulate as relevant will be equally arbitrary. There is something wrong with the logic of the argument. The argument would seem to be a specimen of an uncritical rationalization of the institutions of a particular social system. In this — atomistic — system the individuals are observed to buy bonds and shares. They are also observed not to spend all income on buying securities. With this knowledge at his disposal, the simple-minded economic theorist sits down and works out the eternal rules for rational behaviour. But there is no need that these rules be binding in a different social system, in this case — in a planned economy·

It seems plausible to assume that human beings do not live their lives every day afresh — granting that basic biological needs are satisfied — and even less do they exercise such a continual resurrection annually. Human life is a unique whole which cannot be divided. Since the birth until the death we gradually accumulate knowledge, experience, pleasant and unpleasant memories. The time distribution of this "accumulation" is, *as such*, irrelevant. What matters is the sphere of free choice, i.e., the possibility open to the acting individual to assert himself in his conscious life and it is rational to choose a situation in which the boundaries of free choice are widened. Consider two individuals living on different curves of "life accumulation"; suppose the curves correspond to our Pattern I and II and "life accumulation" is represented by the accumulation of consumption. It follows that everything Individual I does Individual II can do — even better. At first there will be a certain time lag in achieving equal-possibility levels, but if the life as a whole is taken into account, Individual II has a clear advantage. Thus, what matters is the *total* amount of consumption and our growing-economy consumer becomes a general type, of which Schumpeterian stationary-state consumer is a particular case.

Before completing the argument, two potential misunderstandings must be cleared away. What if the "optimum" distribution of consumption involves starvation in the early stages? This eventuality is rendered impossible by the properties of our optimum *IP*-function. Starvation would mean lowering of A and thus, by definition departure from the maximization path. Secondly, we have treated our representative consumer as if he has the same needs in all stages of his life. This treatment was justified because the consumer in question represented the *generation*. Actual consumers, of course, need not be indifferent to the time distribution of their consumption, and still escape the charge of irrationality. The consumption rate of interest seems to be the appropriate device for handling this case (see Ch. 4-d).

Our next step is to postulate that in shaping community's saving policy, every individual, alive at the time when the saving decision is made, has "one vote"; thus the benefits of the majority are considered to be benefits of the community as a whole. In other words, the welfare of the community is assumed to be a function of the welfare of the majority of its members. This is a somewhat crude assumption, but it is not unrealistic, and it is not less realistic than the usual assumptions of that kind. If the assumption is accepted, we can derive the following theorem. Maximization of welfare of *every* generation means maximization of the total volume of consumption in the lifetime of *any* generation consistent with the similar maximization of *any other* generation. Any other policy would lead to diminution of welfare for the generation which undertakes to make the respective saving decision. The characteristics of the world are such that we cannot generalize this conclusion for every single member of the community (unless it pleases us to assume that the referendum in section c-5 has produced unanimous agreement and that the tastes in this respect do not change). But neither is this absolutely necessary. Once we have agreed that investment (saving) decision is inevitably a social decision, it is only necessary to know how it affects the economic welfare of the community as composed of individual members at the time when decision is made. And bearing in mind that, according to our definition, every new-born baby initiates a new generation, the theorem really tells us all we need.

4. The theorem tells us all we need for the purpose of the practical policy. Because, if we take into account the uncertainty range at the end of the planning period, long as a generation's lifetime, and if we assume that after a certain point the *mpi*-curve is rapidly falling, the theorem implies that investment should be increased to the point where *mpi* becomes practically equal to zero (exactly equal to zero would mean a reduction of consumption equal to the amount of investment which will not be reproduced during the lifetime of the present generation).

However, *practically equal to zero* is still different from *necessarily equal to zero*. Does this indicate a flaw in our argument? I believe not. As usually, the solution of the problem is to be sought in the empirical characteristics of the economy we are about to plan. If after a certain point *mpi* decreases rather rapidly, a few additional units of investment will bring it down to zero. On the other hand, the experience in planning indicates that with the extension of the planning horizon beyond 15 — 20 years — in our case even more than 30 years would be needed — the uncertainty increases to such a degree that today's forecasts may be considered adequate only within very wide margins of error. These margins are considerably wider than the difference between the output maximization and the consumption maximization policies. Consequently, *it is technically impossible to distinguish between these two goals*, and therefore, *whichever of the two we choose, our present-day decision remains the same*. Being *operationally impossible*, the juxtaposition of consumption and production maximization policies as two *different* policies, becomes *theoretically meaningless*.

This completes the construction of a new axiomatic system which should rationalize the experience of planned economies more adequately than the axiomatic system which underlies the traditional welfare theory and which represents a rationalization of the experience of an individualist society. The theorem of the preceding paragraph may now be replaced by the following theorem: Given the assumptions about the properties of the economic system it is rational to maximize production.

5. At the end it will be useful to sum up the findings about the empirical basis of our welfare constructs. The principle of output maximization has provided a key for a determinate and practicable solution of the problem of optimum investment and has also provided a basis for an operationally meaningful welfare maximization in a rationally planned economy. As the economy expands, the basic investment decision will soon be reduced to the adjustment of investment to the human

capacity to produce inventions and innovations. This will determine the physical upper limit for the rate of growth and will probably cause a relative stabilization of the share of investment. Judging from the experience so far, this stabilization for the forseeable future may be expected to occur at around 30 per cent (possibly more) of productive investment in social product, which will sustain a rate of growth of output of 10 per cent or more per annum[1]. Thus, doubling or trebling the rate of increase of the population's well-being is what we may expect from the planned economy as compared with the economies we are familiar with. This will mean the exhaustion of the purely economic possibilities of growth and as such represents the limit to which the economist has to say on this subject.

Appendix

MATHEMATICAL CHARACTERISTICS OF THE MODEL

1. Denote gross capital coefficient, i.e., the ratio between gross investment last year and the resulting increment in output in the current year as k, gross investment as G, consumption as C, output as P, rate of growth of gross investment as r, rate of growth of consumption as p, and the share of gross investment in output as s. Gross investment in two successive years is given by

$$G_{t-1} = s_{t-1} P_{t-1}$$

$$G_t = s_t P_{t-1}\left(1 + \frac{s_{t-1}}{k}\right)$$

and the rate of growth in any t year by

$$r_t = \frac{G_t}{G_{t-1}} - 1 = \frac{s_t}{s_{t-1}} + \frac{s_t}{k} - 1 \tag{1}$$

---

[1] It may be worth noting how the naïve though widespread belief, that the rate of growth is bound to decline in a mature economy, proved to be wrong, as the economic history of at least one country, the U.S.S.R., has demonstrated. In the period of the last 85 years, the Soviet economy has experienced the following sequence of the rates of growth of national income: 1870—1900, 3½%; 1885—1913, 4½%; 1928—1937, 7%; 1948—1955, 9%; (14, 101). Similar trends are observable in the Yugoslav economy where the rates of growth for the subsequent periods are as follows: 1926—1939, 2.14%; 1947—1956, 4.85% (15, 358); 1957—1961 (Plan), 9.1%. The post-war Japanese and German economies have displayed high rates of growth. In the last 18 years the American economy is expanding at a rate far higher than the past 80-year average.

If the theory developed in the text is correct, a decreasing *rise* in the rate of growth, and not diminution of the rate of growth itself, is what we may expect in a developed economy. All this, obviously, on the assumption of no obstacles on the part of the institutional set-up. A separate problem arises from the use of "borrowed technology" in the early stage of economic development. Once foreign credit in technological knowledge is basically exhausted, this may depressively influence the rate of growth. However, no such phenomenon seems observable in the Soviet case.

If every year 1 and 2% respectively are added to s, (1) will be expressed by the two respective formulae

$$r_t = \frac{0.01}{s_{t-1}} + \frac{s_t}{k} \qquad (1.1)$$

$$r_t = \frac{0.02}{s_{t-1}} + \frac{s_t}{k} \qquad (1.2)$$

It is evident that the rate of growth of gross investment changes over time. It will be declining when the following inequality holds good

$$\frac{1}{s_{t-1}} - \frac{1}{s_t} > \frac{1}{k} \qquad (2)$$

The inequality holds good up to $s = 17\%$ for 1% additions and up to $s = 24\%$ for 2% additions ($k = 3$). The deviations from an average rate of growth are relatively small within the time interval considered.

2. Similarly, consumption in two successive years will be given by

$$C_{t-1} = P_{t-1}(1 - s_{t-1})$$

$$C_t = P_{t-1}\left(1 + \frac{s_{t-1}}{k}\right) - s_t\, P_{t-1}\left(1 + \frac{s_{t-1}}{k}\right)$$

Therefore

$$\rho_t = \frac{C_t}{C_{t-1}} - 1 = \frac{(1-s_t)\,(k+s_{t-1})}{k\,(1-s_{t-1})} - 1 \qquad (3)$$

The *volume* of consumption will normally be increasing. The condition for this is that the increment of product is not exhausted by the increment of gross investment

$$\Delta P_t > \Delta G_t$$

$$\Delta P_t = \frac{s_{t-1}}{k} P_{t-1}$$

$$\Delta G_t = s_t\, P_{t-1}\left(1 + \frac{s_{t-1}}{k}\right) - s_{t-1}\, P_{t-1}$$

$$s_{t-1}\,(1 - s_t + k) > s_t\, k \qquad (4)$$

If annual addition to s is respectively 1 and 2%, (4) may be expressed as

$$s_{t-1}\,(0.99 - s_{t-1}) > 0.01\, k \qquad (4.1)$$

$$s_{t-1}\,(0.98 - s_{t-1}) > 0.02\, k \qquad (4.2)$$

or, as an approximation

$$100\, s_{t-1} > k \qquad (4.1.1)$$

$$100\, s_{t-1} > 2\, k \qquad (4.2.1)$$

202

This means that, if $k = 3$, the starting share of investment must be greater than 3% in the first case and greater than 6% in the second case in order to prevent consumption falling absolutely in the next year.

The *rate of growth* of consumption is constantly increasing for all feasible values of s and k, as may be found by putting $\rho_{t+1} > \rho_t$.

3. The realistic changes in the assumptions of the model will only slightly change the results described in the text. Thus the smaller the value of capital coefficient k, the greater, *ceteris paribus*, both rates of growth. Further, the smaller k, the smaller the original share of gross investment and the smaller annual additions to it — the sooner the level of consumption of the steady growth Pattern I will be reached. If k decreases from 3 to 2, or if the starting share of gross investment is $s = 9$% instead of $s = 15$%, or if annual additions to investment are 1% instead of 2%, the level of the consumption of Pattern I will be reached one to two years earlier.

4. Finally, consider the changes of the "technological" capital coefficient k on the assumption that the gross capital coefficient k remains constant. If investment maturation period is assumed to be one year and the scrapping of assets is done at the end of the year, technological capital coefficient (see Appendix I-3 to Part IV) is defined as the ratio of new investment made last year to increment in output in the current year,

$$k = \frac{G_{t-1} - R_{t-1}}{\Delta P_t} \tag{5}$$

where R stands for replacement.

In a regularly growing economy with no price and technology changes, replacement is equal to gross investment made n years earlier,

$$R_t = G_t (1+r)^{-n} \tag{6}$$

where n stands for the length of the service life of fixed assets.

In our model Pattern I describes the history of the economy, which is characterized by $r = 5$% and $k = 3$. Assuming $n = 30$, replacement in the year 0 is equal to

$$R_0 = 15 \cdot 1.05^{-30} = 3.47 \tag{6.1}$$

As replacement is function of gross investment made n years earlier, and the period of transition described by the model is shorter than n years, annual replacements will not be affected by changes in gross investment in Patterns II and III. (Strictly speaking, they will be slightly affected because n represents an average and there will be some assets with service life shorter than 10 years.) Thus, in all three patterns replacement will continue to grow at the rate of 5% and by the end of the 9th year will increase to

$$R_9 = 3.47 \cdot 1.05^9 = 5.38 \tag{6.2}$$

Subtracting replacement from gross investment as given in the table in the text, we get new investment in the respective years

$$\text{All Patterns:} \quad I_0 = 15 - 3.47 = 11.53 \tag{7.1}$$
$$\text{Pattern II:} \quad I_9 = 41 - 5.38 = 35.62 \tag{7.2}$$
$$\text{Pattern III:} \quad I_9 = 64 - 5.38 = 58.62 \tag{7.3}$$

From the table in the text take the additions to output in the following years

$$\text{Pattern I:} \quad \Delta P_1 = 5 \tag{8.1}$$
$$\text{Pattern II:} \quad \Delta P_{10} = 14 \tag{8.2}$$
$$\text{Pattern III:} \quad \Delta P_{10} = 22 \tag{8.3}$$

The ratios between new investments and increments in output one year later represent the desired capital coefficients

$$\text{Pattern I:} \quad K = 2.31 \tag{5.1}$$
$$\text{Pattern II:} \quad K_{10} = 2.54 \tag{5.2}$$
$$\text{Pattern III:} \quad K_{10} = 2.66 \tag{5.3}$$

From one pattern to the other the rate of expansion of investment increases and "technological" capital coefficient deteriorates, as it should do. Productivity of investment in Pattern II has decreased by 9%, in Pattern III by 13%.

References:

1. A. P. Lerner, "A Note on Socialist Economics", *Review of Economic Studies*, 1936—37, 72—6.
2. O. Lange, "Mr. Lerner's Note on Socialist Economics", *Ibid.*, 143—4.
3. F. J. Atkinson, "Saving and Investment in a Socialist State", *Review of Economic Studies*, 1947—48, 78—83.
4. J. de V. Graaff, *Theoretical Welfare Economics*, Cambridge, University Press, 1957.
5. W. A. Lewis, "The World's Poverty", in W. A. Lewis and others, *Economics*, London, Odhams Press, 1949.
6. F. P. Ramsey, "A Mathematical Theory of Saving", *Economic Journal*, 1928, 543—59.
7. J. E. Meade, *Trade and Welfare*, London, Oxford University Press, 1955.
8. J. Tinbergen, "The Optimum Rate of Saving", *Economic Journal*, 1956, 603—9.
9. O. Eckstein, "Investment Criteria for Economic Development and the Theory of Intertemporal Welfare Economics", *Quarterly Journal of Economics*, 1957, 56—85.
10. W. Eucken, "On the Theory of the Centrally Administered Economy: An Analysis of the German Experiment", *Economica*, 1948, 79—100, 173—93.
11. R. C. Clemence, F. S. Doody, *The Schumpeterian System*, Cambridge, Mass., Addison-Wesley, 1950.
12. P. A. Samuelson, *Economics*, McGraw-Hill, 1952.
13. J. J. Spengler, "The Population Obstacle to Economic Betterment", *American Economic Review, Papers and Proceedings*, May 1951, 343—54.
14. M. C. Kaser, "Estimating the Soviet National Income", *Economic Journal*, 1957, 83—104.
15. S. Stajić, "Nacionalni dohodak" (National Income), in *Privreda FNRJ u periodu 1947—1956 godine*, Ekonomski institut FNRJ, Beograd, 1957.

VI. PLANNING: OBJECTIVES AND MEANS

We reach the last stage of our enquiry: the borderland between economic theory and economic policy. The situation becomes more and more complex and instead of arriving at clear-cut solutions we shall have to be content with an increasing number of compromises. The nature of these compromises becomes increasingly determined by the features of the actual economy we have in mind. Somewhere in this intermediary no-man's land we have to draw the border-line for the theoretical analysis of a general type. Beyond this border-line the economist is expected to work out specific policy recommendations.

11. THE DEFINITION OF SOCIAL PRODUCT

So far we have been talking about the growth of social product and about the maximization of social product without specifying more exactly the empirical content of the concept. Now it is time to provide an operational definition of the concept. This is by no means an easy task, and a comprehensive discussion of the problem is far beyond the scope of the present chapter. In what follows, I shall be mainly concerned with a clarification of some of the important issues involved and I shall try to derive a solution which is somewhat more satisfactory than those implied in the existing national income accounting practices. The analysis will, of course, be concerned with the conceptual rather than with the purely statistical (in the sense of the compilation of the necessary data) side of the problem. Note also that the single value of the social product we are searching for is not the *only* meaningful overall aggregate. For various other purposes various other aggregates will be more appropriate.

A variety of definitions have been proposed. For our purposes all of them may be classified in three distinct categories represented by three typical definitions. Let us call them the Russian Definition[1], the American Definition[1] and, according to the name of an American economist of Russian origin, the Kuznets Definition.

---

[1] The appelations are chosen for convenience and have no historical implications. The "Russian Definition" was already used before the U.S.S.R. came to existence, and the "American Definition" can be traced back to the work of J. E. Meade and R. Stone in 1941 (1).

(a) The Russian Definition of Social Product

1. The Russian Definition is taken from the last edition of *Politi-českaja ekonomija,* a representative text-book written by a team of competent Soviet economists, and it reads as follows[1]:

> "The total social product is created by the labour of the workers in the branches of material production: industry, agriculture, building, transport when serving production, and also by the labour of the commercial workers representing in their activities extension of the process of production in the sphere of distribution (preservation, finishing, transporting, packing goods, etc.). Along with manual workers, brain workers (scientists, engineers, etc.), engaged in branches of material production, participate directly in the creation of material wealth.
>
> The total social product is not created in non-productive branches. The workers engaged in the non-productive sphere (state administration, culture, welfare, medical service), do not create material wealth. Nevertheless, the labour of the workers of the non-productive branches is indispensable to the socialist society, to material production, it represents socially-useful labour" (2, 542—3).

The above definition has some good properties. It defines social product in a consistent way in the sense that it does not depend on organizational changes within the economy. It is simple and easily manageable. It also provides a good indicator for all those purposes where it is material goods which we are interested in (e.g., for an assessment of the "economic strength" or of the "military strength" of an economy[2]). Thus this aggregate will satisfy a number of uses[3]. However, here we are not interested in the general problems of social accounting, but in the specific problem of an operational maximization of economic welfare. Therefore, every definition of social product must pass the test from the point of view of how successfully it provides an indicator of the welfare content of the activities performed in the society.

---

[1] This definition is commonly called Marxist definition, but that is not correct. It has nothing to do with Marx and in so far as it is attributed to Marx represents an instance of the current vulgarization of Marx's thought. For an explanation see Appendix.

[2] The American Definition is ill suited for this purpose. Cf. S. Lebergott commenting on Gilbert-Kravis's international comparison of national products: "How many officials who compare these GNP totals will understand that one country will have more "economic strength" than another in proportion as it has a more complex financial system (more checks used, more services of financial intermediaries); higher interest rates (more interest paid); more barratry (more legal services); and more residents who take thought of the morrow (more expense on handling life insurance)?" And then: "Comparisons of the economic strength of members of international organizations must reckon with that distinction (committed and uncommitted resources): resources used in making $ 100 worth of automobiles may be available for making $ 100 worth of tanks, but $ 100 worth of vaudeville services may be quite unusable for any other purpose" (Review Article, *American Economic Review,* 1955, p. 440).

[3] A similar definition of social product was used by the Yugoslav Federal Statistical Office. After the Statistical Office published its "Methodology" in 1954, an extensive discussion of the definition took place. For some of the more important contributions written from different points of view see references 3—6.

2. For this purpose, let us postulate three different types of economies of an increasing degree of complexity. Let them be called Az, Buki and Vede. In Az total product consists of 50 tons of potato and 50 tons of wheat, altogether 100 tons of food valued 100 in money terms, say 100 dinars. The working population consists of 100 men.

Total product of Buki consists of the same 100 tons of food, the population is also the same, but because of some innovation, labour productivity (in technical sense) is greater in Buki than in Az. Therefore, Buki society can afford to spare two men, and these two men specialize in teaching and in medicine. How are we to compare Az and Buki in terms of economic welfare?

The Russian Definition is usually derived from the Marxian concept of productive labour in terms of value productivity. Value is determined by the labour time expended (cf. Marx, 7, 178). As in Buki fewer workers are engaged in the production of food, the value of the product in Buki must be smaller. From the point of view of social accounting, the result is meaningless. And it is easy to see why. The Marxian concept implies a social relation, the use of the labour power bought on the market, and has nothing to do with the physical quantity of the product. The social accounting concept, on the contrary, has meaning only in so far as it measures exactly this physical quantity of the product, for what is consumed is product and not value. It follows that the two concepts must not be confused and that the Russian Definition cannot be derived from the Marxian theory of value.

If taken in its social accounting sense, the Russian Definition would indicate that the product of Buki is the same as of Az. But the population of Buki is obviously better off than the population of Az (granting that income distribution is no worse), because, on top of 100 tons of food they are able to enjoy medical and school services. Moreover, in otherwise identical conditions, but equipped with a teacher and a doctor (now in the sense of our A-factors, Ch. 9), Buki economy is likely to grow at a faster rate, providing thus the population with *more food also*. The differential advantage of Buki may be expressed as: 100 tons of food valued 100 dinars plus the services of one doctor and one teacher. But in the same sense food production might have been expressed not in value but as 50 tons of wheat and 50 tons of potato. Once we have decided to aggregate wheat and potatoes in value terms, there is no reason to leave out the services of the teacher and doctor. If the earnings of the last two are the same as the average earnings of the 98 workers in the production of food, total social product of Buki will be 102 2/49 dinars.

3. Thus the Russian Definition does not pass our test. It appears to be arbitrary. And as such it is likely to be misleading as the following statement of Soviet authors shows:

"The systematic increase of the share of labour engaged in the sphere of material production ... promotes the growth of social wealth, the creation of the abundance of products needed for building the communist society" (2, 543).

As it stands, the statement is definitely wrong. The transition from Az to Buki involved a *decrease* of the proportion of labour engaged in the sphere of material production, and yet it was a positive movement both in terms of present welfare and in terms of the potential future welfare (higher rate of growth).

(b) The American Definition of Social Product

1. We now pass on to consider the American Definition as it is formulated by the authors of the official American post-war computations of social product[1]:

"We start with the obvious fact that individuals, non-profit institutions serving individuals, and general government are ultimate buyers in the sense that they do not buy for resale in the market. Accordingly, their purchases are not elements of cost in the value of other output produced for the market. Hence, there is a presumption that their purchases should be regarded as final products in any measure which purports to give a complete accounting of the entire output of the nation" (9, 182).

It is evident that this definition passes the Buki test, so we move on to a more complex Vede economy.

Suppose Vede is in every respect equal to Buki, except that the two non-industrial workers are now one politician and one policeman. If everything else remains the same, it is clear that the Vede community is no better off than the Az community, while according to the American Definition they would be better off. Moreover, the politician and policeman are not likely to remain idle and to justify their existence they may persuade members of the Vede community to divert some resources from the production of food to the production of guns. At best, the guns will be used as a demonstration of force, as a means to instil the necessary respect for the state inside and outside the community. In this case they represent an addition to social capital. But they may also be used and destroyed in a war in the current year — which I assume here for the sake of simplicity — and then they represent current consumption. If the technical substitutability of output is perfect, the aggregate value of potatoes, wheat and guns will again be 100 dinars. According to the Russian Definition social products of Az and Vede economies are the same. According to the American Definition Vede social product is even greater than that of Az. Actually, the Vede community is worse off because the production of armaments is a social waste, or cost, it contributes neither to the present consumption nor to the future consumption of the members of the community.

2. Some other things may happen as well. The politician and policeman, having guns, may decide that they should have higher salaries than the other members of the community. According to the A-definition social product increases. Or, suppose, food growers had a number of private agricultural institutes maintained from the proceeds of the sales of the produce. The politician and policeman, this time more construc-

---

[1] This definition was first applied in the U.S. Department of Commerce national income statistics published in 1947. A lively discussion followed. For more important contributions see references 8—12.

tive-minded, persuade producers to abandon small and inefficient institutes and form a large and well equipped central agricultural institute financed out of taxes (no matter whether direct or indirect). According to the A-definition this organizational change automatically increases social product by the amount of taxation (in addition to the real increment in product due to greater efficiency after the change). This happens because, before the change, private institutes were financed by private industry; after the change the government institute is again financed by private industry (through taxation), but on top of the private product personnel costs of the institute are added once more, now in the form of government product. The same fictitious changes in product occur if the policeman and politician are hired by private firms to perform the jobs of nightwatchmen and legal advisors. Then, their services represent *cost to the firms,* while as members of the government they are supposed to create *product for the nation.* Our pair of government functionaries may become even so constructive-minded as to retire from "public life" into the privacy of their own estates and engage in a leisurely food growing. Taxes being abolished, the A-definition will record a drop in output while there is a clear increase in economic welfare.

It appears that organizational changes, although leaving the total amount of goods and services supplied to the members of the community unchanged, lead to changes in social product if the American Definition is used. These distortions may not be great from the statistical point of view, but they render the A-definition inconsistent and so destroy its theoretical foundation. Also, according to both definitions, war production is likely to increase social product instead of being treated as a social waste.

Despite its limitations, the American Definition has clearly some very useful properties. Registering *all institutional* incomes, it is well suited for many purposes of practical analysis. It is also capable of an interesting theoretical interpretation. Assuming full employment and relative stability of the economic organization, the American concept of product may be interpreted as a measure of the *maximum potential* output in a certain period. In this case, war output indicates the approximate volume of an alternatively possible economic output. Similarly the earnings of government officials and kindred categories of employees show the approximate value of product they would create if they were engaged in producing final goods and services to the consumer. Here even the assumption of full employment may be dropped and the appropriate income may be *imputed* to persons who do not exchange their work for money income (voluntary and involuntarily unemployed on one hand and such persons as housewives on the other). Similarly, the non-wage income may be imputed to idle productive capacities. In this way — we get an apparently useful concept for economic analysis and we shall term it Potential or Statistical Social Product. It represents an absolute maximum of what can be produced, assuming that costs of communal life are non-existent. The difference between potential and actual product may, with proper adjustments for organizational changes, be used as a measure of the efficiency of social organization (thus, for instance, as the politicians and, in planned economy, the economists are responsible for the state of the social organization, this difference will provide an interesting indicator of the efficiency of their labour, which was hitherto difficult to measure).

(c) The Kuznets's Definition of Social Product

1. The two definitions discussed so far have not passed our test, but the discussion has contributed something to our knowledge of the essential characteristics of the problem. It remains to see whether the third, Kuznets's Definition may serve as a basis for generalizations. Kuznets says:

"We assume that the final goal of economic activity is provision of goods to consumers, the final products are those turned out during the year to flow either to consumers or to capital stock (for the ultimate benefit of future consumers), and that everything else, by the nature of the case, is intermediate[1] product whose inclusion in the output total would constitute duplication" (8, 156).

The emphasis of the quotation is on the concept of intermediate product. It is generally accepted that such goods as raw materials (unless exported or added to stocks) are intermediate products. But along with these among intermediate products Kuznets includes also services of courts, government administration and similar other categories. This procedure would seem debatable to many economists and so we have to enlarge upon it.

2. It is often pointed out that all government services should be considered as final product which is consumed collectively. On behalf of the electors, the parliament votes the defence budget with a view to preserve peace, and a court and police budget to ensure internal security and order. Peace and security are therefore commodities which

---

[1] In another paper Kuznets elaborates his idea of intermediate product: "That society as a whole, via the government, decides to devote resources to these intermediate products is no indication that they themselves are used to satisfy ultimate consumers' wants or represent net additions to real capital. The decision indicates only that these products are needed either by business firms or by society at large — that they are necessary for the continuance and improvement of society, including its economic mechanism. It is particularly true of such activities as are directed at domestic peace and the international position of the country that they provide the pre-condition of economic activity; but they themselves cannot be conceived as yielding a final economic product, as if economic product could be imagined without the basic social framework of the economy. (For this reason it seems absurd to speak of the economic value of political liberty or of protection from aggression.)" (15, 8) Social product is an aggregate of *final* products, not of *intermediate products*. The relation between the former and the latter is one of dependency, the output of final products depends on the input of intermediate products; if the former were completely independent from the latter, the latter would be final products too.

In still another paper Kuznets writes: "National income is a measure of net output of economic activity *within* the given social framework, not what it would be in a hypothetical absence of the latter... In other words, the flow of services to individuals from the economy is a flow of economic goods produced and secured under conditions of internal peace, external safety, and legal protection of specific rights, and cannot include these very conditions as services" (10, 193).

result from government activity and are collectively supplied and consumed. This sounds suggestive enough until one starts asking concrete questions as for instance: How much of peace and security do we buy? As Reddaway points out "the periods with large armies were usually those in which the feeling of security was at its lowest" (13, 286). Also, if two countries are equal in every respect, except that one of them has a much larger army, does the latter country enjoy more peace? (History seems to teach us a different lesson.) Similarly, do great police expenditures indicate that the population enjoys a high degree of personal security and freedom, or rather the other way round? Clearly, this sort of argument will not take us very far. Next, if you buy a concert ticket, you will probably enjoy a commodity called singing; thus you feel better off than if you missed the concert. If you *must* go to the court, you will not enjoy security, and after you have paid the lawyer, you will most definitely feel worse off[1]. This is not to say that lawyers are useless. But it is to say that they are not desirable as such but only in so far as they create conditions in which it becomes possible to enjoy singing. The questions and examples can be multiplied at will and they all point at one fact, namely that government services, similarly as business services, are not at all homogeneous. Some of them are in the nature of product, but others are *social cost*, necessary, true, but nevertheless cost. Education and medical services belong to the first category, army and justice to the second.

Extending the notion of intermediate products to government services, we are also able to avoid other inconsistencies of the A-definition. So, for instance, it does not matter whether the agricultural institute in Vede is financed privately or out of taxation. In the first case, the cost of the institute is treated as such by private accountants, in the second case by social product statisticians, and in both cases the value of social product remains unaffected[2].

3. The criticism of the traditional argument may be restated more systematically in the following two points.

(1) Social product is not a collection of physical goods as such, neither does it measure human activities as such; it represents an aggregate of consumers' valuations. In order to be able to treat government expenditures which do not benefit directly individual consumers as collective consumption, one would have to assume that the government represents the majority of the population, that it is a "democratic" government. The activities of a fascist government will not represent a contribution to social product, but a robbery of the population. Thus it follows that the social products of democratic and non-democratic countries would not be comparable. Next, as there is no precise criterion for what is "democratic", it cannot be said with certainty where

---

[1] Even if the case is settled in your favour, judicial service is not productive: "Creation and destruction of rights is not in itself production of final goods, even though such rights may have market value for individuals and firms" (Kuznets, 10, 195).

[2] Another possibility to achieve consistency is to treat services of research institutes as accumulation of intellectual capital. However, there seems to be a general agreement that the concept of intangible capital is not very useful in quantitative economics.

the concept is applicable and where it is not. And finally, since government and state bureaucracy, politicians[1] and army officers, etc., have normally been recruited from social classes which represent a relatively small minority of population, the original assumption (of an identity of government's and subjects' valuations) becomes rather dubious, to say the least.

(2) There is a fallacy in reasoning which from the *physical* fact that government does not buy for reselling deduces the *economic* fact that government is final consumer. For only the individuals are final consumers in an economic sense. The administrative expenses of a firm do not represent product but cost, and the same applies to the nation as a whole. Some of the government activities add directly to the economic welfare of the population, the others add indirectly as intermediate products which are fed into the system, the final product being produced elsewhere. It appears that we can approach our problem in two ways but with identical results. In so far as the administrative activities of a government resemble those performed by a firm, they are not productive (in the sense of increasing final product) and represent cost. If, however, one prefers to say that government produces security, order, etc., then, as Kuznets points out, one must take into account that these "commodities" are not final, because they are pre-conditions of social production and as such are intermediate products. Thus in the case of government not a mechanical criterion of final buying but the character of the service rendered is a meaningful criterion of productivity. In this way, the problem under (1) disappears as irrelevant and we are able to provide a solution which is conceptually more satisfactory.

4. Let us now define the criteria of the Kuznets Definition somewhat more precisely. Its key concept is the concept of social intermediate products or, as I called it, social cost. What is social cost? Or, what is not social cost?

Usefulness can provide no general criterion because raw materials and fuel are also useful and still remain cost in producing final output. Neither is physical finality (no resale) a reliable criterion, since, as we have seen, in the American definition, all government services are considered final. In fact, upon a closer scrutiny, the distinction between cost and income, although so commonly made in everyday life, turns out to be extremely difficult to define precisely and consistently. We must, however, refrain from discussing all the difficulties — largely of a philosophical nature — fascinating as such a discussion would be, and try to provide a simple and workable — if not perfectly satisfactory — solution. The simplest and the most general definition seems to be the following: *All the non-investment government goods and services which do not enter directly into the consumption of individual consumers re-*

---

[1] Just to provide an empirical illustration. W. Miller finds that in the decade 1901—1910 about 86% of leading American politicians came from families of businessmen, politicians and professionals. Only 2% of them were of working class origin (22, pp. 204, 206). For the social origin and valuations of public officials see Chapter 5-c-3-1 and footnotes.

present intermediate products or social costs[1]. Social costs are in fact the costs of social relations, of the social organization. And "not entering directly into the consumption of individuals" means that goods and services in question are not desired as such, but only as inputs in producing further output. The services of physicians are desired for most obvious reasons; the services of bureaucracy are a necessary nuisance. Teachers help to develop the mental and physical faculties of individuals, and so their services undoubtedly have a welfare content; the activity of lawyers is all but desired. Good music, an ably written book, a nice picture — are things always to be desired and we would be most reluctant to dispense with them. But if we could dispense with politicians, policemen, and gunmen in general, we would be too glad to do that.

The concept of social cost is not confined only to the field just sketched with the examples. Together with the cost of the social organization in the narrow sense it also includes intermediate product or cost of economic organization. For instance, the development of industry requires concentration of population, which in turn requires development of towns and municipal services. In so far as short-distance-walking to the place of work is replaced by bus journeys, the services of the local bus company should be considered as a social cost and not as a contribution to social product. The services of banks and other

---

[1] Kuznets suggests three criteria for identifying government services to ultimate consumers:

"(1) rendering the services for no price or for merely a token price — to distinguish them from others in which the government acts as a business enterprise;

(2) the availability of the service only upon direct request or some overt initiative by the individual — to exclude the intangible benefits the government may confer upon society as a whole and upon an individual member who may be quite unconscious of such benefits;

(3) the existence of an analogue to the services, on a fairly substantial scale, on the private markets of the economy — to exclude government acts resulting from an individual's initiative that do not in fact constitute an economic service (balloting, securing services of a court, etc.)" (15, 6; cf. also 10, pp. 192—200).

These criteria are probably not very fortunately formulated. As to (1), every service rendered for less than is needed to cover cost may be treated as a subsidized business service. Compulsory education, compulsory vaccination, etc., will be found to contradict (2). And with respect to (3), the fairly substantial practice to hire and pay private lawyers does not transform their services into positive contributions to social product.

It will also be necessary to indicate in which respect Kuznets's theory has been modified above. Kuznets's statistical definition of social income — private incomes net of taxes plus undistributed profits net of taxes plus final product of government (15, 12, 10, 243) — is not correct if I understand it correctly. According to this definition social income in Vede economy (100 dinars received by food-growers minus taxes to finance the upkeep of the policeman and the politician plus here government final product) would be less than that of the Az economy, while they are clearly equal. There is, further, a difference in my deriving social income from social product by subtracting replacement and not depreciation as Kuznets does. Also, while Kuznets is preoccupied with establishing the identity of national income at factor cost with national income at market prices, to me the above, as an overall aggregate, is a meaningless concept. Factor shares reflect the organizational structure of an economy: social income measures the value of final output. There is no direct relation between the two. Cf. Kuhn (19), Frish (20), Nicholson (21). There are also several other differences in my approach. But in essential points the two approaches coincide.

financial intermediaries provide another example. The upkeep of roads, in so far as they serve business, is also an example of an intermediate product adding nothing to the value of already computed social product. Finally, the product, lost because of underutilization of existing capacity and because of unemployment also represents an item of social cost. Summing up, social cost is cost of the entire social and economic organization of a particular society, the cost of a social system.

6. The way towards a definition of social product has now been paved. *Social product is conceptually and statistically derived from potential (statistical) product by subtracting the cost of the social system*. A statistical estimate[1] of this aggregate will be more difficult than an estimate of either the Russian or American aggregates. However, Kuznets shows that statistical difficulties are not insuperable.

But even if statistical difficulties were so great that statisticians, in their measurements, could not conform entirely to the requirements of the definition, some sort of second best approximation would have to be found. Without this not much meaning can be attached to comparisons between social products (i.e. economically useful production) or between standards of living (individual consumption and socialized services taken together) of various countries or, for that matter, of the same country in a longer period.

(d) The Maximization of Social Income

Having answered the question: What is Social Product? — we have attributed a definite empirical meaning to the maximization problem discussed in the chapters on the optimum rate of investment. Nevertheless, there are still several minor points to be analyzed before we complete the general picture of our problem.

1. Social income is a market category, outside exchange the concept expresses an immeasurable quantity. If one rents a house or hires a car from a business firm, the services of the house and of the car are expressed in the amount of money paid for them. But if one buys a house or a car, their subsequent services are unassessable. It may be argued with some plausibility that a new car renders more satisfaction than it does at some later date and so its amortization is likely to be the greatest in the first year; with the house seems to be the other way round, for the more you get used to it the more valuable it may become to you. It is obviously impossible to say anything meaningful about *this sort* of income. The "psychological income", as it is usually called, is *economically* meaningless.

We need, however, some measure of the services of houses and automobiles when rendered outside the business sector. Now, (1) since they may be used in both sectors, (2) since the bulk of goods and services is obtained through exchange, (3) since the consumer sector pro-

---

[1] Evidently the basic statistical estimate is that of potential (statistical) product. This *statistical* aggregate must be comprehensive enough and detailed enough to allow the construction of various other aggregates necessary for economic analysis.

vides no criterion for measuring social income, and (4) since we are interested in preserving the consistency of estimates, the most obvious procedure would consist in imputing the value to services in the non-business sector according to the same criteria as in the business sector. This means that the value of annual services of consumer durables should be expressed as a sum of depreciation, interest and rent.

2. Next, we must determine the value of capital formation. For activities classified as productive this represents no new difficulty. But the construction of town halls and barracks seems somewhat puzzling. The output of town halls and barracks is considered as contributing nothing to the value of social product. Does not this conception imply that investment in town halls and barracks should also be deducted from the value of social product? It does not. As Kuznets points out (10, 197—8) the treatment should be the same as that of all other fixed capital used in the production of intermediate products. The output of a plant producing semifinished goods is excluded from the value of social product, but fixed capital sunk in the plant was included as a part of social product of the period when the plant was built.

3. The problem of the "psychological income" of paragraph 1 has a somewhat wider significance. Economic welfare is often treated in terms of psychological income, and so is social income itself. The former is logically permissible, the latter is contradictory if social income is to measure the "physical" volume of goods and services. One may assume that the law of diminishing marginal utility holds for every individual and so for the society as a whole. Thus "marginal social welfare" will be diminishing as well. On the other hand, one may assume continuous changes in taste or in the distribution of income resulting in an increasing "marginal social welfare". It follows that a certain relative increase in social income will result in a different — greater or smaller — relative increase in economic welfare. Social income and its changes do not represent economic welfare and its changes in any *absolute* sense directly. But social income does indicate the *level* of economic welfare. Similarly, the statement that per capita consumption income in Britain is about four times as high as in Yugoslavia does not mean that British economic welfare is that much higher. It may be higher more than four times or less than four times. We do not know and, as economists, we are even not interested in knowing it. But the numerical ratio quoted nevertheless gives a valuable information: given the present rate of growth of Yugoslav economy, it is possible to say that Yugoslavia may be expected to achieve the present British level of economic welfare in about fifteen — or whatever the number of — years. The exact reasoning behind this statement is as follows.

We compare the future economic welfare of the Yu-community with the present economic welfare of the B-community. At the time when British and Yugoslav consumption incomes (we do not consider the investment part of income in order to avoid difficulties resulting from the time element involved), valued in the present British prices, become equal, Yugoslav economic welfare from the British point of view will still be smaller. This is so because B-community has spent the available income on the British, and not on the Yugoslav, collection of goods revealing thus preference for the former. Similarly, at the time when British and Yugoslav outputs of consumption goods, valued in future Yugoslav prices, become equal, Yugoslav economic welfare from the Yugoslav point of view will already be higher than the present British welfare. For, by choosing the Yugoslav, instead of the British collection of goods, the Yu-community reveals its preference for the former. Somewhere in the vicinity of these two points lie the points of equality of welfare from one or from the other point of view. As the statistical computations involved are very imprecise, this knowledge suffices for practical purposes. We need only estimate the number of years required for the Yu-economy to attain the specified points. The same reasoning applies, of course, when we allow for the growth of B-income and then try to establish the point of time when the two incomes will become equal[1]. Thus although the statement, that in so many years Yugoslav income will surpass British income, implies a quantification of welfare, it is nevertheless meaningful.

4. This brings us to the problem of evaluation of social income with its familiar index number intricacies[2]. It is outside the scope of this study to discuss this problem systematically. We may content ourselves with the fact that social product has so far been somehow measured.

---

[1] For an attempt to proceed differently in making welfare comparisons between the two countries see J. L. Nicholson, 23.

[2] For an interesting and instructive discussion of this problem see 14—18. In 1940 J. Hicks initiated the debate optimistically. The subsequent contributions tended to be more and more pessimistic, reflecting the characteristic modern trend towards an absolute proof of meaninglessness of economic science. In 1950, the debate ended in a complete nihilism in the hands of P. Samuelson. The collections of goods chosen before and after the change represent the only two observable points, says Samuelson. But each collection of goods could be redistributed among consumers in innumerable ways. If we do this conceptually, we get two infinite series of points representing two utility possibility curves. The curves may easily cross, we do not know, and we do not know whether, generally, the change is to the better. For a general statement that the change increases potential real income it is necessary that there is a uniform outward shift in society's utility possibility function. This is "the only consistent and ethics-free definition of an increase in potential real income of a group..." (18, 19). But if so, there is still some hope left. Although lacking general knowledge, we still know what is happening in the neigbourhood of the two observed points. The next blow of logic destroys this last hope. For the two collections chosen for consumption must also be produced. We repeat the same mental operation now producing various collections of goods which gives us two production-possibility curves. These curves may cross; where — we do not know, the observed price-quantity data do not tell us. Samuelson concludes: "*We shall never be able to infer a genuine change in potential real income as I have earlier defined the term* — no, not even in the simplest comparison of A which shows more of every good than the point B" (18, 16; italics are *not* mine). Now, if nihilism is the appropriate diet of the modern economist — and if economics is about economizing — Samuelson could have had it with much less intellectual effort. We only need to take notice of the following two simple empirical facts: production and consumption choices are not timeless; the members of every human group are mortal. In such a large community as the United States less than a minute is needed for a change in membership. Thus the fundamental assumption underlying real income comparisons based on the index number theory — the assumption of constant taste — breaks down. Here this assumption is not a more or less bad approximation, as in the theory of consumer's behaviour. It is now — the impossibility of interpersonal comparisons being taken for granted — a *logical contradiction*, and so, even before we start theorizing, the theory is already rendered impossible.

If the theory behind these measurements is still intellectually unsatisfactory, this does not change the fact that the available social product estimates represent analytically useful aggregates.

But we can probably say something more than that. In Chapter 6-d the optimum distribution of income was determined. This eliminates the most troublesome variate from the index-number game. In planning the optimum amount of investment for a given period, for the bulk of investment marginal social product will be markedly positive and so the Paasche index greater than one[1]. After that the remaining marginal quantities of investment still to be determined will have no effect on prices, if the degree of precision with which the future price movements can be predicted is taken into account. Consequently index numbers can lead to no contradiction or indeterminacy.

5. Finally, it remains to put together all the pieces which have been worked out so far. We first estimate the value of the potential social product. PSP consists of material product, paid services outside the sphere of material production, imputed unpaid actual and potential services of the members of the community and of underutilized commercial capital, and unpaid services of non-commercial capital (state and private). From this aggregate we deduct social costs, which include imputed items as well. The remainder is social product. We next deduct replacement and maintenance costs. What remains is social income, that welfare indicator which we wish to maximize.

When dealing with the problem of the optimum rate of investment we assumed that it was material product which should be maximized. The assumption was chosen for reasons of simplicity and availability of data. But it provided a reasonable first approximation. For, there is a positive correlation between the increase in production of material goods and of the expansion of social product, and so the maximization of the former is likely to lead to the maximization of the latter. Thus the basic results of Part V hold good. Only the tentative figures — the maximum rate of growth and the corresponding share of investment in product — will change: the former will probably increase slightly (assuming that the non-material part of social product expands faster than the remainder), the direction of change of the latter is not clear *a priori* (because total investment now includes non-commercial investment as well).

One further problem calls for consideration. The maximization of income is not simply a matter of physical volume of goods and services,

---

[1] The current theory is as follows. When Paasche index ($P = \Sigma p_2 q_2 / \Sigma p_2 q_1$) is greater than unity, income has increased (provided that income distribution has not been made worse). This happens because $P>1$ means that in the second situation goods q_2 were chosen although q_1 might have been chosen. When Laspeyres index ($L = \Sigma p_1 q_2 / \Sigma p_1 q_1$) is less than unity, real income has decreased (provided that income distribution is no better). For $L<1$ means that q_2 goods of the second situation were available in the first situation but were not chosen. If $P<1<L$, the situation is indeterminate and an approximation based on both indexes, say $\sqrt{PL}$, should be used. For $L<1<P$ the situation is said to be contradictory.

but is a matter of valuations. This difference becomes important in situations typified by the following alternative: If people worked longer, income would be higher; but they prefer to work less. What should the economist recommend in such a situation? It may be argued that the alternative is specious because historically greater production was positively correlated with greater satisfaction with working conditions. The efficiency of the human machine seems to be an inverse function of the strain and coercion under which it works. Thus the recommendation is obvious. But perhaps a more straightforward answer can be derived from the axiomatic elements of our definition of economics (Introduction 2). If a person, or a community, is offered additional income for additional work and the offer is rejected, then the additional income has a negative value and is something to be avoided. The choice between work and leisure is an elementary economic choice incapable of being further analyzed in terms of efficiency. In the same way as we, *qua economists*, cannot tell the consumer to choose margarin instead of butter, we cannot tell the producer to choose higher income instead of less work. The real difficulty, however, is not in providing logically satisfactory answers. It is in finding out what the genuine valuations of the members of the community *are*. And this is a task to be solved by sociologists and politicians — two professions which, unfortunately, are scientifically even less advanced than the economic profession.

To conclude. What we have done in this chapter consists in providing theoretical criteria for a comprehensive list of empirical items which must be considered when making maximization decisions. With this we reach the border-line of our investigations. The next step, the elaboration of a practically workable scheme, leads already to another field of applied economics.

12. THE ENTERPRISE AND THE PLANNING AUTHORITY

The *enterprise*, together with its social correlate kolektiv, was defined as the basic economic unit of an associationist economy (Chapter 6). At the same time wages and profits were discussed as corresponding categories of economic calculation. Wages and profits, together with interest and rent, play in fact a double role in economic calculus: they are analytical devices by means of which we judge the degree of rationality of resources allocation, but they are also norms by which the kolektivs are guided or instruments by which they are induced to take economically correct decisions. The importance of these impersonal criteria and automatic regulators — *if they can be made to work efficiently* — cannot be overrated. What we have to do now is to discuss the possibility of exactly this fundamental pre-condition: the way in which the autonomous enterprise can be efficiently integrated in the economic mechanism working under the optimum régime.

(a) Social Capital

The means of production in the economy we are concerned with are economically controlled by the kolektivs of the enterprises. Fundamentally two possible institutional frameworks for exercising this control exist. Either the kolektivs own the means of production, or they are owned by the society and so constitute social capital.

1. The first solution represents in fact the familiar capitalist solution in the sense that the technical economic concept of capital retains its full meaning. The main difference from the traditional capitalist solution would consist in the absence of irresponsible private control over the means of production (the absence of the employer-employee relation, public control of book-keeping, absence of patents suppression, absence of cartels, etc.), with socialized banking, and with the Planning Authority preventing large-scale bancrupties and correcting investment decisions. Such a planned, slumps-free economy is perfectly feasible. But the question arises whether it is desirable on economic grounds. To answer this question let us look more closely into the life cycle of a typical manufacturing enterprise.

2. In accordance with the general economic plan of the current year the Planning Authority builds a new factory. After completion, the factory is handed over to the working kolektiv together with the capital debt incurred. If everything goes well, the kolektiv will gradually repay the debt with interest and if this happens, as it normally will, before original assets are scrapped, or if quasi rents exceed repayments, the kolektiv will *ipso facto* appropriate the means of production. Once this has been achieved, the enterprise becomes relatively immune to the financial measures of the Planning Authority. The enterprise accumulates its financial reserves which it may invest whenever and for whatever purpose it finds fit. The Planning Authority may manipulate the interest rate and so try (but not necessarily succeed) to induce the enterprise to choose rationally between putting money in the Bank and using it for an investment project. But the changes in the interest rates violate the principle of equality of opportunity for all firms; or putting it differently, through the resulting capital gains and losses risks are artificially built into the system. Instead of being *productive*-oriented, enterprises become *financially*-oriented. Also, the mere fact that new enterprises have to pay interest on capital, while old enterprises, which finance their investments from their own funds, pay no interest, artificially places the latter in a favourable position. If older enterprises do not use their funds but lend them to the Bank, they will earn interest — an income completely unrelated to the productive effort of the kolektiv — on top of their normal productive profits. If the Bank refuses to pay interest for idle balances, the entire self-regulating mechanism based on interest rate breaks down, and so this possibility must be ruled out.

Apart from the method of a direct repayment of debt, two additional methods are conceivable. The capital assets used by the firm may be considered as a permanent loan on which interest is to be paid, interest being equal to the difference between quasi rents and depreciation quotas. If depreciation quotas are determined according to the "physical" characteristics of the asset — the procedure which is most likely — depreciation will exceed replacement and the difference can be invested at the ruling rate of interest with the same consequences as above. If they are calculated as annuities (see Ch. 7-d-4), every deviation from the prescribed course of events — either that the firm deliberately calculates "reserves", or that the average productivity of investment is greater than the marginal productivity and so greater than the interest rate, or simply that expected and actual results diverge — will be *magnified at compound interest*. In a market economy ownership of capital leads to concentration of capital, to monopoly and to other familiar phenomena which affect the allocation of resources adversely.

Some of the distortions mentioned can, no doubt, be remedied, but fundamentally they cannot be eliminated. For, at the root of them lies *capital*, which is an economic institution conducive to rational financial, not to rational productive choice. All disturbances are magnified through the operation of the compound interest rate, either in its direct form or in the form of profits on investment. To the extent to which profits from purely financial manipulations are likely to be significant, the significance of profits derived from economic (production plus distribution) entrepreneurship must decrease. As profits are assumed to be the driving force, the economic decisions of our entrepreneurs become financially-oriented. Profits being the source of wages and largest financial profits being as a rule different from the most efficient productive solutions, the basis for our optimum distribution of income disappears.

The capitalist solution historically arose from the need to secure a portion of *private* income for *productive* uses. With the abolition of private property the rationale of the system disappears. Investment resources are given — as determined by a social decision — and the only problem is to distribute them among competing firms in the most efficient way. We ask ourselves the following question: If private capital is replaced by social capital, will it be possible to achieve that *financial motivation* leads, at least as a sufficiently close approximation, to the maximization of *productive efficiency?*

3. Consider the same case of a manufacturing enterprise again. The necessary capital is provided by the Bank on the ground that the investment project yields the required rate of interest. Having been built, the factory is handed over to the working kolektiv. Out of the proceeds of production the kolektiv covers costs of production and pays rent. They also pay depreciation contributions into a special account of the enterprise. Depreciation is calculated so as to be proportional to the output achievable with the existing fixed capital. In this way all enterprises, young and old, possessing the same output capacity, are put on the same footing through deducting the same cost item. Next, the kolektiv does not repay the capital loan in the traditional way, but permanently

pays interest[1] on the fixed capital measured by its productive capacity, and pays rent if interest (due to diminishing marginal productivity of investment) does not exhaust net revenue. In other words, when managing the factory the *kolektiv controls a portion of social capital and for this privilege pays a price, similarly as all other kolektivs do*. What is left after all deductions have been made constitutes the *wage fund*. If the wage fund is greater than the sum of standard wages, in whatever way determined[2], the excess represents *profit*. Profit is a reward for the entrepreneurial effort of the kolektiv and as such, an inducement to this effort.

It would seem that the scheme, at least theoretically, eliminates all purely financial — i.e. not related to an increase in production — sources of profit and thus leads to an identification of financial and productive motivations.

4. In practice, of course, the whole problem is immensely more complicated. It is actually *the* problem of market planning. However, I cannot discuss it here in any detail. I may add only a few general observations based on the experience of the first few years of Yugoslav planning, which is the closest existing approximation to the system analyzed in this study.

(1) Profits may be *negative* as well as positive. Small negative deviations, or rather their possibility, is even desirable. But what about large losses? The traditional bankruptcy practices are unsuited for a planned economy, for they result in obvious and unnecessary economic waste. Fundamentally two different possibilities exist.

The enterprise in question may have become *objectively* uneconomic (say, the respective industry is contracting). In such a case some sort of bankruptcy procedure commends itself, because the best

---

[1] If productive capacity does not change and marginal and average productivity of investment are equal, the problem is relatively simple. If capacity changes and there is no equality between the average productivity of capital and the interest rate, the procedure becomes somewhat complicated. In a general case, the Bank may proceed in the following way. Fixed supply of investment finance is confronted with an elastic demand for investment loans. The applications for loans are classified according to the rate of interest they promise and this rate is calculated so as to equalize all future yields (quasi rents) with the capital sum to be lent. Thus we get an index of the average productivity of new capital, which may serve as a very useful first (and in many cases probably final) approximation. In order to establish the marginal productivity, the interest rate must be calculated so as to equalize future yields or losses with the value of the additions to or deductions from the capital sum of the original investment projects. The selection of applications is theoretically made so as to exhaust the available investment fund by a combination of projects all of which have the same marginal productivity of investment. In practice, of course, this criterion will be supplemented by a host of other criteria (import and export contents, structural requirements, etc.). After the loan has been granted, the respective enterprise repays it through depreciation calculated proportionally to the expected output capacity, through interest calculated by applying with the uniform general interest rate on the capital sum varying with the expected output capacity (interest is, therefore, proportional to depreciation), and through fixed annual amounts of rent which represents the balancing item.

[2] In Yugoslavia standard wage-rates for various jobs in an enterprise are fixed by the workers' council and laid down in a document called *Tarifni Pravilnik*. The *pravilnik* must be confirmed by the Trade Unions which see to it that there is a broad uniformity of wage-rates throughout the economy.

thing to do is to eliminate the economic organization which cannot keep up with the existing economic standards. The Yugoslav experience suggests that this case will be found practically only among very small enterprises, such as small retail shops, co-operatives, handicraft shops, where the amount of capital involved is economically negligible.

But one enterprise may fail also for *subjective* reasons, because of lack of entrepreneurship. In this case it seems most appropriate to decide (arbitrarily of course) what percentage of the standard wage fund is to be considered as the lowest tolerable limit below which the level of earned wage cannot be allowed to fall[1]. Once this limit is reached, the Planning Authority automatically resumes the prerogatives of the Workers' Council, reorganizes the enterprise and fills the executive jobs with the best people available in that particular branch of production. In other words, the kolektiv-controlled enterprise is temporarily converted into a government-controlled enterprise. After some time the enterprise will become economically viable and then the control is again handed over to the working kolektiv. By mutual consent the appointed managers may stay or they may leave for another similar intervention. If entrepreneurship is a scarce factor of production, planned economy proves to be able to make the most efficient use of it.

(2) Connected with point (1) is the problem of risk and of its bearing. Some ventures are more risky than others, some are small and other involve huge amounts of capital. In dealing with these problems a socialist bank may learn quite a lot from the capitalist bank, because in both cases the recoupment of the money lent is a rational economic goal. The bank may charge an additional interest rate — Dickinson's uncertainty surcharge[2] — varying from zero, for the most secure industries like those producing stapple foodstuffs and standardized machine parts, to some maximum for the most risky industries like production of fashionable luxuries.

Risk bearing is of fundamental importance. In a completely centralized economy, the risk is borne by the state. This means — taking into account the administrative habits of every bureaucracy — that there is practically no possibility to associate the responsibility with any particular group of persons, and so, in practice, *no-one is responsible for the decision taken.* Taking further into account the unavoidable existence of pressure groups pressing for their sectional interests, the inevitability of huge economic wastes in an administratively run economy becomes obvious. In the associationist economy, the kolektiv bears risk first and foremost. However, for large projects, and also in the case of a brand-new factory, the kolektiv cannot undertake to bear the risk, or at least not alone. In these circumstances the Commune, State or Federation, depending on the size of the undertaking, guarantee the soundness of the capital loan given by the bank and, if the project

---

[1] At the moment, in Yugoslavia, the guaranteed minimum is 80% of standard wages.

[2] "Since the degree of uncertainty will vary as between one branch of production and another, any economic choice ... will be a choice between economic alternatives involving uncertainties of different degrees. A rational calculus of economic costs must reflect this fact" (24, 95).

222

happens to be a failure, are obliged to make good all the losses incurred in an *explicit* way.

(3) This brings me to one of the very sensitive questions of planned economy: the buying and, more importantly, the selling of fixed assets. In the Soviet system, and in the early stages of Yugoslav planned economy, an enterprise could not sell redundant equipment because the proceeds of the sale would distort the results shown by the income account and would undermine the efficacy of the financial indices of the fulfilment of the plan. Therefore the governmental organs had to intervene and *transfer* fixed assets from one enterprise to another. In an associationist economy no such problem exists. If an enterprise sells a piece of equipment, the proceeds are paid into the depreciation account to the amount equal to all as yet unpaid depreciation quotas. The positive or negative difference is balanced with the wage and reserve funds. The enterprise-buyer continues to pay depreciation and interest (proportional to the gross value of the asset) until the machine is scrapped. Various complications are possible, but there is no need to discuss them here. The essence of the transaction consists in a transfer of fixed capital from a less productive to a more productive use without administrative interference and the Bank playing only a passive role of registering the transaction: the enterprise-seller settles its capital debt with the Bank which then lends the same means to the enterprise-buyer reviving thus the original capital loan.

(4) Next, there is the extremely complex problem of the changing basis of calculation. It is clear from the outset that, once the chosen *IP*-curve has been reached, associationist economy has a vested interest in price stability. Unlike a capitalist economy, it can gain nothing from inflation and may lose much by it. On the other hand, a planned economy can easily manage to achieve permanent price stability.

The value of fixed capital represents the basis for depreciation and interest calculation. We have said that fixed capital should be measured by its productive capacity. This is, clearly, easier said than done. Due to declining output capacity proper, to increasing maintenance costs, and to obsolescence, output capacity may be expected to decline gradually over the life period of fixed assets. On the other hand, the manual skill of operatives and the efficiency of the whole organization may be expected to rise sharply over the first year of a new enterprise, with corresponding effects on output. All this is certainly not something which can be dogmatized about but is a matter of reasonable empirically founded compromises. Taking into account the findings of Chapter 8, the Planning Authority will have to classify industries and fixed assets they use in certain groups and then prescribe such fixed capital accounting rules, which will approximate best to the theoretical ideal.

(5) Some enterprises, for instance hydroelectric power stations, may operate under permanently or semipermanently unalterable conditions. The highly inelastic supply of important factors of production makes for differences in capital productivity which are unrelated to the entrepreneurial efforts of the kolektivs. This disturbing influence must be eliminated by charging the appropriate amount of rent.

Closely related is the case of fluctuating prices due to changes in demand conditions. A fall in prices, resulting in heavy losses, may be dealt with the device described in point (1). A rise in prices, resulting in extraprofits, must be tackled differently. Generally, extraprofits are profits no more conducive to an increase in productive efforts, which means that profit shades into the familiar category of rent. In some cases this rent may be taxed away by means of indirect taxes. But a more regular procedure will be to apply a progressive income (profit) tax.

(6) Finally, Depreciation, Rent, Interest, Wage and Profit as parts of the allocating mechanism are not sufficient in themselves to provide for the good working of it. For, being an *economic* mechanism, it needs continual readjustments. And the stuff for these readjustments is provided by what we may call the Reserve Fund of the enterprise. In years more favourable than the average the kolektiv will accumulate financial resources to draw on in bad times. Oscillations around an average will occur because depreciation allowances do not reflect changes in output capacity exactly, and because the market conditions are not perfectly stable and predictable (because of the changes in prices and as certain inputs might cease to be available and certain outputs to be saleable, possibly because of the extra-business factors). However, in the last case the Planning Authority will intervene whenever fluctuations transgress the boundary of what is considered to be normal. The financial resources in the Reserve Fund do not bear interest and neither is interest being paid for them because they do not represent real capital. Their aggregate value for the economy as a whole and also the ways enterprises use them, are bound to display certain regularities thus permitting the Bank to make reliable forecasts.

It has been said that the enterprises pay interest on all capital in use and that investment loans are granted by the Bank. Now, it is not always possible to identify a certain outlay as an investment expenditure, neither is it possible to draw a sharp dividing line between new investment and replacement. Moreover, small investments are made all the time and the obligation to contact the Bank in every particular instance would lead to an unnecessary bureaucratization of the economic process. The Yugoslav experience suggests that it is absolutely vital that the enterprise has under its command a certain amount of financial resources with which it disposes in the way it thinks fit. The necessary amount of these resources is a matter for empirical investigation; for institutional and psychological reasons it may perhaps be determined as the sum of depreciation and reserve funds (or as a fixed percentage of this sum depending on the rate of expansion or the particular industry). These Enterprise Funds may be used to finance an investment program independently. The only condition to be fulfilled is, of course, to pay the Bank interest on the capital invested at a given rate. Again the aggregate use of resources of the Enterprise Funds is likely to show certain regularities which the Bank will be able to foresee.

(b) The Planning Authority

1. Throughout this study the term "Planning Authority" has been used to denote the organs of economic co-ordination above the level of individual enterprises. These organs are by no means uniform; they perform a great variety of tasks and, consequently, differ from each other in many respects. They may be thought of as servomechanisms of a complicated self-regulating machine of planning which must be designed in such a way as to keep the economy on the path of production maximization. It is outside the scope of the present study to undertake a description of construction details and performance characteristics of the planning machine. But on the other hand it seems inadmissible to leave the subject of the theory of planned economy without at least indicating what are the institutions through which the planning is actually done. These few concluding paragraphs will, therefore, be used to systematize some basic principles and to survey the main institutions of planned economy by summing up and supplementing the conclusions and suggestions scattered throughout the text.

2. We have found that, in order to avoid the evils of bureaucratism — the pure and direct technical inefficiency as well as the far-reaching sociological consequences — initiative and responsibility have to be transferred downwards and kept close to the place of direct work. Consequently the enterprise, personified by the working kolektiv, becomes the basic economic (decision-making) unit of an efficiently planned economy. The enterprise enters into three different kinds of relations with the rest of the system.

First, it enters into impersonal market relations with other enterprises and with consumers. Providing that market imperfections can be kept within certain tolerable limits, the market becomes an extremely useful part of the co-ordinating mechanism. It registers consumer preferences accurately, quickly and cheaply. It supplies information vital for price-output decisions. It provides strong incentives for everyone concerned with avoiding waste and increasing productivity. These three characteristics of the market constitute the basis for feasibility of having *independent* enterprises in a *planned* economy. The market simply does the greater part of planning automatically.

Unlike market relations the other two types of relations are not impersonal. They reflect the need for horizontal co-ordination — on a certain territory — and for vertical co-ordination — of an industry or the economy as a whole· For essentially the same reasons as the enterprise — the avoidance of bureaucratic polarization resulting in inefficiency the basic politico-administrative unit must be small enough to enable direct participation of the citizens in the organization of their social life. It has been suggested that the Commune is such a unit. "The Commune is a social-territorial community of citizens bound together by the common interests as producers as well as consumers" (Gerško-vić, 26, 22). On the territory of a Commune there are many enterprises and non-commercial institutions whose kolektivs — and similarly individual citizens as producers and consumers — have common or conflicting interests. To satisfy the former and to resolve the latter, the

Commune must set up a technical co-ordinating apparatus and establish a representative body whose valuation will be superior to that of a single kolektiv or an individual in matters concerning the interests of other kolektivs and individuals.

The third relation, concerning vertical co-ordination, is that which is usually regarded as *the* planning. It is a rather complex relation including a whole structure of decisions taken on various levels above the enterprise. Compared with the first two relations, this one is comparatively unimportant for the daily life of a kolektiv. It is, however, vital for the economy as a whole. Its main component parts are, perhaps, the following five.

3. First, enterprises will find it necessary to create associations according to industries. The purpose of these associations is to tackle the problems affecting the respective industries like those of introducing new techniques, selecting new locations, training workers and technicians, foreign trade, standardization of products, constant technological and economic research (cf. 27). The Association represents its members before the State organs, considers and gives suggestions on proposed bills affecting the industry. It may be arranged that a representative of the higher Planning Authority attends the meetings of the Association with the power to approve on the spot of the conclusions, transgressing in their effects the boundaries of the industry. The Association sets up an information office and a research institute which prepare the factual basis of the alternatives to be evaluated by the member-enterprises. The institute carries out technological and economic research and prepares drafts of annual and perspective plans for the industry.

Secondly the drafts of overall economic plans for the entire economy are made by a body of experts in the Planning Bureau which is responsible to the Parliament. The Planning Bureau provides factual basis for decisions to be taken by the Government and for laws to be discussed by the Parliament. The Social Plan itself is a law (in that it obliges the Government to carry out certain specified activities, in that it fixes financial instruments like taxes and interest rates and assigns financial means for development of backward regions, in that it determines certain key projects to be undertaken, etc.). In preparing Social Plans, the Planning Bureau gets valuable help from the industrial Associations, which, in turn, have access to all information accumulated in the Bureau.

Thirdly, there will be an institution whose primary task is to determine the structure of wage-rates and to protect individual workers. Trade Unions are traditionally qualified to assume the task of such an institution.

Fourthly, the supreme planning authority is vested in the Parliament and its executive committee, the Government. The Parliament passes the law on Social Plan and determines the legal framework within which the economy is to operate. The Parliament is a body whose valuation is superior to any other in any respect. The Government is primarily a technical executor of the will of the Parliament (though this more in theory than in practice, and in fact here lies the main danger of a bureaucratic degeneration). Unlike the Planning Bureau, the economic departments of the Government are *operative* planners. They manipulate reserve stocks and other devices of price control in order to stabilize prices. They apply special treatment to enterprises whose problems do not fit into the general legal framework. They negotiate foreign loans and regulate foreign trade. They approve or veto the decisions of various Associations on specific questions.

The activities of the Government departments fall into two groups. Those like selling reserve stocks represent *economic* interventions. Those like fixing the prices, represent *administrative* interventions. Economic *inducements* are not objectionable in themselves, but administrative *orders* are, because of their ostensible arbitrariness. In general, the better an economy is organized, the smaller is the need for administrative interventions. An extremely useful — and the last in my list — institution in eliminating much of administrative intervention is the Bank. The Bank is first of all a market institution. But in a planned economy it is more than that. If it is desired that certain industries — say those whose output has high export content — are expanded more quickly, this aim may be achieved by allocating necessary resources directly to specified firms. But the same aim can also be achieved by instructing the Bank to apply selectivity in its credit policy. Similarly, foreign exchange allocation may be centralized and administratively carried out. But it is also possible to leave the Bank to create a foreign exchange market. Finally, it is the business of the Bank to register all day-to-day transactions of the enterprises and the collection of data obtained provides a useful guide for the current economic policy of the Government. The "Bank" like the "Planning Authority", is not a single institution. The term stands for an institution comprising a number of different banks which specialize in various businesses but whose activities are co-ordinated.

4. With this I complete the picture of the institutional structure of a planned economy as I see it. The decisions affecting the daily lives of men and women in their capacities as producers and citizens are made by the organizations in which they participate directly. The co-ordinating decisions made on higher levels are already to a great extent technical in their nature. The traditionalization of the institutional system is likely to lead to routinization of the activities of the co-ordinating organs. Increase of economic welfare with corresponding increase in leisure time and equalization of incomes, elimination of class antagonisms with the corresponding equalization of opportunities, and scientific progress — including the progress of the economic science as well — are likely to diminish the need for valuations in economic matters above the level of the enterprise. In such conditions rational economic choice becomes feasible and consequently the scientifically planned economy becomes a fact.

Appendix

MARX'S CONCEPTION OF PRODUCTIVE LABOUR

According to one of the current definitions, social product represents the value of material goods produced in a specified period; services are declared unproductive and as such are excluded. It is commonly held, by both Marxist and non-Marxist (cf. e.g. Seers, 28) economists, that this is a Marxist definition of social product. The remarkable fact that on this issue otherwise theoretically antagonistic people find themselves in agreement; the fact that this belief is so widely shared; and the presumption that "Marxist" means the theory developed or implied by Marx — justify a brief excursus into this field. For this belief is — as beliefs mostly are — wrong. Marx was a more serious thinker than both camps would have him.

1. Marx, being a Marxist, was not concerned with the theory of productive labour *in general*. Nowhere in his voluminous opus is one able to find an attempt to formulate such an eternally valid theory. He was interested in the problem of productive labour only in connection with the economic epoch he was studying and for which he tried to formulate a comprehensive political economy. It was the epoch of *capitalist* production. His starting point was that of a typical capitalist-entrepreneur. A capitalist is interested in the *profitability* of his business, he tries to maximize the difference between price and cost. If this is the typical *behaviour* of the typical productive agent in the capitalist system, this must be taken as a criterion for the productivity of labour in this system. Labour is productive when it produces surplus value.

What from the point of view of society is income is *gross* income from the point of view of the capitalist. What the latter considers as net income corresponds to income minus wages. However, "this is an abstraction to the extent that the entire society, on the basis of capitalist production, places itself upon the capitalist standpoint and considers only the income divided into profit and rent as the net income" (29, 668).

The above two paragraphs show the Marxian problem in the nutshell. In what follows we shall consider more systematically some of the more important aspects of the problem. The only place where Marx discusses the problem systematically is the chapter on productive and unproductive labour in the first volume of the *Theories of Surplus Value* (the critique of Smith) and in the appendix to this volume (Marx's positive views). Hence these two chapters will provide the necessary quotations. As I am here swimming against the stream, it will be necessary to undertake some measures of precaution. To escape the charge of reading my own thoughts into Marx, I shall confine myself to brief comments leaving Marx to speak for himself.

2. Marx takes over his theory from Smith[1]. Smith, as frequently happened to him, had in fact two and mutually inconsistent theories.

---

[1] Hence it would seem that not only Marx needs protection against Soviet economists, but also Smith needs to be defended against their Western colleagues. That has been done by A. W. Lewis. Incorporating the fundamentals of the classical

According to the first, labour is productive when it produces capital. According to the second, the criterion is the production of material commodities (as against unproductive labour expended on personal services). This second definition of Smith is today called the Marxist definition of social product. Needless to say, Marx, together with other economists, criticized the second Smith's definition for its obvious weakness.

In a system of simple commodity production the producer exchanges his products for the means of subsistence. The capitalist mode of production cuts the ties between labour and ownership of productive instruments, and between the exchange of work for consumer goods interposes the machinery of *capitalist* production. The goods produced may remain the same but the social content of production is now different.

"The result of the capitalist production process is neither a mere product (use value), nor a commodity, that is, a use value which has a definite exchange value. Its result, its product, is the creation of surplus value for capital, and hence the actual transformation of money or commodity into capital ... And it (capital) achieves this *specific product* of the capitalist production process only in exchange with labour, which is therefore called *productive labour*" (7, 185).

The definition of the productive labour follows straightforwardly:

"*Productive labour* is therefore — in the system of capitalist production — that which produces *surplus value* for its employer, or which transforms the objective conditions of labour into capital and their owner into a capitalist; and therefore labour which produces its own product as capital. When therefore we speak of *productive labour*, we speak of *socially determined* labour, labour which implies a quite precise relation between the buyer and the seller of the labour" (7, 181).

Obviously, from this point of view it is irrelevant whether labour results in a material good or in an immaterial service:

"It follows from what has been said that the designation of labour as productive has absolutely nothing to do with the definite content

---

approach in two admirable papers (30; 31), Professor Lewis shows explicitly and implicitly that Smith's concepts are both meaningful and useful tools for economic analysis. Lewis's interpretation of Smith is identical with that of Marx, as may be seen from the following passages: "As Adam Smith set out the distinction, there are two elements to productive labour. First, its output consists of wage goods, and excludes services. Secondly, productive labour produces a surplus over wages, and has therefore a larger average product than unproductive labour. The distinction was made and used only for the purpose of analyzing capital accumulation." Footnotes: "Strictly Smith's definition is between commodities and services. But our modern distinction between wage goods and other output seems really to be what he was striving after, and fits his analysis best." "Neoclassical economists have attacked the distinction from the standpoint of value theory, but since it was not intended for that context, the attack is irrelevant." And finally: "The classical economists approached the analysis of accumulation *via* the consumption of wage goods. They divided consumers into three classes: (1) capitalists and landlords, (2) producers of services and luxuries and (3) producers of wage goods. In the wider sense, the consumption of the producers of non-wage goods was part of the consumption of capitalists and landlords, since they regarded class (2) as being maintained by class (1) for its amusement, etc., out of the surplus extracted from class (3). Thus, when they spoke of the capitalists saving they sometimes meant reducing their personal consumption of wage goods, but more often they meant merely having fewer servants, and so reducing the numbers maintained in class (2)" (31, 4—5).

of the labour, with its special usefulness, or with the particular use value in which it manifests itself. The same kind of labour may be productive or unproductive..." (7, 186).

Thus, for instance, a tailor employed by a tailoring firm is a productive worker. "On the other hand the journeyman tailor (who works for me at home) is not a productive worker, although his labour provides me with the product, the trousers, and him with the price of his labour, the money" (7, 187). But what about classical unproductive workers, such as artists, for example? Marx's answer is unequivocal:

"A singer who sells her song on her own is an unproductive worker. But the same singer, commissioned by an entrepreneur to sing in order to make money for him, is a productive worker. For she produces capital" (7, 186).

We may now summarize:

"It is characteristic of all unproductive labours that they are at my disposal — as is the case in the purchase of all other commodities for consumption — in the same proportion as that in which I exploit productive workers... *Vice versa*, however, my power to employ productive workers does not at all increase in proportion to the extent that I employ unproductive workers, but on the contrary falls in the same proportion" (7, 191).

3. This is then the Marxian theory of productive and unproductive labour. However, Marx makes an additional step. He is now interested in finding out whether and to which extent the second Smith's definition might be considered as an approximation to the first one. If this could be done, his model of the capitalist system would be somewhat simplified without losing any of its essential characteristics. He starts by generalizing the empirical evidence of his time:

"For it is also a law that economic development divides out functions among different persons, and the artisan or peasant who produces with his own means of production will either gradually be transformed into a small capitalist who also exploits the labour of others, or he will suffer the loss of his means of production... and be transformed into a wage worker. This is the tendency in the form of society in which the capitalist mode of production predominates. In examining the essential relations of capitalist production it can therefore be assumed that the whole world of commodities, all spheres of material production — the production of material wealth — are subordinated (formally or really) to the capitalist mode of production... On this premise, which expresses the goal (limit)... all workers engaged in the production of commodities are wage workers, and the means of production in all these spheres confront them as capital. It can be said to be a characteristic of productive workers, that is, of capital-producing workers, that their labour is realized in commodities, in material wealth. And so productive labour, along with its determining characteristic — which takes no account of the content of the labour and is independent of that content — would be given a *second, different* and *subsidiary* definition" (7, 193—4; my italics).

It remains to see whether any tendencies are observable in the realm of "intellectual" production.

230

"The production of immaterial things, even when it is carried on purely for exchange, that is, when it produces commodities, may be of two kinds:

(1) Its result is commodities, use values, whose form is different from and independent of producer and consumer; they may therefore exist during an interval between production and consumption, and in this interval circulate as vendible commodities, as in the case of books, pictures, in a word all artistic products which are different from the artistic performance of the artist producing them. Here capitalist production is applicable only to a very limited extent: as for example when a writer of a joint work — say encyclopedia — exploits a number of others as hacks ...

(2) The production cannot be separated from the act of its producer, as is the case with all performing artists, actors, teachers, doctors, parsons, etc. Here too the capitalist mode of production is met with only to a small extent, and from the nature of the case can only occur in a few spheres ... All these manifestations of capitalist production in this sphere are so insignificant compared with total production that they can be left completely out of account" (7, 195).

Marx does not draw explicit conclusions from the above considerations. But if any conclusion is to be drawn, it will read as follows: The essential features of the capitalist mode of production may be established by an analysis of the production of material goods in this system. And that is all.

4. Yet another interpretation is still possible. Marx might have been so confused as to fail to realize the inconsistency of this particular theory of his with his own more general theory of development of socio-economic systems. This assumption is implicitly made by all those writers who derive the "Marxist" conception of social product from the Marxian theory of the relation between the *basis* and *superstructure*. The most elaborate version of that doctrine known to me is that of the Soviet economist J. A. Kronrod, from whom I shall borrow a couple of quotations for an illustration:

"Social product is a result of material production, a result of productive labour. The results of human labour, whose task is reproduction of the material conditions of the life of the society, are expressed in product ... But precisely for that reason the results of mental production do not create the product in an economic sense, but are only a reflection of the process of material life ... The confusion of material and mental production leads to a non-Marxist elimination of the difference between the basis and the superstructure, leads to an identification of the results of material production, which create product, with the results of mental production which represent the reflection of the material process of life" (32, 9).

Marx taught that the relations between men in production — economic relations — provided the most important determinant of the structure of any known society. We speak of feudal, capitalist, etc., societies because of the feudal, capitalist, etc., economic relations in these societies. The ideologies, or even more generally, the cultures in these societies reflected their economic bases and as such represented superstructures. In every class society the culture is the culture of the ruling, i.e., of the owning class. The owning classes create their culture either directly, as "mental producers", or indirectly, as buyers. In either case the owners and the persons dependent on them live on the work of havenots. All that follows from this desperately simplified materialistic conception of history is a fundamental sociological difference between the "economic sphere" and the "ideological sphere" of life. It provides no criterion for distinction between goods and services — which is the basis of the "Marxist" definition of social product. Where should one classify the services of barbers, nurses and street-cleaners? Kronrod seems to be aware of the difficulty and suggests that in such cases one should "analyze the concrete function of labour with respect to its productivity" (p. 15), but gives no hints how this is to be done.

However, much more important is the fact that the economy-ideology relation has no necessary bearing on the relation between productive and unproductive labour. As we have seen, according to Marx's definition the mental labour of artists and writers, if organized on capitalist lines is equally productive as that of manual workers, while manual work of an artisan tailor is — in a capitalist system — unproductive. Unless we pretend to teach Marx what he should have thought, we are bound to accept the definition of productivity in the sense in which he himself used it. And from the above quotations it is obvious that Marx defined productivity in terms of *accumulation of capital*, i.e., in terms of social relations existing under the capitalist mode of production. This has nothing to do with the problem of the basis-superstructure relation.

5. Once the first inconsistency is incorporated, the others necessarily follow. The contradiction between the Marxian product of value productivity and the Ostrovitjanov-Kronrod concept of social product has already been mentioned in the text (Ch. 11-a-2). Further, we saw that in Marx's opinion, when "we speak of *productive labour*, we speak of *socially determined* labour". It follows that the *same* physical aggregates of goods and services will have *different* contents of productive labour depending on whether the economy is capitalist or socialist. Defying this straightforward logic, the protagonists of the "Marxist" definition of social product prescribe the *same* statistical rules for the computation of social product in *both* economies, namely the inclusion of material goods and the exclusion of immaterial services. In this respect one refinement deserves a brief comment. Some writers endeavour to develop their "Marxism" one step further, and in doing so they postulate a slightly different formula for a socialist economy. This brings me to the next point.

6. Since the days of Adam Smith — the end of XVIIIth century — the distinction between productive and unproductive labour has always had a strong moral overtone. As Marx put it, Smith had in fact classified state officials, lawyers and parsons in the same category with clowns and servants. This procedure could not fail but produce strong protests on the part of the former. Malthus was a case in point. Upper social strata had to be made productive.

We might expect that apologetics will reappear in the mid-twentieth-century discussions of the subject. Kronrod provides us readily with the wanted piece of theory:

"On the other hand, socialism creates new productive functions ...
The function of the Socialist State and the function of the Party, as
leading forces of socialist society, are directly productive functions
because the State and the Party plays an economic-organizational
role, *directly* leading and organizing the whole process of material
production in a Socialist society" (32, 39).

For Marx, of course, the state apparatus was a prototype of social
parasitism and the proposition of "withering away of the state" in socialism is famous enough to need any further evidence. The quotation
serves to illustrate the fact that "Marxism" and "Marx's theoretical
heritage" are not necessarily the same thing.[1]

7. It remains to answer the question about the origin of the
"Marxist" definition of social product and to explain the unique solidarity
of two antagonistic camps with respect to this issue. Among the various
possible explanations, I choose to base my own on the good old Marxian
approach of considering the theory as socially determined.

As the "Marxist" definition is either arbitrary or leads to meaningless
results, the anti-Marxist writers could have nothing against it.[2] Social
pressure — or bias — of the last proposition of Kronrod is evident. For
the rest the identification of product with material product may be partly
due to the influence of J. Stalin and his primitive philosophical materialism.[3] But primarily it is, I believe, the result of the particular economic conditions of the Soviet Union in the time when planning was
established in that country. For people engaged in the process of rapid
industrialization seemed to be obvious that what mattered were steel and
coal, i.e., tangible material goods by which they sought to increase the
productive wealth of the country.[4] Consciously or unconsciously the
labour engaged in this field of social activity was attributed an aura of
special usefulness and dignity. The suggestive Smith-Marxian term "productive labour" met the emotional requirement of the situation extremely
well and the authority of Marx's name could only reinforce the total
impression. Once you undergo this process, the proposition becomes
self-evident and as such escapes logical analysis. You just *know* that
factory workers are productive and university teachers unproductive and
living from the labour of the former. The last two sentences generalize
the author's personal experience.[5]

---

[1] Another instance of the doctrine propounded by Kronrod is a somewhat
more carefully phrased statement by Notkin (33, 83n). One should add, however,
that Soviet statisticians have not followed the advice of their fellow economists and
do *not* compute Government and Party services as an addition to social product.

[2] As P. Wiles, an Oxonian economist, put it on one occasion, Marxism means
"the holding of silly views on a number of subjects" (*Encounter*, Dec. 1957, p. 12).

[3] Thus Kronrod supports his views by quoting Stalin's philosophical reflections
of the following kind: "In order to live men must have food, clothes, shoes, shelter,
fuel, etc., in order to have these material goods it is necessary to produce them"
(32, 3).

[4] Kronrod says: "The great tasks set by the new Five Year Plan to our
country require that the share of productive labour, engaged in the sphere of
material production, be increased even further ..." (32, 40).

[5] It is one of those phenomena for which a counterpart among Western economists may be found, curiously enough, in the same field. "National income
total at factor cost" is so evidently a meaningless concept. And yet how many
economists and national income statisticians are aware of that?

8. As we have dealt with the three aspects of the problem — as defined at the beginning of this appendix — our task is now over. We may conclude by stating explicitly the relation between Marx's conception of productive labour as labour producing surplus value and the social accounting conception of social product as an aggregate of all useful goods and services produced in a specified period. This may be done in two points:

(a) The two problems are conceptually completely different and

(b) even quite apart from that, the Smith-Marx conception of productive labour has no meaning for a socialist economy. In the strict logic of Marx's assumptions in a socialist economy surplus value is non-existent; therefore, all work is unproductive, and social product is equal to zero. One can agree or disagree with Marx's theory, one may find it useful or useless, but one cannot make nonsense of it. Or, at least, one would need a considerable amount of ignorance and courage to attribute such a nonsense to Marx. On the other hand, if we insist on extending Marxian analysis to a socialist economy, this may be done in the following way. In so far as planning may be assumed to be directed towards the satisfaction of needs of the members of the society, it provides a direct link between the expenditure of labour and the appropriation of the consumption goods. Capital is no more an intermediary agent responsible for the organization of production, and so profit-producing ceases to be the criterion of productivity. The *immediate and ultimate purpose of production* is the production of use values and so every labour, which produces goods and services for the satisfaction of the needs of the members of the community is a productive labour. This definition of productive labour implies exactly that definition of social product which was elaborated in the text. We thus get a monistic theory. It is outside the scope of this appendix to develop the theme further.

References:

1. J. E. Meade, R. Stone, "The Construction of Tables of National Income, Expenditure, Savings and Investment", *Economic Journal*, 1941, 216—33.
2. K. V. Ostrovitjanov and others, *Političeskaja Ekonomija* (Political Economy), Moskva, GOSPOLITIZDAT, 1955.
3. Savezni zavod za statistiku, *Metodologija za obračun narodnog dohotka u 1954 godini* (The Methodology for the Computation of National Income in 1954), Beograd, 1954.
4. G. Grdjić, *Narodni dohodak* (National Income), Beograd, Ekonomski institut NR Srbije, 1955.
5. A. Bajt, "Marxove sheme reprodukcije društvenoga kapitala i društveni bruto proizvod" (Marxian Schemata of Reproduction of Social Capital and Social Gross Product), *Ekonomist*, 1956, 423—55.
6. B. Horvat, "Društveni proizvod" (Social Product), *Ekonomist*, 1957, 69—78.
7. K. Marx, *Theories of Surplus Value*, London, Lawrence and Wishart, 1951.
8. S. Kuznets, "National Income: A New Version", *Review of Economics and Statistics*, 1948, 151—79.
9. M. Gilbert, G. Jaszi, E. F. Denison, C. F. Schwartz, "Objections to National Income Measurement, A Reply to Professor Kuznets", *Ibid.*, 1948, 179—95.
10. S. Kuznets, "Government Product and National Income", in *Income and Wealth*, Series I, Cambridge, Bowes and Bowes, 1951.

11. R. T. Bowman, R. A. Easterlin, "An Interpretation of the Kuznets and Department of Commerce Income Concepts", *Review of Economics and Statistics*, 1953, 41—50.
12. J. Mayer, "Proposals for Improving Income and Product Concepts", *Ibid.*, 1954, 191—201.
13. W. B. Reddaway, "Some Problems in the Measurement of Changes in the Real Geographical Product", in *Income and Wealth*, Series I, Cambridge, Bowes and Bowes, 1951.
14. J. R. Hicks, "The Valuation of Social Income", *Economica*, 1940, 105—24.
15. S. Kuznets, "On the Valuation of Social Income — Reflections on Professor Hicks's Article", *Economica*, 1948, 1—16.
16. J. R. Hicks, "The Valuation of Social Income — A Comment on Professor Kuznets' Reflections", *Economica*, 1948, 163—72.
17. I. M. D. Little, "The Valuation of the Social Income", *Economica*, 1949, 11—26, 369—70.
18. P. Samuelson, "Evaluation of Real National Income", *Oxford Economic Papers*, 1950, 163—72.
19. J. W. Kuhn, "The Usefulness of the Factor Cost Concept in National Income Accounting", *Review of Economics and Statistics*, 1954, 93—99.
20. R. Frisch, "Market Price versus Factor Cost in National Income Statistics", Sankhya, 1955, 1—8; cf. also the discussion H. Ezekiel — R. Frish, *Ibid.*, 1956—57, 245—46.
21. J. L. Nicholson, "National Income at Factor Cost or Market Prices?", *Economic Journal*, 1955, 216—24.
22. W. Miller, "American Historians and the Business Elite", *Journal of Economic History*, 1949, 184—208.
23. J. L. Nicholson, "The International Comparison of National Products", *Economic Journal*, 1955, 352—9.
24. H. D. Dickinson, *Economics of Socialism*, London, Oxford University Press, 1939.
25. E. Lindahl, E. Dahlgren, K. Kock, *National Income of Sweden 1861—1930*, Part One, London, P. S. King, 1937.
26. L. Geršković, *Društveno upravljanje u Jugoslaviji* (Social Self-Government in Yugoslavia), Beograd, Savremena administracija, 1957.
27. B. Horvat, "Ekonomika industrijske grane" (Economics of a Branch of Industry), *Ekonomski pregled*, 1955, 488—507.
28. D. Seers, "A Note on Current Marxist Definitions of the National Income", *Oxford Economic Papers*, 1949, 260—8.
29. K. Marx, *Capital*, Vol. III, Calcutta, Saraswaty Library, 1946.
30. W. A. Lewis, "Economic Development with Unlimited Supplies of Labour", *Manchester School*, 1954, 139—91.
31. —————, "Unlimited Supply: Further Notes", *Ibid.*, 1958, 1—32.
32. J. A. Kronrod, *Fundamental Questions of Marxist-Leninist Teaching on Productive Labour in Capitalism and Socialism*, Zagreb, Naprijed, 1948; a Serbo-Croat translation of the article originally published in *Izvjestija Akademiji Nauk SSSR*, Otdelenie ekonomiki i prava, No. 1, 1947.
33. A. I. Notkin, *Očerki teoriji socialističeskogo vosproizvodstva* (An Outline of the Theory of Socialist Reproduction), Moskva, OGIZ, 1948.

Subject Index

Accumulation 20, 56, 64, 78, 140, 156, 161, 168—169, 175, 199, 229, 232

Alienation 11, 80

Allocation 18, 28, 41, 121—122, 187
— of foreign exchange 227
— of labour fund 13, 15, 120—121, 130
— of resources 18, 23, 27, 43, 55, 218, 220, 227
— optimal 21, 56, 62

America 3, 76—77, 100, 105, 109, 115, 118, 126—128, 133, 176, 201, 216

Analitic concepts, instruments 38, 148, 153, 159, 178

Austria 103, 105

Axiomatic system 197—198, 200, 218

Bank 119, 213, 219, 224, 227

Basis and superstructure 231

Belgium 106

Bureaucracy, bureaucratic organization 82, 97, 105, 111—112, 117, 212—213, 222, 224—225, 227

Capacity 128, 191, 214, 220, 223, 224
— absorptive capacity of the economy 177—178, 181—184, 187—188, 191—194, 199
— productive capacity of the economy 139—141, 143, 146, 151, 156—160, 162, 165—168, 171, 178, 221, 223

Capital 12, 16, 49, 73, 95, 109, 141—145, 148—155, 160—171, 179, 186—187, 194, 195, 210, 215, 217, 219, 222, 224, 229, 234
— constant 168
— fixed 16, 20, 24, 144, 154—155, 161, 168—169, 191, 215, 220—221, 223
— marginal efficiency 63, 68, 71, 178
— private 217, 220
— productivity 55, 156—157, 159, 175, 181, 185, 187, 192
— saturation 68
— social 62, 187, 194, 208, 219—221

Capital coefficient 160, 166, 184, 188, 191, 197, 204
— gross 190—191, 197, 201—203
— technological 140, 166, 191, 203—204

Capitalism 75, 114, 228—232
— cf. also : economy
— liberal 77, 81, 93
— private 2, 80, 82—83, 115, 118, 130
— state 4, 77, 79—80, 82—83, 93, 95, 118, 130

Category
— economic 13
— sociological 13

China 116, 182

Choice 32, 176—177, 184, 188, 195—199, 216, 218, 222
— rational 1, 5, 12, 220, 227
— social 1, 178

Class struggle 98

Commune 97—98, 100—101, 120, 175—176, 222, 225—226

Consumer 10, 19, 21, 31, 60—61, 115, 128—129, 175—176, 190, 196, 199, 209, 214, 218, 225, 229, 231
— sovereignity of 31

Consumption 1, 54, 65, 123, 132, 175—179, 182, 186, 188, 190—194, 197, 200—203, 208, 211—216, 229—231
— maximization 2, 60, 122, 123, 151, 178, 195—199

Cost 209, 211—214, 217, 220, 222—223, 228
— average 18—19, 24—25
— full 17—18, 25, 27—29
— maintenance 141, 155—157, 159, 167—168, 217
— marginal 18—21, 23—28, 40, 45, 187
— of fixed assets 139—140, 148, 150—153, 157—161, 169—170
— opportunity 48
— primary 26, 155, 157—158, 161—168
— replacement 69, 153—157, 159—161, 166—168, 217
— variable 18, 24—26

237

INDEX BY AUTHORS